The Ironic Spectator

In memory of my mother, Thomais

The Ironic Spectator

Solidarity in the Age of Post-Humanitarianism

LILIE CHOULIARAKI

polity

First published in 2013 by Polity Press

Polity Press
65 Bridge Street
Cambridge CB2 1UR, UK

Polity Press
350 Main Street
Malden, MA 02148, USA

ISBN-13: 978-0-7456-4210-9
ISBN-13: 978-0-7456-4211-6(pb)

A catalogue record for this book is available from the British Library.

Typeset in 11 on 13pt Adobe Garamond Pro
by Servis Filmsetting Ltd, Stockport, Cheshire
Printed and bound in Great Britain by MPG Books Group Limited, Bodmin, Cornwall

For further information on Polity, visit our website: www.politybooks.com

Contents

Detailed Contents

Figures

Acknowledgements

In writing this book, I have been privileged to be surrounded by excellent colleagues, whose scholarly passion has been a constant source of inspiration for me. I have also been fortunate to direct my Department's PhD Programme and be challenged by a number of talented and dedicated students who always pushed me beyond my intellectual comfort zone. I thank them all for this. Furthermore, I am grateful to the participants of various seminars, symposia and conferences, within and outside the LSE, who offered me invaluable feedback in the process of working out the argument of this book. These include the LSE's Atrocity, Suffering and Human Rights group, the Gender Institute's reading group and the Centre for the Study of Global Governance, as well as intellectual encounters at Lancaster, Loughborough, Leicester, Cambridge, Brunel, Sussex, the Institute of Education, University of London, CELSA-Sorbonne in Paris, Utrecht, Stockholm, Copenhagen, Helsinki, Chicago and Boston.

Let me also thank those who offered their permission for the use of various visual and linguistic texts in the empirical chapters of the book. These include the Estate of Audrey Hepburn and photographer John Isaac for the UNICEF picture of Audrey Hepburn; PLAN, Oxfam, Amnesty International and UNWFP for visual material from their campaigns and the BBC for permission to use their linguistic texts on earthquake news.

Last but not least, I am grateful to Daphne and Elias for always being there for me. Without their love and support, this book would not have been possible.

1 Solidarity and Spectatorship

Introduction: 'Find Your Feeling'

> 'Get involved. Feeling inspired? ActionAid's supporters experience incredible feelings of happiness, warmth and pride all the time. There's no limit to the scale of amazing feelings you can get by getting involved. To discover what your feeling might be, take the ActionAid interactive quiz today.'[1]

'Find Your Feeling: How Could ActionAid Make You Feel?' is a 30-second quiz that invites us to explore what our 'true feeling' towards this major humanitarian brand might be by clicking on a number of questions: which picture moves us most, for instance? The child 'next door' happily swinging away? A group of protesters in Latin America or a couple of women hugging and smiling at the camera? Depending on our choice of emotions towards these distant others, we are offered a certain self-description: we might be 'warm and fluffy' or 'inspired and excited', and, having been in touch with our emotions, we are then invited to 'click on the link' and 'find out more about ActionAid'.

It is the relationship between 'how I feel' and 'what I can do' about distant others, so clearly thrown into relief in the ActionAid appeal, that concerns me in this book. There is no doubt that emotion has always played a central role in the communication of solidarity, yet, I argue, there is something distinct about the ways in which the self figures in contemporary humanitarianism. This is obvious when we consider earlier Red Cross appeals, for instance, where the question of 'what can I do?' is raised through shocking images of emaciated children, or Amnesty International ones, where the question is answered through a call to personalized letter-writing for the liberation of prisoners of conscience. Neither of these two examples returns the imperative to act on vulnerable strangers to ourselves, asking us to get in touch with our feelings in order to express our solidarity with them.

Taking my point of departure in this new emotionality, I explore the ways in which the communication of solidarity has changed in the course of the past four decades. A crucial period for humanitarianism, the 1970–2010 time-span, is characterized by three major, seemingly unconnected but ultimately intersecting, transformations: the instrumentalization of the aid and development field; the retreat of the 'grand narratives' of solidarity; and the increasing technologization of communication. Whilst each transformation has been extensively explored in its own right, the co-articulation of the three and, importantly, the implications of this co-articulation for the changing meaning of solidarity, have remained relatively untouched.

In drawing attention to the new emotionality of the 'Find Your Feeling' appeal, then, what I propose is that the meaning of solidarity today should be approached as simultaneously defined, or overdetermined, by the branding strategies of ActionAid, by a generalized reluctance to accept 'common humanity' as the motivation for our actions and by the interactive possibilities of online media. It is, I argue, only when we examine solidarity as a problem of communication, that is, as a moral claim seeking to reconcile the competing demands of market, politics and the media, that we can better understand how the spectacle of suffering is subtly but surely turning the West into a specific kind of public actor – the ironic spectator of vulnerable others.

Irony refers to a disposition of detached knowingness, a self-conscious-suspicion vis-à-vis all claims to truth, which comes from acknowledging that there is always a disjunction between what is said and what exists – that there are no longer 'grand narratives' to hold the two together (Rorty 1989). Whilst irony is often translated into 'postmodern' postures of cool cynicism that reject moral attachment in favour of playful agnosticism, the spectacle of vulnerable others, I argue, complicates this posture in that, by virtue of confronting us with their suffering, it continues to raise the question of 'what to do' – it continues to call upon us as moral actors. The ironic spectator is, in this sense, an impure or ambivalent figure that stands, at once, as sceptical towards any moral appeal to solidary action and, yet, open to doing something about those who suffer. How has, then, the ironic spectator emerged through the communicative structure of solidarity, across time? And how does this twilight figure manage today to negotiate and resolve the tensions (political, economic, technological) of solidarity that our times press upon us?

The story of this book is, in this sense, a story of the communication of solidarity in the West at a historical turning point. This is the point when the expansion of the field, the end of the Cold War and the explosion of the media came together and ushered a paradigmatic change in the ways in which we are invited to perceive ourselves as moral actors. Even though the West cannot be regarded as a homogeneous sphere of safety, just as the global South cannot equally be seen as one single sphere of vulnerability, my use of these terms preserves nonetheless a historical and political distinction that is crucial to my story: the global division of power that, in unequally distributing resources along the West–South axis, reproduces the prosperity of the former whilst perpetuating the poverty of the latter. In the light of this division, the communication of solidarity becomes simultaneously the communication of cosmopolitan dispositions – public dispositions towards vulnerable others shaped by the moral imperative to act not only on people close to 'us' but also on distant others, strangers we will never meet, without the anticipation of reciprocation (Calhoun 2002; Linklater 2007a,b).

If I look at humanitarian communication as the main carrier of this imperative, this is because humanitarianism has successfully incorporated into its self-description a series of distinct altruistic claims, from the religious tradition of *agape* or care towards the stranger-in-need to the secular requirements to save lives or protect rights, which, despite their differences, have managed to create a relatively coherent moral order that defines our times as an 'empathic civilization' (Rifkin 2009). Instead of understanding humanitarian communication in a narrow manner, as institutional appeals strictly emanating from the field of international organizations, however, I treat it as involving a range of popular practices beyond appeals, such as celebrities, concerts and news. I consider these practices to be humanitarian to the extent that each uses its distinct aesthetic logic, for instance the personifying power of celebrity, the enchantment of the rock concert or the professional witnessing of the journalist, so as to confront us with the spectacle of distant sufferers as a cause that demands our response. In so doing, these practices form part of a dispersed communicative structure of cosmopolitan ethics that mundanely acts as a moralizing force upon western public life – what, in chapter 2, I introduce as the 'humanitarian imaginary'.

In following the mutations of these communicative practices across time, the story of the book is essentially a story of how changes in the aesthetics of humanitarian communication are also changes in the ethics of solidarity. It is a story about how the move from an objective representation of suffering as something separate from us that invites us to contemplate the condition of distant others towards a subjective representation of suffering as something inseparable from our own 'truths' that invites contemplation on our own condition, is also a move from an ethics of *pity* to an ethics of *irony*. This is an epistemic shift[2] in the communication of solidarity, I contend, in that it signals the retreat of an other-oriented morality, where doing good to others is about our common humanity and asks nothing back, and the emergence of a self-oriented morality, where doing good to others is about 'how I feel' and must, therefore, be rewarded by minor gratifications to the self – the new emotionality of the quiz, the confessions of our favourite celebrity, the thrill of the rock concert and Twitter journalism being only some of its manifestations.

Whilst all ethics of solidarity involves an element of 'egoistic altruism', ironic solidarity differs from other versions in that it explicitly situates the pleasures of the self at the heart of moral action, thereby rendering solidarity a contingent ethics that no longer aspires to a reflexive engagement with the political conditions of human vulnerability. The decline of grand narratives has undoubtedly contributed to the rise of the ironic disposition, but, as I show below, this contingent ethics of solidarity has a more complex history that forces us to examine all three dimensions of its emergence – not only the political, but also the professional and the technological. In telling the story of humanitarianism's four key communicative practices, I, therefore, choose to focus on the various ways through which appeals, celebrities, concerts and news have, in time, come to accommodate the tensions of the field by increasingly relying on the marketing logic of the corporate world as well as the digital technologies of media culture – and, in so doing, they have also come to respond to the political collapse of narratives of common humanity with the celebration of a neoliberal lifestyle of 'feel good' altruism.

At the heart of these aesthetic and ethical transformations, I conclude, lies a fundamental mutation in the communicative structure of humanitarianism. This is the retreat of the theatrical structure of solidarity, where the encounter between western spectator and vulnerable other takes place as an ethical and political event, in favour of a mirror structure, where this encounter is reduced to an often narcissistic self-reflection that involves people like 'us'. Any radical alternative to this dominant ethics of solidarity, I propose, needs to start by reclaiming the *theatricality* of the public realm, the sense of the world beyond the West as a really existing, albeit different, world, which confronts us with the uncomfortable but vital questions of power, otherness and justice and, in so doing, keeps the possibility of social change in the global divisions of our world alive.

But first things first. In this introductory chapter, I set the scene for the exploration of solidarity as a problem of communication by introducing each of the three key dimensions of this communication: the *institutional*, where I discuss the implications of the increasing expansion and concomitant instrumentalization of the aid and development field; the *political*, where I address the end of grand narratives and the ensuing rise of individualist morality as a motivation for action; and the *technological*, where I show how the new media have facilitated an unprecedented explosion of public self-expression, thereby also changing the premises upon which solidarity is communicated. It is, as I have said, only in the light of these three dimensions that we can begin to make sense of the shift from the objectivity of the theatre to the new emotionality of the mirror as a paradigmatic shift in the very meaning of solidarity.

The instrumentalization of humanitarianism

The 'Find Your Feeling' appeal is informed by an emphasis on 'inspiration' that, as Richard Turner, ActionAid's ex-head of fund-raising, put it, focuses on making people 'feel great if they give, but [doesn't] make them feel rotten if they don't'.[3] Leaving the needs-based iconography of poverty behind for inducing negative feelings of guilt, the inspiration-based approach is about inducing positive, warm feelings and, in so doing, aims at motivating longer-term support for the organization's cause: 'we'd like to think', as Turner continues, 'that the kind of supporters we attract are likely to give to us for longer and give more than if we'd increased our response rate with hard-hitting, more needs-based advertising.'[4]

Reflecting a general tendency in the aid and development field, this is the language of corporate communication that, instead of traditional strategies of dissemination, prioritizes the strategy of branding: the cultivation of a deep emotional attachment to a particular commodity, the NGO brand, with a view to guaranteeing customer loyalty to this brand. Whilst the emotional focus of branding deprives humanitarian communication of an argumentative rationale for solidarity, an issue I explore in chapter 3, what concerns me here is the broader point that our moral encounter with human vulnerability is now cast in a particular logic of the market.

Humanitarianism has, of course, never been antithetical to the market and has, in fact, been theorized as a quintessentially liberal idea born out of capitalism, for instance as the benign face of the expansion of labour markets beyond the West (Friedman 2003; Bajde 2009). Yet, the contemporary articulation of humanitarianism with the market is a rather recent development that reflects a shift within capitalism from, what Boltanski and Chiapello call, a classical liberal to a neoliberal conception of public morality (2005). In the light of this shift, we may argue that, whereas modern humanitarianism was grounded on the crucial separation between a public logic of economic utilitarianism, applicable in the sphere of commodity exchange, and a private logic of sentimental obligation towards vulnerable others, applicable in the sphere of individual altruism and increasingly in institutionalized philanthropy, late modern humanitarianism, what I here theorize as *post-humanitarianism*, increasingly blurs the boundary between the two. In so doing, it manages both to turn the ever-expanding realm of economic exchange into a realm of private emotion and self-expression and, in a dialectical move, to simultaneously commodify private emotion and philanthropic obligation.

Starting in the 1980s and gaining full momentum in the early 1990s, two developments have brought about this shift towards what Cheah (2006) calls the *instrumentalization* of the aid and development field – that is, the subordination of the other-oriented aims to save lives and change societies to the self-oriented imperative of profitable performance in the humanitarian sector itself. These are the *marketization* of humanitarian practice and the *production of administrative knowledge* in the discipline of Development Studies.

The *marketization of humanitarian practice* is a consequence of the explosion of international organizations (IOs) and international NGOs (INGOs) in the aid and development sector. Aid agencies, for instance, expanded their operations by 150 per cent in the 1985–95 decade whereas, in the USA alone, their numbers rose by a hundred in the 1980–90 decade (from 167 to 267) and almost doubled in the subsequent one, 1990–2000 (from 267 to 436).[5] Marketization has, in this sense, emerged from these organizations' strong competition for survival in a sector that has not only become more densely populated[6] but has also come to depend primarily on project-based funding by transnational intermediaries and state donors. In the 1990–2000 decade, to give an example, funding levels rose nearly threefold, from $2.1 million to $5.9 million, reaching more than $10 million by 2005–6, whilst the distribution of these funds has increasingly shifted to depend on bilateral aid and state budgets' earmarking, thereby rendering strong state interests a key criterion for INGO fund-raising (Smillie & Minear 2004: 8–10, 195; Barnett 2005: 723–40; Barnett & Weiss 2008: 33–5).

Even though the proliferation of humanitarian agencies has been hailed as contributing to the cosmopolitan ethos of global civil society, in that INGOs 'breed new ideas, advocate, protest, and mobilize public support', as Mathews argues, and, in the process, further 'shape, implement, monitor, and enforce national and international commitments' (1997: 52–3), we can clearly see that such proliferation entails a major risk. Insofar as it takes place within an economy of scarcity, where many agencies bid for limited funding, the competition for resources inevitably tends to foster compliance with the rules of the western donor market rather than with real priorities in the global South. Indeed, despite the expansion of the field and the provision of 'more aid than ever before', as Barnett and Weiss claim, 'the bulk of resources [are] controlled by a few donor countries that [are] more inclined to impose conditions and direct aid towards their priorities' so that, they conclude, 'the least fortunate [are] getting the least attention' (2008: 34).

The aims of humanitarianism, to provide relief and secure sustainable development in the global South, are thus made possible by a regime of economic relations that simultaneously subjects these aims to the priorities of western entrepreneurship – sustainable funding and renewable contracts for the organizations themselves. This paradox at the heart of the field, the 'inhuman conditions' of humanitarianism, ultimately serves to reproduce rather than change the economic relations of subordination between the wealthy West and the poor South: 'while a degree of mass-based cosmopolitan solidarity has arisen in the domestic domains of Northern countries,' Cheah argues, 'it is unlikely that this solidarity will be directed in a concerted manner towards ending economic inequality between countries because Northern civil societies derive their prodigious strength from this inequality' (2006: 494).

Despite, therefore, its benign objectives of maximizing efficiency and increasing accountability to donors, the financial regime of the aid and development field ultimately legitimizes a neoliberal logic of governance that turns the cosmopolitan aspirations of humanitarianism into the corporate aspirations of the West and, in so doing, not only fails to serve the ideal of global civil society but delivers harmful effects on vulnerable others. Drawing on three different case studies of INGO project implementation, for instance, Cooley and Ron (2002) persuasively demonstrate how 'agency problems, competitive contracts, and multiple principals generate incentives promoting self-interested behaviour, intense competition, and poor project implementation' (2002: 18); the competitiveness built into this system, they conclude, is 'deeply corrosive'.

If the instrumentalization of humanitarianism is enacted through institutional practices on the ground, it is primarily legitimized through the *scientific knowledge produced in the field of Development Studies*. Born in the 1960s as a response to the need to study the processes of decolonization and the evolution of the new states, Development Studies has always been marked by a key tension between normative theory, showing what ideal societies or states would look like, and best practice, making concrete policy recommendations that are applicable in the here and now (Schuurman 2009). Even though this has historically been a productive tension that propelled critical research in the field, there has recently been, according to theorists, a definitive tip in the balance towards policy rather than normative theory (Biel 2000; Kothari 2005).

This means that Development Studies is today largely abandoning the critical perspectives of political economy, which thematized inequality as a systemic cause of underdevelopment and linked inequality to non-economic issues – thus further connecting Development Studies to the disciplines of Politics, Sociology or History and Anthropology. Instead, what today dominates the field is what Fine (2009) calls 'new development economics': the neoliberal economics of the (post-)Washington Consensus, which favours micro-economic, rather than macro- or structural economic, approaches to development, and methodologically positivist, rather than critical reflexive, research designs.

The former, micro-economic approaches, favour an emphasis on the logistics of capital circulation within specific markets, whilst ignoring 'big picture' questions of injustice and redistribution that are specific to the contexts of development. In treating the market as a 'universal' language of science that can be variously applied to particular states, 'new development economics' not only sidelines non-economic factors that affect development but further subsumes all development under a specific brand of administrative research – one that focuses on 'individual incentives' as responses to 'market failures' (Krueger 1986: 62; Mansell 2001, 2002).

The latter, positivist research designs, come to rely almost exclusively upon quantitative methodologies of measuring impact and assessing outcomes at the expense of more qualitative approaches that emphasize the histories, contexts and actors of development. Even though the academic field of Development Studies is admittedly complex, with voices such as Amartya Sen's on economics and moral philosophy (1999, 2009) or Joseph Stiglitz's (2002) on critical economics seeking to articulate more holistic alternatives to the economic reductionism of the neoliberal approach, the fact remains that dominant methodologies have imposed a purely technocratic agenda in the field. In so doing, they have marginalized the moral and political content of development: 'neoliberal thinking', as Schuurman puts it, 'is having a growing influence on determining the research agenda of development studies, making it increasingly difficult to maintain a critical research tradition' (2009: 832).

Following the mainstream epistemology of their field, INGOs similarly adopt a modus operandi that depoliticizes questions of development in favour of a focus on 'impact' and 'measurable indicators': 'humanitarian organizations', as Barnett argues, therefore 'define "impact", specify their goals and translate them into measurable indicators, gather data in highly fluid emergency settings, establish baseline data in order to generate a "before and after" snapshot, control for alternative explanations and variables, and construct reasonable counterfactual scenarios' (2005: 730). Development knowledge production remains, in this way, tightly linked to the managerial priorities of major IOs, such as the UN, IMF, and the World Bank, that, in regulating the traffic and distribution of project funding, also come to define the object and methodology of development research: 'the World Bank', Fine says, 'has both increased its influence on the social science of development and the influence of such social science (and economics within it) on development thinking' (2009: 895).

This discussion clearly, albeit sketchily, illustrates the institutional logic of contemporary humanitarianism – a neoliberal logic of micro-economic explanations that ignores the systemic causes of global poverty and turns humanitarianism into a practice of depoliticized managerialism. What this discussion further suggests, however, is that, whilst substantial critical work on the instrumentalization of both the practice and knowledge production of humanitarianism already exists, there is little that has been said about the impact of instrumentalization on the communication of solidarity itself.

Grounded on the working hypothesis that the communication of solidarity cannot but participate in this broader process of instrumentalization, as the 'Find Your Feeling' appeal already shows, my aim is to address the question of *how* instrumentalization came to be enacted through a range of key practices of humanitarian communication and, crucially, *which implications* this instrumentalization bears on the dispositions of solidarity that become available in our public culture. There is, I propose, an ambivalent cosmopolitanism inherent in the communicative structure of humanitarianism today (Yanacopulos & Smith 2007) – one that both hints at the possibility of solidarity today and simultaneously undermines this possibility. Let me, now, turn from the institutional to the political dimension of humanitarianism in order to discuss how the meaning of solidarity itself has been changing as a result of the post-Cold War collapse of ideologies.

Solidarity without 'grand narratives'

The 'Find Your Feeling' appeal employs a branding strategy that aims at 'inspiring' solidarity. Its instrumental character granted, it is nonetheless committed to cultivating a cosmopolitan disposition among its publics – the moral disposition to act benevolently on distant others without asking back. Far removed from the heroic iconographies of the Good Samaritan or the comrade-in-arms, which traditionally portray solidarity as involving strong emotions or a self-sacrificial attitude, the 'Find Your Feeling' quiz illustrates, among other things, the plasticity of solidarity as a concept that can also be portrayed in terms of minor emotions and a 'feel-good' approach to virtue. What does this plasticity tell us about the historical mutations of cosmopolitan solidarity in late modernity? What are, in other words, the meanings of solidarity and how have they changed in time?

The idea of solidarity has a long and complex genealogy (Rorty 1989;

Boltanski 1999; Eagleton 2009). In its contemporary secular form, however, solidarity dates back to the eighteenth century 'culture of sympathy', when the rise of modern capitalism generated a new moral discourse on the inherent goodness of human nature and on the importance of treating distant others not as enemies but as 'cordial strangers' (Hutchinson 1996; Hyde 1999). The founding father of the economic liberalism of modernity, Adam Smith, is an instrumental figure in this discourse in that he both celebrated benevolence towards vulnerable others as a fundamental moral property of the human psyche, in his *Theory of Moral Sentiments* (1759), and advocated the regulation of society by the amoral 'invisible hand' of commercial activity, in his *Wealth of Nations* (1776/1999; and see Shapiro 2002 for the 'Smith effect' upon western modernity).

Often referred to as 'the Adam Smith problem', this seeming contradiction between universal morality and amoralism can, in fact, be seen as a condition of possibility for modern humanitarianism, insofar as it is precisely because of the violent dynamics of market circulation, exploitation and expansion that a theory of human goodness as constitutive of the moral tissue of social life becomes not only significant but also necessary in the legitimization of colonial modernity. Indeed, Smith's economic theory, far from being a purely mathematical matter, was, as Phillipson notes, 'deeply embedded in a system of moral philosophy, jurisprudence and politics', always seeking to link economic behaviour with 'the natural wants and demands of mankind' and their consequences 'for the progress of civilization and the human mind' (2010: 217). Even though, therefore, the moral emphasis in Smith's philosophical oeuvre remains undecidedly suspended between other-oriented sympathy and self-love, what is significant about this foundational discourse on western morality is that it situates the instability of solidarity at the heart of modernity itself.

It is, I argue, this instability between humanity and inhumanity, between benevolence and violence, that has propelled the historical variations of the meaning of solidarity in the course of modernity. Two of these variations are relevant to my discussion on humanitarianism: *solidarity as salvation*, or the humanitarian solidarity of the Dunantean project, and *solidarity as revolution*, or the political solidarity of Marxian militantism. Whereas the former is associated with humanitarianism 'proper', in that it was born as a moral response to the atrocities of war and aspired to save lives and comfort suffering humanity, the latter is associated with a social critique of the conditions of suffering and aspired to change the social relations of economic exploitation that made suffering possible in the first place.

Even though both variations share a reference to the benevolent humanism of the 'culture of sympathy',[7] they differ in that solidarity as salvation remains resolutely apolitical, grounding humanitarianism on the principles of neutrality, impartiality and independence (Slim 1997, 2003; Barnett 2005), whilst solidarity as revolution is a profound radicalization of the 'culture of sympathy' that keeps the faith to human goodness but challenges the bourgeois benevolence of its capitalist roots, seeking to replace it with a new world order – one that is not regulated by self-interested markets but by the just redistribution of resources across social groups (Sen 1989; Nussbaum 1997).

Solidarity as salvation is reflected in a long tradition of humanitarian practice that today constitutes the operational infrastructure of aid in the global South. Prototypically expressed in the institution of the Red Cross (founded in 1862 after the Battle of Solferino) and subsequently the League of Nations and the United Nations (founded in 1919 and 1945 respectively), humanitarian solidarity has now come to encompass a diverse body of agencies that go beyond solidarity as relief from suffering so as to include sustainable development in their priorities (Barnett 2005; Calhoun 2009).

Solidarity as revolution, in contrast, follows a different trajectory of political struggle for social justice within and beyond the West. If solidarity in the West was institutionalized largely through the establishment of Marxist political parties and their networks of collaboration, notably the Communist International (or Comitern, 1919–1943) and the Socialist International (1889–today), solidarity beyond the West was reflected in the anti-colonial movements of the global South, in the post-WWII period up to the mid-1960s (Moyn 2010: 84–119). Articulating a political vision of emancipation from the West, which system of wealth accumulation relied on the impoverishment of colonies, the solidarity of revolution offered a powerful alternative to humanitarianism proper in that it thematized the demand for justice and hence the vision of a suffering-free humanity as an indispensable part of the moral imperative to act on vulnerable others.

Despite their profound differences, these two forms of solidarity, salvation and revolution, are nonetheless informed by similarly universal norms of morality. Humanitarian solidarity is informed by a morality of altruistic benevolence, which had both Christian and secular roots (Boltanski 1999), whilst political solidarity is informed by a morality of social justice, which relied on Marxian and anti-colonial theory (Calhoun 2009; Moyn 2010). Like all forms of universalism, however, neither of the two solidarities was ultimately able to avoid the accusation that its moral certainties were doing more harm than good to the societies they were applied to: 'solidarity', in Gilroy's words, became 'suspect' (2006: 70).

The solidarity of salvation, to begin with, has been accused of perpetuating the very suffering it sets out to comfort: 'Dunant's legacy', as Gourevich puts it, 'has hardly made war less cruel. As humanitarian action has proliferated in the century since his death, so has the agony it is supposed to alleviate' (2010: 109). Two main reasons lie at the heart of this self-defeating diagnosis of humanitarian solidarity. The first reason has to do with political interest, namely that aid agencies, despite their neutrality principle, have all too often made inappropriate compromises with corrupt regimes in order to remain operational in specific world regions (Ignatieff 2001; Terry 2002); more recently, the resort to moral argument for the use of military violence in 'new humanitarian wars', for instance in Yugoslavia, Afghanistan and Iraq, has further profoundly challenged the integrity of humanitarian ethics (de Waal 1997; Duffield 2001; Wheeler 2003; Douzinas 2007).

The second reason has to do with institutional inertia, namely that these agencies traditionally rely on organizational self-monitoring without external assessment and, therefore, tend to enjoy total immunity from accusations of failure – even in the face of evidence about their complicit participation in humanitarian catastrophes – for instance, the Congo (1993–2003) or Rwanda atrocities (1994). Insofar as all evaluations rely on their own accounts of events, no formal distribution of responsibility to aid agencies can take place: 'As far as I am aware,' Polman has recently remarked, 'no aid worker or aid organization has ever been dragged before the courts for failures or mistakes, let alone for complicity in crimes committed by rebels or regimes' (2010: 106). The consequence is, as Kennedy argues, that, despite its often harmful practices, 'humanitarianism tempts to hubris, to an idolatry about our intentions and routines, to the conviction that we know more than we do about what justice can be' (2004: xviii).

The solidarity of revolution, in a different manner, also turned out to perpetuate the injustice it sought to eliminate and, in so doing, it has also ultimately reproduced the structures it promised to change. Critiques of Marxism, on the one hand, focus on the ways in which its totalizing narratives of social change construe the non-West as a savage 'Other' and, thereby, reproduce the symbolic domination of the global South by its western 'saviours' – even as the latter claims to liberate the former (Said 1993, 2002). A reflection of broader scepticism towards Marxian universalism, this orientalist critique draws on postmodern sensibilities that celebrate difference and locality to challenge the ways in which Marxism becomes divorced from the particularities of non-western contexts and, in so doing, tends to impose rather than co-construct projects of change in the South: 'most Marxists', as Corbridge puts it, echoing the sceptical argument, 'trade an armchair understanding of development issues for a commitment to local development initiatives born of a participatory research framework' (1993: 454). Critiques of neocolonialism, on the other hand, similarly emphasize the political violence inherent in revolutionary universalism but tend to focus less on the biases of Marxian theory and more on the failure of its emancipatory project itself and the continuing dependence of the South on the West. Their emphasis falls, in particular, on the ways in which the new regimes of the decolonized South perpetuate structures of western domination, whilst safeguarding the 'grotesque' power of the local sovereigns in these newly founded states (Mbembe 1992, 2001; Abrahamsen 2003).

Ultimately, what these critiques of universalism towards both forms of solidarity – salvation and revolution – problematize is the traditional relationship between politics and solidarity. The former, the critique of salvation, points to the fact that there can be no pure humanitarianism, in that all choices to save lives are ultimately political choices about which suffering is worth alleviating and who is to blame for it: 'the humanitarian act', as Orbinksi put it, upon receiving the Nobel prize for Médicins Sans Frontières, 'is the most apolitical of all acts, but if action and its morality are taken seriously, it has the most profound of political implications. And the fight against impunity is one of those implications.'[8] This politicization of the solidarity of salvation, echoed in MSF's 'ethics of refusal' to remain silent in the face of injustice but also reflected in the post-Cold War implication of armed conflict in humanitarian projects, has today undermined the moral certainty of humanitarianism as a pure ethic of salvation: 'humanitarianism's "politics" are now more visible', as Barnett and Weiss say, 'and the relationship between humanitarianism and power is now more complex' than ever before (2008: 38).

It is, at least partly, in response to the redefinition of the morality of salvation as ultimately a political morality that the field has sought to instrumentalize its institutional practices through scientific methodologies and, in so doing, to sustain the claim that its practices remain neutral, beyond political interest. Rather than succeeding, however, humanitarianism is today accused of a double compromise – not only of being 'undertaken in a variety of circumstances that challenge its moral clarity' but, as Calhoun observes, also of being undertaken 'in complex organizations that demand instrumental orientations to action' (2008: 96).

In parallel to this attempt to defend the depoliticization of the solidarity of salvation, there is a simultaneous marginalization of the politics of justice in the solidarity of revolution. Symptomatic of the post-Cold War decline of narratives of social change, the retreat from justice has its roots in the New Left, which, already in the late 1960s, challenged its 'Marxist predecessors' precisely for being 'guilty . . . of inhumane behaviour in the name of the revolution and the better society that awaits humanity in the far-off, distant future' (Rifkin 2009: 416). The significance of this position, to be radicalized in the post-Cold War era, is not only historical, in that it produced a scathing attack on the inhumanity of the Soviet model of social justice, but, importantly, intellectual, in that it replaced the Marxian critique of class injustice with a new focus on the human condition – what Boltanski and Chiapello call, a 'critique of authenticity' (2005).

Fully resonating with, albeit not restricted to, the postmodernist celebration of the death of meta-narratives, this intellectual shift towards 'authenticity' rather than social justice further signals a new political focus not on the suffering society as a pathology of the capitalist system but on the suffering self as a generalized pathology of all systems of power: 'Loneliness, estrangement, isolation describe the vast distance between man and man today . . . We oppose the depersonalization that reduces human beings to the status of things. If anything, the brutalities of the twentieth century teach us that means and ends are intimately related, that vague appeals to "posterity" cannot justify the mutilations of the present . . .' (Roszak 1995: 58, cited in Rifkin 2009: 416).

What this move from justice to authenticity suggests is that solidarity as a vision of a suffering-free society is now replaced by a humbler vision of simply managing the present, in a non-heroic pursuit of pleasures for the self. Our moral disposition towards vulnerable others, we may hypothesize, consequently also changes orientation from 'the worldwide ideological struggle that called forth daring, courage, imagination and idealism', as Fukuyama had put it, towards an orientation to 'economic calculation, the endless solving of technical problems . . . and the satisfaction of sophisticated consumer demands' (1989: 2). The instrumentalization of the solidarity of salvation, in other words, may today be combined with an equally forceful instrumentalization of the solidarity of revolution, where self-interest and individual pleasure take precedence over the demand for justice.

Yet, even though contemporary solidarity may depart from the moral certainties of saving lives or changing society, it nonetheless retains a deep commitment to the suffering of distant strangers. The 'Find Your Feeling' appeal, let us recall, may be focusing on our emotions but does so in order to invite us to engage with ActionAid's proposal for solidarity. The question of this book becomes, in this light, a question of how the solidarity of neoliberal capitalism, a solidarity without moral certainties but with a continuing commitment to act on human vulnerability, may look today.

Drawing on Moyn's historical argument, I hypothesize that this void of universal ethics produces a new morality of solidarity that is resolutely 'anti-political', in that it replaces the other-oriented solidarities of the past with an individualist morality of 'feel good' activism. Moyn approaches this post-Cold War morality from the perspective of human rights, so as to argue that the neutral character of human rights has now conveniently replaced the impasses of salvation and revolution with a new discourse – one that relegitimizes humanitarianism as a series of 'individual entitlements' at the cost, however, of ignoring 'the relevance of economic and larger structural relationships for the realization of those entitlements' (2010: 225).

Similarly to Moyn's subjects of solidarity, who are treated as individual holders of rights disembedded from structures of injustice, I argue that the publics of solidarity, too, are today called to enact solidarity as an individualist project of contingent values and consumerist activisms – ironic solidarity being precisely a solidarity that, in recognizing the limits of its own legitimacy and efficacy, avoids politics and rewards the self. Even though, as I discuss in my concluding chapter, the philosophical contours of this emerging practice of solidarity has been imaginatively conceptualized in Rorty's seminal treatise on irony as a condition of solidarity as early as 1989, the precise content of this practice, its articulation with the market and technology as well as its implications for public morality, have not as yet become the focus of critical inquiry.

In order to explore this new practice, I take my point of departure in the two key historical moments of the communication of solidarity – the Cold War moment, which I flexibly define as the period between the late 1970s to the end of the 1980s, and the contemporary moment, which I define as the period between 2005 and now – and ask the question of how the proposals to solidarity that each moment of humanitarianism puts forward differ from one another and how they remain similar. It is, as I argue in chapter 2, in this search for discontinuities as well as continuities in the communicative logic of appeals, celebrities, concerts and news that the question of solidarity can become the object of our reflexive analysis and critique.

The technologization of communication

The question of solidarity and its historical mutations, it follows, cannot be examined separately from the communicative structure that has made this moral discourse available to us in the first place. The 'Find Your Feeling' appeal, to return to our example, is interesting precisely because its structure does not resemble earlier proposals to solidarity in at least two ways. First, it uses the interactive affordances of the internet so as to talk about distant others, yet it ultimately communicates something about 'us', and second, it invites us to connect with the ActionAid website as a response to the question of 'what to do', yet it avoids the question of 'why we should act'. It is these two features, the invitation to self-expression and the absence of normative morality which, I suggest, define the technologization of humanitarianism today. Let me address each of them in turn, before I reformulate anew the main concerns of my research.

The first, the *invitation to self-expression*, is a key feature of new media, in that digital technologies have provided the necessary infrastructure to turn media users into producers, rather than only consumers, of public communication. Whereas the ActionAid appeal capitalized on the interactive potential of online sites to generate personalized profiles of its users, other practices of humanitarian communication rely on mobile phones, blogs and convergent journalism platforms to involve increasingly more people in the production of their messages. The technologization of solidarity refers, in this sense, to the capacity of digital media to incorporate the moral imperative to act on vulnerable others within digital platforms that render solidarity a matter of tweeting personal emotion, downloading the message of our favourite celebrity, web-streaming our preferred Live 8 bands, clicking on the donation link of ActionAid or clicking 'like' on a Facebook wall (Fenton 2007, 2008 for the ambivalence of new media solidarity).

It is this capacity of the new media to engage people in unprecedented forms of public self-presentation that, according to Rifkin, has defined our 'empathic civilization' as simultaneously the age of a 'new dramaturgical consciousness' – the consciousness of our capacity to act ourselves out in front of unknown others (2009: 555–60; see also Thumim 2009). Dramaturgical consciousness becomes, in this account, paramount in the formation of cosmopolitan dispositions, precisely because the planetary connectivity of the new media have now turned the world into a new *theatrum mundi* – a theatre whose moralizing force lies in the fact that we do not only passively watch distant others but we can also enter their own reality as actors: 'the whole world might be a stage,' Rifkin says, echoing the Shakespearean metaphor, 'but during the twentieth century most of the people were in the audience, whereas in the twenty-first century everyone is onstage and in front of the spotlights, thanks to YouTube, MySpace, Facebook, the blogosphere, etc.' (2009: 555).

Whilst the quality of cosmopolitan dispositions that the digital media are able to mobilize is fiercely debated, what interests me here is the fact that the cosmopolitanizing potential of these media relies on their capacity to act both as sites of self-expression *and* as sites of spectatorship: 'Young people today', Rifkin continues his description of the West as an empathic civilization, 'are *in front of the screen or on the screen*, spending much of their waking day in virtual worlds where they are scripting multiple stories, directing their own performances, and choreographing virtually every aspect of their lives – hoping that millions of others will log on and follow along' (2009: 558, emphasis added; see Livingstone 2008 for adolescent self-expression in new media).

In blurring the boundaries between watching and acting, self-expression challenges the modern, theatrical conception of moral education that, grounded as it was on the Enlightenment idea that virtue is to be cultivated through secular institutions, depended precisely on the act of watching and presupposed a strict separation between those who act and those who observe the actors (Marshall 1984; Gullace 1993). This new challenge of self-expression resonates well with the orientalist critique of the theatre, which similarly claims that the spectacle of the vulnerable other reproduces objectified perceptions of the non-West and operates as a site of western domination: 'the Orient', as Said has argued, 'seems to be, not an unlimited extension beyond the familiar European world, but rather a closed field, a theatrical stage affixed to Europe' (2002: 27). It is, partly, in response to such theoretical critiques of humanitarian communication as a mechanism of 'othering' that self-expression has emerged, thematizing the self as a key dimension of its moral discourse.

At the same time, this humanitarian turn to self-expression is also a practical response to compassion fatigue, the public's apathy towards traditional iconographies of suffering. Demonstrating a high degree of institutional reflexivity, as Vestergaard (2010) argues, major INGOs are today experimenting with a new aesthetics of solidarity that, in line with market research, is driven by the preferences of public polling – as, for instance, in ActionAid: 'The charity's direction', as Richard Turner said in 2009, speaking of the new emotionality of appeals, 'is the result of extensive consultation with donors and focus groups.'

Self-expression is, in this sense, an ambivalent development. From the perspective of theoretical critique, it is welcome in that it introduces an inclusive, *anti*-theatrical (though by no means non-theatrical), model of moral education, which allows for a radical fluidity of theatrical positions and so enables a new plurality of voices and images to be heard and seen, in the West. This anti-theatrical model avoids the risks of 'othering' in that, as ActionAid puts it, it 'is leading us to a place where when we show a photograph we want to be able to tell you who that person is, what the context is and get across that they are having to get through quite extraordinary issues related to poverty – but in a way that's inspiring' (Turner).[9]

However, self-expressive communication is simultaneously driven by the interests of the aid and development market, which takes the emotionality of the donor, rather than the vulnerability of the distant other, as a key motivation for solidarity – and isn't 'Find Your Feeling' an 'inspiration'-based appeal that evokes the need of others by speaking about us? In reproducing the asymmetry of the digital divide in the distribution and use of new technologies, this market can be accused of setting up a predominantly western stage of mass self-communication (Castells 2009), which simply confronts us with multiple images of people like 'us'.

In the context of a highly instrumentalized field of humanitarianism, my hypothesis is, therefore, that the invitation to self-expression may claim to be about challenging orientalism, yet, insofar as it does not allow the other to be seen and heard, it may primarily serve its own ends – sustaining consumer loyalty and, in the longer run, steady profits for its agencies: 'Long-term results from ActionAid and Save the Children strategies will be a long time coming, but for now both organizations are optimistic that their approach will keep their donors on board'.[10]

My approach to the technologization of solidarity is, consequently, one of sceptical optimism, enabling me to explore the communicative structure of humanitarianism in terms of the fundamental ambivalence I have just outlined. On the one hand, I accept that the new media habituate us into mundane cosmopolitanizing acts, by enabling us to get selectively engaged with momentary but efficient forms of online activism – from signing a petition to donating money; in so doing, they may be encouraging what Schudson calls 'monitorial citizenship', a mode of citizenship that no longer relies on our physical presence or sustained commitment to common affairs but on a more fragile and fleeting public sensibility characterized by simply being 'watchful even while [we are] doing something else' (1998: 311).

On the other hand, I suspect that the new media may simultaneously undermine cosmopolitan morality in that, by rendering the West both the actor and the spectator of its own performances, they marginalize the voice of distant others in favour of a narcissistic indulgence in the authenticity of the self. In a similar vein, Papacharissi draws upon Williams's (1984) definition of mobile privatization, that is, the ability of the media to bring the unfamiliar into the comfort zone of our home, so as to argue that cosmopolitanism today may be enacted as part of a private sphere of individual self-expression – 'a technologically enabled mobile private sphere of thought, expression and reaction' that, rather than facilitating our encounter with human vulnerability, is primarily, 'in search of our ultimate autonomy and expression' (2010: 136).

This ambivalence of technologized solidarity becomes a politically significant object of study if we simultaneously approach the reflexive aesthetics of humanitarianism as also a manifestation of the ethical impasses of solidarity, in both its narratives – salvation and revolution. Relevant here is *the absence of an explicit message of solidarity* in the 'Find Your Feeling' appeal – the second feature of technologization I wish to address. A key characteristic of this appeal, as I said, is not only that it relies on self-expression and marginalizes the voice of vulnerable others but also that it invites us to visit the ActionAid website and, in so doing, it engages us with a brand rather than the cause of solidarity.

Motivated, again, by the diagnosis of compassion fatigue, this focus on the brand capitalizes on the mature market of humanitarianism, so as to take our familiarity with major INGOs for granted and avoid explicit messages of solidarity that may fuel suspicion towards grand narratives – for instance, towards the solidarity of salvation through iconographies of starving babies (McLagan 2003; Vestergaard 2010). Yet, even though branding builds upon a rather confident view of western publics as already familiar with the morality of solidarity, the engagement of these publics with specific humanitarian brands can by no means be taken for granted. This is because, as recent UK-based research shows, western publics may accept that helping the poor is our 'human obligation' but, at the same time, appear reluctant to prioritize poverty in the South over poverty at home and, in fact, provide support, albeit limited, to cuts in humanitarian aid; such results, as Henson and Lindstrom put it, 'are, on the one hand, quite heartening. Even in times of austerity' they argue, 'there are quite strong views that we have a moral obligation to help the poor in the world. On the other', they continue, 'when it comes to support for spending on aid, such values appear to be undermined by domestic priorities . . . the view seems to be that when times are tough, we cannot afford to waste money and must focus on problems closer to home' (2010: 3).

In the context of this fragile 'existing cosmopolitanism' (Beck 2006), it is crucial, I believe, to explore the practices by which the instrumentalization of humanitarian communication, including product branding like ActionAid's, but also the use of rock stars in 'Make Poverty History', the recruitment of Hollywood celebrity in the UN's Millennium Development Goals and the promotion of citizen journalism in the BBC's disaster reporting, may be contributing to changing the meaning of solidarity, today. It is, I hypothesize, by promoting Angelina Jolie's confessions, Bono's charisma, the personal opinion of a citizen 'produser' or the 'warm and fuzzy' emotions of the ActionAid consumer as the new messages of solidarity that contemporary humanitarianism may deprive us not only of the voice of vulnerable others but also of moral discourse that would link vulnerability to justice.

The process of technologization is, in this context, no longer simply a matter of the media platforms that carry the message but also a matter of what Foucault calls the 'technologies of the self' that the publics of solidarity are invited to engage with – that is the practices of feeling, thinking and acting that these publics are mundanely socialized in so as to become certain types of citizens rather than others (1988).

One of the most pervasive technologies of the self, the theatre, has historically functioned as a force of moral education, precisely through what Aristotle calls the force of 'habituation' – the subtle but sustained socialization of its audience into the civic dispositions of the polis (Aristotle, *Nicomachean Ethics*, Book II). Organized around the historical figures of the sufferer, the persecutor and the benefactor, the theatrical model, let us recall, articulates the moral discourses of solidarity by mobilizing a politics of pity (Boltanski 1999) – strategic choices of representation, where the spectacle of distant suffering either evokes the tender-heartedness characteristic of the solidarity of salvation, by focusing on the benefactor who alleviates the suffering, or induces indignation characteristic of the solidarity of revolution, by focusing on the persecutor.

The contemporary shift from theatrical to anti-theatrical communication is, in this context, also a shift in the technologies of the self through which humanitarianism habituates its publics into the civic disposition of solidarity. Rather than a minor mutation, however, I argue that this is an epistemic shift that challenges the foundations of the 'culture of sympathy' and its politics of representation. It is, as I show in chapter 7, a shift from the paradigm of *pity*, where solidarity is anchored on the spectacle of the other, inspiring the normative moralities of salvation or revolution, towards the paradigm of *irony*, where solidarity is anchored instead on the spectacle of others like us, inviting our capacity for self-reflection. Even though the paradigm of irony is in no way ruptural, in the sense of fully replacing the paradigm of pity (traditional iconographies coexist, indeed, with more novel ones), the proliferation of anti-theatrical practices does suggest that a different process of moralization is becoming available, if not dominant, in the humanitarian imaginary of the West – one that abandons issues of otherness and justice in favour of a new emotionality of the self.

The question that this book addresses becomes, in this sense, a question of *how* the technologization of humanitarian communication, both as digital platforms and as proposals for moral subjectivity, changes the ways in which the West is today invited to perform solidarity. If, following Henson and Lindstrom's recommendations for INGO communication, 'longer-term and concerted efforts are required to raise awareness of global issues and reorientate value systems towards personal responsibilities' (2010: 3), then it is urgent to explore how exactly the anti-theatrical model might be contributing to the reorientation of our value systems and what this might imply for our public morality. The ironic solidarity of self-expression may be our historical response to the decline of grand narratives, yet, we must wonder, does solidarity need to collapse into narcissistic spectatorship, under the seductive pressure of a global market of aid, or can we still imagine new ways of being cosmopolitan citizens?

The ethics of objectivity

The historical transformation of solidarity, I have argued so far, is a complex matter that should be approached in its institutional, political and technological dimensions. Whilst it is impossible to produce a perfect narrative that encompasses all three in equal measure, my ambition is rather to study the communicative practices of humanitarianism as sites of articulation, where all three dimensions intersect with and overdetermine one another, in ways that variously come to define solidarity, at different points in time.

Exercising a hermeneutics of suspicion, albeit one that looks upon power as a productive rather than a purely negative force of public life, this book takes its point of departure in key popular practices of humanitarian communication through which solidarity is performed in our culture. It aims to trace down the ways in which changing performances of solidarity also reflect changing articulations of the market, politics and technology.

This focus on communication is of course not new. The humanitarian field has always focused on the impact of its messages on public attitudes to solidarity – for instance, in the reflexive aesthetics of inspiration-oriented rather than needs-based discourse. More often than not, however, such concerns have failed to go beyond the instrumental question of how to maximize donor funding and address the real question of how the communication of solidarity may shape longer-term perceptions of the West as a moral actor. This neglect of the performative force of humanitarian communication, not only in the direct sense of acting out dispositions of solidarity but, in so doing, also in the sense of producing the publics it addresses rather than simply referring to them as pre-existing bodies of spectators, has given rise to a 'persistent problem' in the field: the problem of engagement. Whilst, according to research, INGO donations have today reached an all-time high, the quality of public engagement with questions of development appears to have fallen to its lowest point ever: 'the disjuncture between the two sets of data [donations/ engagement]', Darnton comments, 'sparks some serious questions about how long the prevailing business model for development NGOs can continue, and what the implications are for the quality of public engagement' (2011: 13).

The humanitarian field rightly approaches the problem of engagement as a communication problem, seeking to replace the 'transaction' model of communication with a 'values' model and so to introduce new interpretative 'frames' for its messages of solidarity (Darnton with Martin 2011). My view is, however, that the paradox of engagement cannot be addressed simply by shifting around the wording of messages or moving across a continuum of given values. Far from underestimating the power of words, what I suggest is that the morality of solidarity requires a more holistic understanding of humanitarian communication – one that takes its point of departure in the historical shift from the solidarity of pity to the solidarity of irony.

At the heart of this historical account lies a deeper concern with the systemic paradox of humanitarianism, that is, the fact that global inequality, which humanitarianism seeks to alleviate, is simultaneously its very condition of possibility – or its inhuman condition, to recall Cheah's formulation. Whereas this systemic paradox forcefully brings up the demand for a new world order that is founded on the principle of justice, a demand extensively explored in critical scholarship on development, my own argument is that this demand for justice needs to be reintroduced in the communicative apparatus of humanitarianism, too. The paradox of public engagement with vulnerable others, in other words, should be addressed not through the neoliberal strategies of branding or show business but through a new morality of solidarity that challenges the systemic paradox of humanitarianism and seeks to change its inhuman conditions.

Crucial to the formulation of such morality is the *theatricality* of humanitarian communication, that is, the capacity of this communication to stage human vulnerability as an object of our empathy as well as of critical reflection and deliberation. Theatricality, as I explain in chapter 2, refers to a communicative structure that does not necessarily belong to the theatre but operates in line with the conventions of theatrical performance – namely by distancing the spectator from the spectacle of the vulnerable other through the objective space of the stage (or any other framing device) whilst, at the same time, enabling proximity between the two through narrative and visual resources that invite our empathetic judgement towards the spectacle: 'More than a property with analyzable characteristics,' as Feral argues, 'theatricality seems to be a process that has to do with a "gaze" that postulates and creates a distinct, virtual space belonging to the other' (2002: 97). If, following my hypothesis, humanitarian communication today capitalizes on late modernity's capacity for thoughtful contemplation of the human condition only in order to collapse the other onto the self, then, I argue, we must now insist on reclaiming the objectivity of the theatre – and, with it, the irreducible otherness of distant suffering that exists beyond us and makes a demand not in the name of an authentic self but in the name of justice.[11]

This is important. Given that the global South is primarily known to us through acts of communication, which themselves rarely originate outside the West, we need to fully recognize the performative power of humanitarianism – its power, that is, to constitute vulnerable others as worthy or unworthy of our emotion, reflection and action. It is precisely this power to speak in the voices of distant others, what Chandler calls 'democracy by articulation' (as opposed to 'democracy by representation'; 2009: 7), which obliges us to reflect on the close relationship between the market, the politics and the technology of humanitarianism. 'Finding our feeling' or following celebrities-on-Twitter may enable some contact with these others but such practices may also mislead us to believe that we can become cosmopolitans simply by getting in touch with ourselves. *Pace*, then, Rifkin's claim that the dramaturgical consciousness of the new media places this demand for authenticity, for expressing one's own feelings about others, at the heart of our empathic civilization (2009: 564), I would insist that it is not authenticity but objectivity, seeing suffering others as human others and recognizing ourselves as actors upon their suffering, which must become central in our public culture.

To this end, I take my point of departure in Arendt's metaphor of the public realm as an agonistic 'space of appearance', where different performances of vulnerability are played out, so as to make a case for the importance of the theatre in the moral experience of modernity. It is precisely this possibility of seeing and being seen, central not only in Arendt but also in Smith's theatrical morality, that ultimately defines how we relate to distant others. Despite their difference around the role of emotions in catalysing civic dispositions, both agree that theatrical spectatorship mobilizes the faculty of imagination – namely our capacity to see the world from other people's standpoints as well as our capacity to imagine how we might act on these others' predicament.

Unlike Arendt, however, who rejects empathy as a private emotion in favour of reflexive judgement (1958/1998), I would insist, with Smith, that empathy is a constitutive dimension of public life that enables, rather than corrupts, civic sensibilities – provided that it is combined with judgement so as not to collapse into narcissistic emotion (Chouliaraki 2006). It is Smith's theory of 'sympathetic identification' that comes, therefore, to flesh out my theatrical conception of humanitarianism, based, on the one hand, on our imaginative capacity to feel for vulnerable strangers (Smith's involved spectator) and, on the other, on our imaginative capacity to observe ourselves as actors upon their suffering (Smith's impartial spectator and Arendt's reflexive judgement).[12]

Rather than stories about us, I conclude, humanitarian communication should open up this space of performance, where distant others can be seen and heard but also where we are all able to consider the question of why we should act on their vulnerability – a question that makes the critique of power and the pursuit of justice a part of our public practice of solidarity. This proposal still draws on the legacy of the 'culture of sympathy', but without relying on its moral certainties, salvation or revolution. Instead of attaching to solidarity a specific kind of truth, the agonistic paradigm treats justice as our minimum 'common pursuit' that recognizes certain shared presumptions about what it is like to be a human being and conceives of solidarity as a political, rather than a consumerist, project: 'We could have been creatures incapable of sympathy, unmoved by the pain and humiliation of others, uncaring of freedom and – no less significant – unable to reason, argue, disagree and concur,' Sen argues; yet, he continues, 'the strong presence of these features in human lives . . . does indicate that the general pursuit of justice might be hard to eradicate in human society, even though we can go about that pursuit in different ways' (2009: 415). Anchored on our fundamental human abilities both to empathize and to judge, then, my view of solidarity is less about branding and more about our systematic and explicit engagement with the voices of vulnerability and the values that may inform our action upon it.

Conclusion: on this book

This is a book that strongly defends the role that humanitarianism continues to play in sustaining a public ethos of solidarity with vulnerable others beyond the West. It is, simultaneously, an equally strong note of caution against the increasing instrumentalization of the humanitarian field and the neoliberal hegemony of its morality of solidarity. Such caution is not meant to advocate a return to the grand narratives of solidarity, an impossible argument today, but seeks to rethink the relationship between humanitarianism and politics.

Even though humanitarianism has long been suspended between apolitical benevolence, in the solidarity of salvation, and radical militantism, in the solidarity of revolution, I have argued that it is today becoming more politicized than ever. If the instrumentalization of solidarity is an individualist response that denies this politicization, agonistic discourse is an alternative response that replaces the solidarity of irony, so readily incorporated in the neoliberal rhetoric of the media market, with a persistent pursuit of the meaning of justice. My own contribution to this proposal is to provide a critical analysis of the solidarity of irony, in its major public manifestations, and to offer a fresh theorization of the theatre as a crucial communicative structure of our culture. It is to this theorization of the theatre that I now turn before I begin telling the story of the four key practices of the imaginary: appeals, celebrity, concerts and news.

2 The Humanitarian Imaginary

Introduction: communicating vulnerability

From the Korem camp in Ethiopia to the Abu Ghraib prison and from the Asian tsunami to the Haiti earthquake, ongoing debates about how vulnerable others are represented in the West illustrate the significance of spectacles of suffering in our public culture. By problematizing the ways in which human misfortune is mediated in this culture, such debates presuppose that spectacles of suffering have the power to move us into action; and in posing the question of 'what to do' in the face of mediated suffering, these debates further work on the assumption that not only is it good but also possible to do something for those others who, by virtue of being mediated, will remain forever strangers to us (Silverstone 2007). In this dual sense of moral obligation, not only as something desirable but also as something 'doable', the spectacle of human vulnerability raises the question of cosmopolitan solidarity – of the disposition to act towards vulnerable others without the anticipation of reciprocation.

It is this focus on the vulnerability of the human body as the clearest manifestation of our common humanity that has historically informed the emergence of humanitarianism in the West (Halttunen 1995). A catalyst in the establishment of global justice structures, the discourse on corporeal vulnerability has also been instrumental in the long-term civilizing process of western modernity, contributing to the formation of solidarity bonds within and beyond the West (Cmiel 1999). Indeed, if solidarity articulates our moral commitment to act on vulnerable others by reference to our communities of belonging, *cosmopolitan* solidarity, in particular, relies upon the *universality* of vulnerability to broaden its conception of community beyond particular bonds of belonging and towards the human species as a whole (Gilroy 2004, 2006; Linklater 2007a,b).

Yet, whereas the mediation of vulnerability, in the age of global technologies, has been regarded as a catalyst for the cosmopolitanization of solidarity, as I argued in chapter 1, mediation has simultaneously been held accountable for failing to represent vulnerability as a cause for solidarity beyond the West. The proliferation of technological images and stories about vulnerable others, critics argue, deprive suffering of its moral urgency and ultimately leads to generalized suspicion or even apathy amongst media publics (for an overview, see Chouliaraki 2006). This scepticism towards mediation comes to contribute to a dystopian argument on the possibility of solidarity, which rests on the diagnosis that the media commodify distant suffering and, in so doing, transform other-oriented dispositions to action into a cynical hyper-individualism (Moeller 1999; Cohen 2001).

My own argument is that, even though solidarity is undergoing profound transformations under new economic, political and technological pressures, the question of what solidarity comes to look like today is still an open matter that urgently requires our analytical attention. To this end, I take my point of departure on humanitarianism as a historically specific articulation of cosmopolitan solidarity, which acts directly on the global South through specialized institutions (IOs and INGOs), yet seeks legitimacy in the West through a communicative structure that disseminates moral discourses of care and responsibility.

It is, in particular, the communicative structure of the theatre that functions as a form of moral education in the West, by mundanely mediating the foundational moral claim of solidarity through a variety of spectacles of suffering. And it is, I argue, by analysing these spectacles of human vulnerability available in the theatrical structure of solidarity that we may be able to say something important about transformations of solidarity in our times and about the implications of such transformations for cosmopolitan ethics. I develop this argument in three moves.

I first introduce a historical account of the theatricality of humanitarianism as a constitutive element of western public culture and, as a second move, I provide a critical overview of dominant social and cultural theories that, in their *tout court* denunciation of mediation, prematurely deny the moralizing potential of spectacles of suffering. In response, I formulate an alternative account of mediated public life, what I call the 'humanitarian imaginary', which proposes a different analytical approach for the study of humanitarian communication – one that allows both for subtler understandings of the historical transformations of solidarity and for more effective forms of critique towards these transformations.

The theatricality of humanitarianism

Humanitarianism has traditionally been founded on a theatrical arrangement that separates safe spectators from vulnerable others and communicates its moral message through the staging of spectacles of suffering. This is because humanitarianism derives its force from the heartbreaking spectacles of human suffering (think, for instance, of Goya's 'Disasters of War', 1807–14, or Ut's 'Vietnam Napalm', 1972), which are made available for all to witness as potential benefactors. Contemporary citizenship largely depends on this moral acknowledgement of unfortunate others who, in being shown to suffer, mobilize the West as a public – a collectivity with the will to act. On the other hand, by virtue of the gap between zones of suffering and western publics, these spectacles of suffering simultaneously separate those who watch at a distance from those who act on the spot.

Reflected in the global distribution of labour between an acting body of institutions involved in humanitarian work and a monitoring civil society, this theatrical arrangement, far from being inevitable, arose as a historically specific response to the management of suffering as a problem of modern western polity (Calhoun 2009). And even though the current world order may be unthinkable without it, this conception of humanitarian politics remains fragile insofar as the ethics of vulnerability at the heart of its constitution suggests that, whilst action remains in the hands of the few, it is the millions who watch at a distance that confer upon it its true legitimacy (Alleyne 2005; Albrow & Seckinelgin 2011).

It is this arrangement of separation that tends to organize the social relationships of humanitarianism around a theatrical conception of communication. Rather than inviting these publics to engage in direct action, which is inevitably impossible, theatrical communication invites us to engage in performances, that is, staged images and stories about action and, thereby, enables us to imagine ourselves as citizens who can act at a distance, by speaking out (through protest or petition) and by paying (through donation) in the name of a moral cause (for a discussion, see Chouliaraki 2006). By the same token, it is this repertoire of staged images and stories about distant suffering that comes to legitimize the imperative to act on vulnerable others as the moral order of modernity – what I later theorize as its 'humanitarian imaginary'.

A constitutive dimension of the theatrical structure of humanitarianism, the imaginary relies, therefore, on 'aspirational' practices of emotion and action: practices that, *performed* as they are by those few who already appear to act within the zones of suffering, become, simultaneously, *performative* of the many who watch at a distance, in that they ultimately seek to shape the moral dispositions of those many towards the misfortune of vulnerable others.

Mapped onto the broader asymmetry between the affluent West and a developing South, what I earlier called the systemic paradox of humanitarianism, this theatrical arrangement renders the mediation of suffering itself a paradoxical affair that threatens to undermine the ethical dispositions it intends to cultivate. The first paradox of humanitarian communication is grounded on the claim that, whereas the spectacle of suffering aims at inviting a moral response, its mediated nature weakens the truth of suffering and may undermine rather than intensify moral commitment. The second paradox of humanitarian communication is grounded on the claim that, whilst it speaks the language of common humanity, the spectacle of vulnerability simultaneously evokes the language of power, and thus tends to reproduce existing global divides rather than propose bonds of solidarity beyond the West. To both these paradoxes, critical theory responds with a pessimistic narrative that leaves little or no ground for the promise of cosmopolitan solidarity.

It is the nature of these paradoxes and the interventions of critical theory that I review in the following two sections, entitled respectively 'Theatre and moral education' and 'Solidarity and political power', before I conclude with the need to revisit the paradoxes of humanitarianism as productive tensions that may open up a new imagination of cosmopolitan solidarity.

Theatre and moral education

The theatricality of humanitarianism is anchored on the view that the spectacle of suffering mobilizes a certain array of emotions that are constitutive of the moral tissue of western public life (Marshall 1984; Nussbaum 2003). Emerging, though not originating, in eighteenth-century Europe, this view is informed by a sceptical epistemology of spectatorship, according to which the disposition of solidarity does not automatically arise as a consequence of the sight of suffering as such, but inheres instead within a particular communicative structure of suffering – a structure that manages to incite the spectators' 'sympathetic identification' with the sufferer and make specific proposals as to what we can do to alleviate the sufferer's pain. It is, in other words, only certain spectacles that can act as a moralizing force on western publics.

This is a view that originates in the classical conception of Greek tragedy as 'dramatic action' seeking to evoke 'pity and fear' amongst those who watch the 'misfortunes of men [sic]' (Aristotle, *Poetics*, book XIV) and reappears with a vengeance in early modern Europe through a renewed, though not uncontroversial, appreciation of the role of staged action as a catalyst for solidarity – for example, in Smith's *Theory of Moral Sentiments* (1759) and Hume's 'Of Tragedy' (1777/1993). It is our capacity for imagination, the argument has it, that sets in motion the moralizing process amongst viewing publics. This is because imagination, that is, the capacity to momentarily place ourselves in the sufferer's condition, enables a fleeting transfer of emotion as if the suffering were our own, and can potentially lead to action: 'by the imagination,' as Smith argued, 'we place ourselves in his [sic] situation, we conceive ourselves enduring all the same torments, we enter as it were into his body, and become in some measure the same person with him' (1759: 9).

This moralizing potential of sympathetic identification constitutes, indeed, the most important legacy of the theatre as a pedagogic institution, ever since the tragic plays of classical Athens exposed citizens to spectacles of suffering with a view to cultivating virtuous modes of being in the 'polis' (Wasserman 1947; Marshall 1984; Williams 1973). The pedagogical principle of these spectacles is that 'the viewing of pitiable and fearful things and our response of pity and fear themselves', as Nussbaum puts it, 'can serve to show us something of importance about the human good' (1986: 388).

Despite the role of the theatre in teaching us something about the human good, however, the theatre has always been the object of intense controversy. This is, sceptics claim, because the theatrical evocation of emotion may exhaust itself to the experience of feelings of 'pity and fear' without promoting moral virtue – sentimental education, in other words, may not necessarily lead to moral education. This opposition, which was originally formulated between Plato's anti-theatricalism and Aristotle's defence of tragedy, reappears in early modern Europe, where it is now played out upon a parallel (though not similar) conception of publicness as *theatrum mundi* – a metaphor that has been both intensely celebrated and fiercely opposed (Christian 1987). The early modern theatrical controversy is best illustrated in the exchange between D'Alembert's optimistic view of the theatre as providing exemplary modes of behaviour in everyday life and Rousseau's sceptical view of the inauthenticity of theatrical acting as leading to the corruption of moral sensibilities (for a discussion, see Sennett 1977). More recently, the twentieth century rise of anti-theatricalism, through Nietzsche, Fried and Benjamin, marks yet another moment of controversy around the moral value of the theatre, pointing, as Puchner claims, 'towards a larger, if also more diffuse, anti-theatrical tendency operative within the period of modernism' (2002: 3–4).

What these controversies suggest is that the ambivalence over the theatre, which continues to inform debates of humanitarian spectacle to date, is not simply the outcome of a persistent disagreement that happens to emerge at different points in time. Ambivalence is, rather, an inherent property of the communicative structure of the theatre, caught as it is in an impossible duality: both responsible for cultivating the ethico-political dispositions of the polis and simultaneously culpable of producing narcissistic emotion; in Boltanski's words, offering both 'a way of looking which can be characterized as disinterested or altruistic, one which is oriented outwards and wishes to see suffering ended, and one which is, selfishly, wholly taken up with the internal states aroused by the spectacle of suffering: fascination, interest, excitement, pleasure, etc.' (1999: 21).

Contemporary debate on the spectacle continues to be defined by this ambivalence, what I below refer to as the *paradox of authenticity*, thereby placing theatre under the constant pressure of inventing new narrative repertoires, new genres of representation and new claims to legitimacy (Puchner 2002). The historical trajectory of the theatricality of suffering includes, indeed, an ever-expanding repertoire of communicative practices, such as the painting, the pamphlet or the novel, which complicate the function of the spectacle beyond the acting stage and, thus, enhance the communicative panoply of humanitarianism in contemporary public culture (Boltanski 1999; Cmiel 1999). The mediation of suffering through electronic and digital media has further recontextualized such practices in the screen technologies of photography, cinema, television and the internet, thereby contributing to the proliferation of spectacles of suffering on a planetary scale.

Even though they are not theatrical in the strict sense of the word, such practices can be considered as theatrical insofar as they rely on an arrangement of separation between those who watch and those who suffer and use the aesthetic resources of language and image so as to mobilize the power of imagination. Given the impossibility of direct action upon mediated suffering, let us recall, this communicative repertoire, organized as it is around the presence of the two paradigmatic figures of suffering (the persecutor who inflicts pain or the benefactor who seeks to alleviate it) invites spectators to identify with the moral claim each figure represents: denunciation against the injustice of suffering, in the presence of a persecutor, or care and tenderheartedness towards the victims, in the presence of a benefactor (Boltanksi 1999: 46–8). In this manner, sympathetic identification capitalizes on the key moral emotions of indignation and empathy in order to enable us to imagine ourselves as public actors either by speaking out, through protest or petition (in the solidarity of revolution), or by paying, through donation (in the solidarity of salvation; see also Chouliaraki 2006, 2008a).

The theatrical apparatus of moral education consists today of this repertoire of performative practices, which now includes the multiple mediations of twentieth-century crimes against humanity: the Holocaust, world wars, torture and terror. In a cumulative manner, such practices have come to be regarded as indispensible in late modern pedagogy, acting both as commemorative claims, enacting the 'never again' imperative (Zelizer 1998; Wells 2010), or as solidarity claims, gently albeit constantly urging us to enact the imperative to care for vulnerable others without asking back (Hodgkin & Radstone 2006).

Yet, similarly to earlier critiques of the theatre, the legitimacy of such practices is undermined by a recurring suspicion towards the staging of human misfortune. If earlier arguments expressed scepticism regarding the authenticity of professional acting per se, contemporary ones focus on a new risk for the theatre of pity, namely the market relations of technology which threaten to manipulate the spectacle of suffering and thereby deprive suffering of its authenticity and moral gravity – and as we shall see, both the market and technology play, indeed, an instrumental role in the struggles that define the practice of solidarity today.

In summary, the first paradox of humanitarian communication draws upon a historical tradition that treats the spectacle of suffering as, at once, a source of moral education and a force of moral corruption – capable of both humanizing and desensitizing its publics. The second paradox of humanitarian communication, to which I now turn, treats solidarity as, at once, a site of domination and a force of social change, raising questions about action on distant suffering – the paradox of agency.

Solidarity and political power

The theatricality of humanitarianism, which places suffering at the heart of the moral education of the West, simultaneously situates the communication of solidarity within a particular conception of politics as pity.

Pity is a form of politics that relies on the spectacle of vulnerability so as to put forward the moral claim to common humanity, in salvation or revolution, as a cause for our action (Arendt 1958/1998; Boltanski 1999). Rather than a modern invention, the genealogy of pity goes back to the Aristotelian definition of tragedy, where it is defined as a response to 'undeserved' suffering that comes about from an unfortunate 'twist of fate' (Nussbaum 1986: 186). A similar definition of pity is also echoed in the modern conception of humanitarianism, where benevolence towards 'undeserved' suffering emerges as a cornerstone of the moral universalism of the Enlightenment.

Modern pity, in this sense, constitutes the dominant response to 'pauperism', the problem of the poor, which turned into a challenge for Western European states between 1795 and 1845 and established philanthropy as the dominant practice for the management of poverty (Dean 1991). Preexisting, as it were, the birth of political economy as a discipline of government, the paradigm of pity did not recede with the early development of public policies on poverty. On the contrary, it defined the moral philosophy of such policies, which now prioritized the relief of 'undeserved' misfortune, rather than addressing questions of 'a just wage or just price' (Himmelfarb 1984: 41). Even though it shifted the responsibility of the poor from charity to the state, Himmelfarb argues, pity continued to sustain 'the primacy of morality in the formulation of the social problem and in the making of social policy' (1984: 12).

Whilst Arendt's modern scepticism towards pity refers specifically to the morality of salvation as an inadequate political principle that draws on 'the Christian religion of mercy' (1963/1990: 65), Boltanski, following Arendt, extends this scepticism to the morality of revolution, which may not appeal to mercy but similarly draws on the morality of common humanity so as to denounce societal wrong-doings; the indignation inherent in revolutionary projects, he argues, 'clearly has its source in pity. In the absence of pity for the sufferer, there would be no reason to be indignant about his suffering' (2000: 9).

Like welfare policies, then, the two versions of humanitarianism are also founded upon a moral conception of community, although community is now not a national but a transnational collectivity of universal humanity – 'a series of equivalent individuals' bound together by a sense of obligation to one another (Calhoun 2009: 78). As moralities of salvation and revolution waned during the post-Cold War retreat of ideologies, it is today the idea of human rights that grounds this secular sense of moral obligation (Sznaider 2001; Moyn 2010). This is because the legitimacy of human rights similarly derives from their appeal to the irreducible materiality of the body, which subsumes all difference under the hyper-category of the human species: 'our species is one', as Ignatieff puts it, 'and each of the individuals who compose it is entitled to equal moral consideration' (2001: 3–4). Echoing the classical idea of 'natural right', which originates in a Stoic conception of moral obligation as the non-negotiable imperative to care for others beyond the 'polis', the contemporary idea of rights (albeit following a different genealogy) similarly expands the reach of obligation beyond our proximal encounters with people like 'us' to encompass distant relationships of unreciprocated giving in the 'cosmopolis' (deChaine 2005: 42).

The significance of the idea of human rights for cosmopolitan solidarity lies, in this sense, not simply in postulating the individual as a universal bearer of rights, but in recognizing that this bearer of rights is simultaneously a figure of inherent benevolence, a moral subject with a natural inclination to care for others. Emerging in eighteenth century moral philosophy, as I argued in chapter 1, this conception of natural 'goodness' places solidarity without reciprocation at the heart of modern humanitarian subjectivity: 'How selfish soever man may be supposed', Adam Smith claimed, 'there are evidently some principles in his nature, which interest him in the fortune of others, and render their happiness necessary to him, though he derives *nothing from it except the pleasure of seeing it*' (1759/2000: 3, emphasis added).

The spectacle of suffering is significant in this conception of moral subjectivity in that, properly staged, it activates the latent potential to care inherent in all and orients it towards purposeful action on distant suffering – what Ainley refers to as the presupposition of 'perfectibility' in humanitarian subjectivity (2008). Inclination thus turns into obligation through this exposure to the theatrical performances of suffering, which mundanely communicate the imperative to act on vulnerable others in the West (Williams 1973). *Pace*, then, the dominant distinction often drawn between utilitarian and deontological approaches to humanitarianism, which locate the source of obligation either in rational argumentation or in the maximization of individual benefits (Hutchings 2010), the theatricality of pity suggests another possibility. It suggests that moral action on distant suffering may be informed by what Aristotle calls the force of habituation: the cumulative formation of dispositions of solidarity through repeated stagings of human misfortune (McIntyre 1981/2006: 113–15).

Whilst this position does not necessarily exclude the part that individual rationality or self-interest may play in the decision to act, it does locate the source of morality in the public realm, *inter homines*, rather than within the self, *in interiore hominis* (Gullace 1993). What this public conception of morality suggests is that pity, rather than pre-existing the performances of suffering, emerges instead through these performances, which are there for everyone to witness as potential benefactors. By the same token, contemporary citizenship should be seen as depending upon this acknowledgement of distant suffering, which mobilizes the western world as a collectivity with the will to act – a public.

An ethics of virtue, then, underlies the politics of pity, insofar as the latter's proposals for action on vulnerable others seek to contribute both to some conception of well-being amongst those others, the beneficiaries of humanitarian action, but also, importantly, to the cultivation of dispositions of solidarity amongst the community of benefactors. Far from implying that the meaning of solidarity is unified within this moral order, the politics of pity operates, let us recall, on a flexible definition of well-being which has included both a minimalist version of obligation as the saving of human life, in salvation, and a maximalist version as social change, in revolution – today converging around the moral obligation to human rights. Differences between these versions granted, my point is that a moralizing vocabulary has currently hegemonized the public domain, reconstituting the political, economic and military rationalities of the global world order along the lines of an ethics of humanitarianism (Chandler 2002). As a consequence, Kennedy argues, the vocabulary of solidarity 'has become the mark of civilization and participation in a shared ethical and professional common sense community' (2004: 271).

Despite much celebratory rhetoric, however, humanitarianism introduces into the politics of pity yet another controversy, beyond that around the corrosive impact of technology and the market. This is now a controversy that revolves around the tension of humanitarianism as an act of benevolence or as an act of power. Informed by a deep scepticism about the inherent goodness of 'man' (sic) at the heart of the idea of human rights, this argument postulates instead that all acts of solidarity are acts of domination and that the concept of rights functions precisely as a device of social regulation. Rather than positively promoting solidarity in the name of human flourishing, human rights work by defining the limits of the subject and perpetuating hierarchies of human life on a global scale (Douzinas 2007).

This ambivalence of solidarity is reflected in the semantic instability of the 'gift', a key metaphor in the virtue ethics of benevolent giving. The humanitarian 'gift' is seen, on the one hand, as instrumental in establishing bonds of solidarity beyond the sphere of intimate relationships by extending the circle of benevolent giving to an imaginary community of distant others (Bajde 2009). It is simultaneously seen, on the other, as responsible for misrecognizing the subordination of the global South by the West as a relationship of unreciprocated giving, which allows the West to appear as a benefactor of those whose extreme deprivation it has originally caused: 'the primary purpose of the gift', as Hattori puts it, 'is not the resources extended but the social relationship created or reinforced' (2003b:161).

This 'dark side' of humanitarianism, then, draws attention to an equivalent asymmetry between the structure of pity and the structure of the theatre. Just as the theatre may be claiming to educate through moral imagination, yet risks to turn suffering into pure spectacle, similarly solidarity may be claiming to be a manifestation of benevolence in the cosmopolis, yet it ultimately contributes to reproducing an unequal world order founded on the colonial legacy of the West. Following directly from the systemic paradox of humanitarianism, then, the paradox of agency raises the question of what kind of action towards vulnerable others might be possible and desirable in the West.

To summarize, modern humanitarianism operates as a force of moral education for western publics by relying on the theatre of pity – spectacles that raise the question of action on the basis of salvation or revolution. The communication of solidarity, through pity, however, is far from straightforward; it takes place on the basis of two paradoxes: the paradox of *authenticity*, which entails the possibility that the mediation of suffering numbs rather than mobilizes moral sensibilities, and the paradox of *agency*, where acts of benevolent giving are seen to legitimize the systemic asymmetry between West and the global South. How does critical theory respond to these paradoxes?

Critiques of the theatricality of humanitarianism

Critical theory responds to the two paradoxes of humanitarian communication by providing a rather bleak confirmation of the sceptical narrative. Under 'Spectacle' below, I explore how influential strands of critical theory in the fields of social and cultural analysis engage with humanitarian communication in order to address the implications of the market for an 'authentic' ethics of solidarity. Under 'Empire', I discuss how an equally influential strand of political theory engages with humanitarianism in order to argue for the complicity of solidarity in the reproduction of an unequal global order.

Spectacle: the inauthenticity of representation

The scepticism of critical theory towards the role of mediation in cultivating solidarity is not new. Early critiques of spectatorial sympathy treat the act of viewing human misfortune as a dubious act – one that contributed to educating the eighteenth-century European middle class into the newly found sensibility of secular care, yet, at the same time, fostered a sense of delight in juxtaposing the vulnerability of distant others with the safety of the middle class (Halttunen 1995). Even though it appears to challenge the benevolence of the humanitarian actor, inherent in the conception of politics as pity, this critique in fact places the blame on the structure of the spectacle rather than the morality of the spectator.

The staging of human misfortune, the argument has it, does not bridge the moral distance between those who watch and those who suffer, but ultimately intensifies such distance. This is because spectators are subject to the manipulating power of acting, which removes suffering from the realm of the real into the realm of fiction, and so triggers a response to suffering only to then immediately disconnect it from action outside the theatre itself.

Rather than cultivating dispositions of solidarity towards distant others, then, mediation produces instead an inauthentic sense of reality and, ultimately, rehearses private emotion without public impact.

If stage acting has been historically responsible for the corrupting potential of the spectacle, from Plato onwards, it is the market of media technologies that has today become the main source of suspicion in critical theory. Guy Debord's theory of the spectacle is a paradigmatic discourse of such suspicion with a deep and lasting impact within and beyond academic scholarship. The spectacle, for Debord, differs from previous modes of theatrical representation precisely because of the intervention of media technologies, which drastically reconfigure the ways in which spectators interact with images: 'the spectacle', Debord writes, 'is not an ensemble of images; it is a social relation between people mediated by images' (1967/2002 para 4, 4/6).

Grounded on the Marxian critique of capitalism, this influential view on the spectacle extends the thesis of 'alienation' from the material realm of labour to the cultural realm of representation. Just as capitalist relations of production mediate between people and things to turn human labour into commodity, so the spectacle mediates between people and their reality to turn human experience into an illusion: 'when the real world is transformed into mere images, then mere images are transformed into real beings' (Jappe 1999: 107). In lamenting the fusion of boundaries between image and real life, the critique of the spectacle is, essentially, a critique of inauthenticity, that is, a critique of reality experienced not in its 'natural state' but as 'the inevitable outcome of a technical development perceived as natural' (Debord 1967/2002: para 24).

Reminiscent of the early modern suspicion of the theatre as corrupting public sensibilities, Debord's thesis shares, indeed, with Rousseau a nostalgia for the lost authenticity of the public realm, yet it is inspired less by Rousseau's communitarian moralism and more by Adorno and Horkheimer's critique of the culture industry. It is, specifically, inspired by the latter's claim that the complicity between technology and capitalism, what they call the 'technological veil', has today subordinated autonomous art to the logic of commodity (1942/1991: 55). Under the pressure of this destructive synergy, Horkheimer and Adorno argue, a new ideology of mass culture emerges which perpetuates social inequality no longer by 'misrecognizing' the revolutionary role of the working class, but by weakening the revolutionary role of the arts in capitalist societies. Rather than acting as a catalyst for social change, the arts of mass culture have instead managed to turn the real world or 'the world outside' into 'a seamless extension of the one which has been revealed on screen' (Horkheimer and Adorno 1947/2002: 99).

This pervasive critique of the spectacle as inauthentic representation that compromises the capacity of spectators to distinguish fact from fiction is also reflected in critiques of humanitarian communication. Despite their internal variations, such critiques similarly point to the failure of the spectacle of suffering to establish the morally crucial distinction between image and reality (Boltanski 1999). Specifically, whereas the *commodification critique* seeks to defend the authenticity of suffering against its corrosion by the market, the *simulacrum thesis* goes as far as claiming that there is no authentic suffering beyond its representation on screen.

The commodification of suffering thesis, the most influential problematization of mediated suffering to date, builds upon Debord to set up a relationship of complicity between spectacle and the market that produces and disseminates it (Habermas 1962/1989; Debray 1995; Best and Kellner 2007).[1] The mediation of suffering, this argument has it, follows the logic of commercial exchange in that it subordinates the moral imperative to act on vulnerable others to the capitalist principle of the maximization of profit (Kennedy 2004; de Waal 2008). What this subordination of morality to the market implies is that the spectacle of suffering fails to raise the demand for practical action and seduces us, instead, into a contemplative consumption of its sensual (and sensational) properties – the planes crashing onto the WTC or the panorama of Baghdad in flames. The spectacles of commodification propose, in other words, a voyeuristic or even 'pornographic' disposition towards suffering, insofar as they remove the urgency of its circumstances and place suffering in the realm of fiction (Sontag 2003).

It is precisely this link between suffering as fact and suffering as spectacle that is altogether abandoned in Baudrillard's critical theory of the simulacrum. A radicalization of Debord's critique, the theory of the simulacrum announces that, through a movement of implosion, reality today is not simply dominated by spectacle but is altogether displaced by it: 'today's violence', Baudrillard says, 'is a simulacrum of violence, emerging less from passion than from the screen: a violence in the nature of the image' (1993: 74). The displacement of reality is, here, evident in Baudrillard's definition of 'violence' exclusively as a reference, an infinitely reproducible imagery of violence without a referent, a 'simulacrum' that lacks the 'passion' of violence in unmediated exchanges. As a consequence of blurring the distinction between what we see and what might exist, Baudrillard redefined the real as 'that of which it is possible to give an equivalent reproduction' (1983: 146).

Even though this breakdown of the referential function of the spectacle is attributed to technology itself, that is, the capacity of technology to reshape the image through techniques of montage or retouching, the detrimental effects of this breakdown are seen as originating, again, in the market. It is, specifically, the new 'intellectual-political market' that is responsible for manipulating the image at the service of the most aggressive interests of mature capitalism (Baudrillard 1994). Unlike the commodification thesis, however, where the reality of violence beyond the screen is not only possible but also desirable for social critique, the simulacrum thesis posits that violence does not exist outside the screen but is inherent 'in the nature of the image' itself. This suffocating overtake of the social by the market, the thesis has it, renders obsolete the possibility of mediated communication to refer to anything other than itself.

Extending this Baudrillardian critique of technological capitalism, Virilio goes on to discuss the live mediation of war as nothing more than a manifestation of the 'virtual theatricalization of the real world' (1995: 33). Ironically, however, Virilio's evocation of the theatre echoes the early modern metaphor of the world-as-stage (a *theatrum mundi*) only to reverse the role of the theatre in the formation of moral collectivities and argue for the opposite. The theatricalization of 'hypermodernity', he says, contributes not to the formation but the disappearance of new collectivities: 'today there remains nothing but the cathode ray screen, with its shadows and specters of a community in the process of disappearing' (1986: 23).

In summary, the critique of the spectacle challenges the claim that the theatricality of human misfortune may act as a force of moral education, on the grounds that the technological market turns content into aesthetic form – into spectacle. As a consequence, the spectacle cancels the authenticity of suffering, that is its urgent matter-of-factness beyond the screen, rendering suffering an object of inactive contemplation rather than a cause for action. Even though, as we shall see, this critique of authenticity has today informed an unprecedented surge of mediated self-expression as the new truth of suffering, Virilio's quote on the 'disappearing' community goes beyond challenging such truth to further suggest a failure in the performance of solidarity, too. It is this critique of the theatre as 'empire' that I explore next.

Empire: the bio-politics of solidarity

Expanding upon earlier critiques of colonialism, which denounce the hegemony of the West for emerging at the cost of the sovereignty of non-western peoples, the critique of humanitarianism as empire develops a novel critique of post-colonialism as *bio-power*. This term is inspired by the

Foucaldian juxtaposition of two systems of power, namely sovereignty, the centralized power of pre-modern rule, and discipline, the capillary power of modern institutions (Foucault 1977). If sovereignty is about the absolute authority of the ruler, exercised through brutal spectacles of colonial domination, discipline is about the subtle control of welfare, exercised through invisible interventions on the human body. In modernity, therefore, the body becomes a site of power not through its subjection to raw violence but through a benign logic of protection, which subjects this body to new, ever-expanding regimes of regulation (hence the 'bio-political' character of modern power; Rose 1999).

In evoking the vulnerability of the body as the moral cornerstone of solidarity, critics say, humanitarianism should not, then, be seen as a noble project of cosmopolitan morality but as a crucial mechanism of the bio-political apparatus of modernity (Edkins 2000). This is so in the sense that the appeal to the biological body as a manifestation of our common humanity does not work to cultivate the virtue of solidarity but, rather, to institute a strategic distinction between forms of human life. This is the distinction between *zoe*, or 'bare life', and *bios*, or political life, which ultimately defines distant sufferers as pre-political subjects striving for survival whilst relegating the status of the citizens to the benefactors of the West (Agamben 1998). This 'ontological' classification of vulnerability reproduces the existing global order in that, even though bio-politics is exercised upon individual bodies, it is nonetheless responsible for the production of the global South as a passive or agentless body politic (Douzinas 2007).

Informed by this view of power as bio-politics, critical theory on empire moves beyond the Marxian morality of revolution to offer a more complex understanding of the processes by which the power relations between West and the global South are today sustained. Unlike traditional empires, which were organized around the imperialist superpower of a nation-state, bio-political empire does not necessarily occupy a bounded territoriality but rather situates its strategic calculations on life and death within a 'deterritorializing apparatus of rule' that has no centre, yet relies on global media spectacles to legitimize the divisions of place and human life that the new empire reproduces (Hardt and Negri 2001: xii; Yrjölä 2009).

Far from the early modern spectacles of colonial violence that reflects such divisions, humanitarianism has indeed developed its own theatrical practices to signify the asymmetries of the new global order: 'it takes only a glance', says Agamben, 'at the recent publicity campaigns to gather funds for the refugees from Rwanda to realize that human life is exclusively considered . . . as bare life – which is to say, as life that can be killed but not sacrificed – and that only as such is it made into the object of aid and protection' (1998: 133–4).

At the heart of this rejection of the humanitarian spectacle as the exercise of bio-political power is Arendt's critique of dehumanization. The recognition of vulnerability as a human right, she argues, is used by totalitarian nation-states in order to reduce certain groups of people to 'nothing but men', precisely in order to be able to subject these groups to various forms of violence: 'a man [sic] who is nothing but a man', Arendt says, 'has lost the very qualities which make it possible for other people to treat him as a man' (1951/1979: 300). It is this problematic of dehumanization that, as I mentioned in chapter 1, is central to the contemporary critique of solidarity as empire. Whereas not unrelated to the problematic of authenticity, dehumanization shifts the focus of critique from the distinction between fact and fiction, which is central to the theatre as spectacle, to the distinction between the human and the non-human, which lies at the heart of solidarity as empire. The problematic of dehumanization, in this sense, draws attention to the ways in which the communicative structure of solidarity selectively mobilizes the concept of 'humanity' so as to forge bonds of solidarity with certain populations rather than others and, ultimately, to legitimize a new imperialism of the West as a self-congratulatory community of benefactors (Hattori 2003b).

Drawing upon the cases of the 2003 Iraq war and the 2004 Abu Ghraib prison scandal, Butler shows how mediated suffering operates as bio-political power by instituting a metaphysical distinction between 'good' and 'evil', which demonizes non-western others and justifies the imperialist logic of 'new humanitarian wars' against those 'others' (2006). What is at stake in this Manichean relegation of 'pure evil' to the West's others, this critique has it, is not only the political hegemony of the West but the very conception of the human: 'it is not', as Butler puts it, 'just that some humans are treated as humans, and others are dehumanized; it is rather that dehumanization becomes the condition for the production of the human to the extent that a "western" civilization defines itself over and against a population understood as definitionally illegitimate, if not dubiously human' (2006: 278).

Sharing a similar suspicion of the effects of mediated suffering, Rancière further links the critique of dehumanization with the ways in which bio-political modernity, what he calls 'the age of the humanitarian' (1999), has brought about a moralization of politics that collapses the political question of global justice with the moral question of responding to the urgency of bodily needs. What the spectacle of dehumanized others does, he argues in an Arendtian spirit, is that it elevates 'the wordless victim' into a paradigmatic figure of the global political scene: 'the ultimate figure of the one excluded from logos, armed only with a voice expressing a monotonous moan, the moan of naked suffering, which saturation has made inaudible' (1999: 126).

Unable to go beyond the 'monotonous moan' of the sufferer, not only does the spectacle of suffering dehumanize vulnerable others but, by the same token, it also exhausts itself in 'a pure defense of the innocent and the powerless against power' without offering an alternative political vision (Žižek 2005: 9). This is a kind of anti-politics that blocks the possibility of a political community of solidarity to extend beyond the West and to encompass distant others. Even though, as we shall see, humanitarianism today responds to this critique by further marginalizing the question of politics, my point here is that, for the theorists of empire, the call to solidarity masks, in fact, the unchanged power relations of the 'new' empire. In this critique, humanitarian communication cancels not so much the authenticity of suffering but the potential for action that might make a difference in the developing world. Rather than enabling solidarity, the bio-politics of empire both produces dehumanized others and undermines the possibility of cosmopolitan agency, even if it claims to institute it.

A critique of the critical school

Critical theory, in its various disciplinary versions, responds in a negative way to the two paradoxes of humanitarianism. On the one hand, in theorizing the theatre as spectacle, that is, as part of a culture industry whose images blur the boundary between fact and fiction, critical theory treats mediated suffering as inauthentic and forecloses the capacity of humanitarianism to have a moralizing influence upon its publics. On the other hand, in theorizing solidarity as bio-political power, critical theory further treats humanitarian communication as inherently dehumanizing and, therefore, unable to forge cosmopolitan solidarities in the West.

It is evident, then, that critical approaches to humanitarian communication take their starting point in the pessimistic diagnosis of the theatre as Debordian spectacle – as part of a broader aesthetic system which, in entering the technological circuit of mass production, not only loses its capacity to transform the social world but becomes complicit to its depoliticization – or to, what Horkheimer and Adorno call, the thoroughgoing 'aestheticization' of the public realm. As a consequence, the critical school may theoretically acknowledge the political significance of a cosmopolitan ethics of distance in that it denounces the global hierarchies of suffering, nonetheless it cannot analytically go beyond a communitarian ethics of proximity, insofar as it one-sidedly rejects the cosmopolitanizing role that the theatre may play in forging bonds of commitment and care beyond the West.

If we wish, however, to affirm the possibility of cosmopolitan solidarity in our public culture, I argue that the task of going beyond the spectacle in order to recuperate a positive view of the theatre as moral education becomes of paramount importance – a view that, as we saw, has already been dominant at different historical moments. What this recuperation involves is keeping separate two important epistemological dimensions in the study of humanitarianism. The first is the sphere of critique, which asks how humanitarianism should look and, therefore, provides normative accounts of humanitarianism either as inauthentic spectacle or as bio-political power; the second is the sphere of analysis, which asks how actual practices of communication work and provides empirical accounts of humanitarian performance at specific moments in time (see Chandler 2009 for a critique of post-territorial politics along similar lines).

The aim of this differentiation between critique and analysis is to open up a space wherein to approach the theatricality of humanitarianism in its full ambivalence – that is, to treat its paradoxes not as a priori disabling facts that define the meaning of solidarity once and for all but as productive tensions that may settle the meaning of solidarity in different ways, at different moments in time. What does this mean in the context of this study? It means that, on the one hand, I approach the paradox of authenticity not as a predetermined diagnosis of the spectacle of suffering as fiction but as a site of struggle, where the mediation of suffering may or may not appear as fiction – a struggle that inevitably translates into a range of various authentication strategies across a number of communicative practices available in our culture. On the other hand, I approach the paradox of agency not as a definitive act of dehumanization but as a struggle over the moralizing strategies of humanitarian communication that may or may not enable the humanization of distant others. The advantage of this approach is that it opens up the possibility for subtler analyses of historical change in the communicative structure of humanitarianism and, ultimately, allows for more effective forms of critique on its political and moral implications. It is to the theoretical account of this structure as the 'humanitarian imaginary' that I now turn.

The humanitarian imaginary

A theoretical account that places the educative function of the theatre at the heart of contemporary public culture starts with due attention to the concept of the imagination. It is, as we saw, the power of the theatre to imaginatively engage us with someone else's position that renders imagination a pedagogical catalyst in the theatrical experience. Indeed, ever since Aristotle's conception of tragedy as imitating an 'important and finite act' that inspires pity and fear (Nussbaum 1986), imagination is seen to rely on the capacity of image and language to represent suffering as a cause of sympathetic identification that may lead to action.

Whereas contemporary theatrical spectacle has come to encompass a wide range of mediated practices, from television to the mobile phone, what remains important through time is the reliance of imagination on the aesthetic qualities of these practices and their ability to propose different positions of engagement to their spectators. This dependence of the imagination on imagery, however, should not be seen exclusively as a historical feature of our media-saturated culture, but should also be regarded as an epistemic property of imagination (Thompson 1984).

Radical imagination, as Castoriadis argues (drawing on Aristotle's distinction between inventive and radical imagination; Aristotle, *De Anima*, Book III), presupposes that the image, that is, some form of figural signification of human thought or affect, is not the empirical manifestation of these pre-existing interiorities but the very condition of possibility for the emergence of thought and affect in the first place: 'The imaginary of which I am speaking is not an image of. It is the unceasing and essentially undetermined (social-historical and psychical) creation of figures/forms/images, on the basis of which alone there can ever be a question of "something". What we call "reality" and "rationality" are its works' (1975/1987: 3).

The realm of the imaginable, and hence the thinkable or the affect-able, cannot thus be exhausted to a description of any singular visual culture, but needs to be conceptualized as a socially instituted sphere of communicative practices that uses specific 'imaginal' cultures, with their own aesthetic possibilities, in order to regulate the production of particular moral imaginations at particular historical moments.[2]

Despite its normative function in seeking to domesticate imagination within the boundaries of the possible, the imaginary refers neither to prescriptive codes of conduct nor to canonical theoretical arguments about what the public should think or feel. Rather than such forms of authoritative morality, I argue, the imaginary works performatively through a morality of virtue, that is, it draws upon familiar practices of aesthetic performance so as to engage spectators with images and stories about our world and, thereby, to socialize us into those ways of feeling and acting that are legitimate and desirable in a specific culture.

Insofar as it sets up an arrangement of separation between these aesthetic performances and their spectators so as to habituate western publics into positions of sympathetic identification, the communicative structure of the imaginary can be defined as theatrical – a definition that also lies at the heart of Taylor's conception of modern social imaginaries as spaces of communication consisting precisely of 'those images, stories and legends' through which 'people imagine their social existence, how they fit together with others, . . . and the deeper normative notions and images that underlie these expectations' (2002: 106).

In a similar way, we may define the humanitarian imaginary as that configuration of practices which use the communicative structure of the theatre in order to perform collective imaginations of vulnerable others in the West, with a view to cultivating a longer-term disposition to thinking, feeling and acting towards these others. Such practices of performance, which include the early genres of posters, paintings and novels but today also appeals, celebrities, concerts and the news, make up a theatrical structure that mundanely produces imaginations of solidarity – a sense of what Arendt calls 'our common shared world' as a field of our action (see Tester 2010 for a similar view of what he calls 'common sense humanitarianism').

This virtue-oriented normativity of the imaginary, as theatrical practices that mobilize image and language in order to sustain collective self-descriptions of the West as an altruistic community, points to the fact that such practices, rather than simply educating their publics, in fact *constitute* these publics as moral subjects at the moment that they claim to address them. The force of habituation that, as I mentioned earlier, is instrumental to the function of the theatre as moral education is, in this sense, not a simple corrective to a pre-existing public morality but, let us recall, bears a performative force on this morality, as it routinely calls an ethics of solidarity into existence through the theatrical performance of stories about suffering (Butler 1993, 1997 for a theoretization of the performative; Chouliaraki 2006 for the performativity of spectacles of distant suffering).

Yet, just as habituation is never only the mindless repetition of habit but requires a reflexive engagement with the particular context of its use and hence an always renewed performance (Aristotle's practical wisdom or 'phronesis'; Aristotle, *Nicomachean Ethics,* Book VI), similarly, the theatrical iterations of the norms of the imaginary do not uniformly repeat themselves but demonstrate an inevitable variation that may subvert these norms in the act of reproducing them – a dialectics of change that I have elsewhere theorized as 'conditional freedom' (Chouliaraki 2008a). It is this dialectics of change, whereby the imaginary is transformed through the very theatrical practices that reproduce it, that bears the potential for a more nuanced critical account of the humanitarian imaginary.

Between, then, the instrumentalized knowledge produced in the field of humanitarianism, mentioned in chapter 1, and the pessimistic accounts of critical scholarship, described earlier in this chapter, my dialectical account seeks to understand how the synergies between spectacle, politics and the market may change humanitarian communication and, with it, the proposals to solidarity available to us at various moments in time. Let me conclude the chapter with brief descriptions of the two analytical challenges involved in this account.

The critical analysis of the humanitarian imaginary

Unlike the critical school, which assumes specific causal links between politics, the market and technology and ends up prematurely lamenting the inauthenticity of mediated suffering and the decline of solidarity, I start instead from a position of informed agnosticism. I approach, therefore, the humanitarian imaginary as a space of regulated undecidability – a space where the links between the three may always exist in bounded relationships to one another, yet these relationships cannot be fully predetermined and, in a crucial way, depend upon the specific historical contexts of their emergence and use. Far from arguing, then, that humanitarian performance prefigures a necessary relationship between such performance and its public appropriations, a question that warrants separate empirical investigation, the focus on performance emphasizes instead the complex and dynamic ways in which particular moral imaginations of solidarity come to be articulated as public norms at different points in time.

This privileging of performance as the object of a critical inquiry into the humanitarian imaginary draws attention to two dimensions of analysis: the *historicity* of the imaginary, which looks at how the performances of the imaginary change in time, thereby making different claims to authenticity and agency, and the *performativity* of the imaginary, which looks at how these changes of performance produce, in turn, different truths of suffering and different moral imaginations of solidarity beyond the West.

The historicity of the humanitarian imaginary

The humanitarian imaginary cannot be described in unequivocal terms. As moral education, it is undermined by its inscription in technology and the market, whilst, as a form of solidarity, it is equally undermined by its historical complicity with empire. What this instability reflects, let us recall, is a concomitant instability in the structure of the theatre which, rather than existing in a state of 'pure' publicness, has always been defined by its complicity to the economic and political relations of modern capitalism.

Operating in this complex context, modern theatre, as I argued in chapter 1, has always sought to reconcile the pursuit of profit, an amoralistic endeavour, with the cultivation of virtue, an ethics of solidarity that may turn the *homo economicus* into a 'man of sentiment' (Marshall 1984). As part of the pedagogic apparatus of the West at the age of imperialist expansion, the theatre of colonialism played, in this sense, a pivotal role in reproducing stereotypes of distant others as exotic objects of fear and desire whilst simultaneously raising awareness of the injustices of suffering that eventually led to the abolition of slavery (Said 2002; F. Nussbaum 2005).

Despite major differences, contemporary humanitarianism points to a similar configuration of tensions between the public morality of solidarity and the commercial morality of branding and show business. Now as much as then, the educative force of the imaginary, suspended as it is between moral habituation and capitalist legitimization, cannot be settled in advance. The study of the historical transformations of solidarity, it follows, needs to begin from this fundamental instability in order to trace the different ways in which humanitarianism stages the spectacle of suffering and provisionally stabilizes its claims to solidarity at different moments in time.

It is Foucault's approach to 'historicity' that best helps us capture the ambivalence of the humanitarian imaginary as both a source of profit and a source of critical enlightenment. Differentiating traditional history, a mode of narration that perceives the past as a readily available reality that can be unproblematically compared to an equally transparent present, from 'historicity', a mode of narration that sees the past as always emerging through performative acts of meaning-making, Foucault places the comparative study of such performative acts at the heart of critical inquiry. His study of historicity, as Thompson puts it, consequently 'works not by uncovering the sense history, the traditionality of the sciences with which it is concerned, but by excavating the empirical surface of words and things so as to lay bare the stratum of rules, the layer of savoir, that governs the fields within which scientific discourses operate' (2008: 16). Historicity, in this Foucaldian sense, enables us to recount transformations in the humanitarian imaginary, not as a linear narrative of facts that moves from past to present, but as a conceptual narrative that focuses on the ways in which the tensions of the imaginary come to be provisionally settled in key performances of solidarity at two distinct moments in time – its emergence and its contemporary state.

My analysis focuses, in this sense, on four performative genres of the imaginary – appeals, celebrities, concerts and news – then and now, with a view to identifying change in the strategies each genre employs so as to claim *authenticity* in its representations of suffering and to propose to the West forms of *moral agency* upon this suffering. Whereas, as I said, these two strategies, *authentication* and *moralization*, are inherent dimensions of the humanitarian structure, each comparative moment introduces into this structure its own particular historical pressures and, in so doing, necessarily inflects these strategies into concrete aesthetic and moral choices, characteristic of each moment. Far from being a narrative of continuity that illuminates the present in the light of its past, it follows, mine is a narrative of discontinuity that renders past and present intelligible through an analysis of their uniquely differentiated strategies of aesthetic performance – 'the present becomes', in this way, 'intelligible as it is aligned with a past moment with which it has a secret affinity' (Peters 1999: 3).

It is the time-span of the past forty years (1970s–2010s), following as it does the end of colonialism and the subsequent synergy of humanitarianism with market and technology, that delimits the historical boundaries of the humanitarian imaginary in my study. In this trajectory, today's theatre of humanitarianism should be seen as emerging through Red Cross photojournalistic images of emaciated poor in India (1958), the rock concerts to end the war in Vietnam (George Harrison, 1973) or famine in Ethiopia (Live Aid 1985), as well as through UNICEF's early celebrity advocacy (Audrey Hepburn, 1988) and the journalistic reports that speak of the Biafra famine (1968) or the deadly earthquakes of the 1970s.

Each of these genres refers to a configuration of relatively stable performative practices, for instance the appeal or the concert, which are recognized as constitutive of the humanitarian structure but, at the same time, are permeable enough to become infinitely hybridized by new technologies and their aesthetic registers (Chouliaraki & Fairclough 1999: 139–49). Humanitarian appeals, for instance, change from an early aesthetics of photojournalism, where suffering appears as 'raw' reality, to a contemporary aesthetics of textual gaming, where photojournalistic immediacy gives way to the advertising techniques of graphic animation or hyper-realism. Both belong to the genre of appealing, marked as this is by the evocation of a cause and a call to action, but the performance of solidarity available in each genre and the dispositions to act upon its cause radically differ at these two points in time.

By approaching such generic shifts as manifestations of the paradoxes of humanitarianism, always rearticulated, I am able to tell the story of the humanitarian imaginary as a change in the relations of the field – political, economic, technological. The shift from photorealism to textual games in appeals, to carry on from the previous example, makes sense in the context of a shift from 'scientific aid' or 'sustainable intervention', as key strategies of the field in earlier decades, towards an increasing instrumentalization and technologization of INGOs, where the dominant strategy now is to maintain consumer loyalty under conditions of compassion fatigue.

In order to engage with such issues, the analytical chapters that follow frame each genre of the imaginary within a historical controversy that both touches upon the genre's state of the art and reveals its complicities with the past. The controversy around appeals, again, exemplifies how long-term debates about the truth value and moral force of photorealistic depictions of suffering have informed the aesthetic transformation towards today's self-reflexive styles of appealing and their predilection for low-intensity, fleeting sensibilities of a 'feel good' altruism – what I later return to theorize as an ironic morality.

The value of historicity lies here in reminding us that we should not analyse the humanitarian imaginary one-sidedly, that is, in ways that force our analysis towards one or the other side of its communicative paradoxes and so prematurely reduce it to an unambiguous political or moral position – for instance, by deploring the fictionalization of suffering in appeals as Debordian spectacle. Rather, historicity alerts us to the fact that every humanitarian performance, despite the appearance of permanence, always emerges within a context of controversy and, therefore, remains a provisional construct that captures the specific moral imagination of its time. It is the contours of various controversies regarding appeals, celebrities, concerts and news, then, that the historicity of the imaginary urges us to reconstruct, thereby setting the scene for an exploration of the specific ways in which each genre strives to reconcile the paradoxes of the imaginary at its own particular moment.

The performativity of the humanitarian imaginary

If historicity draws analytical attention to the value of historical controversy in the humanitarian imaginary, performativity focuses on the manifestation of change in the aesthetic properties of specific humanitarian performances. Drawing on a post-structuralist view of communication as constitutive of the social, this focus is grounded on the assumption that humanitarian genres nurture moral imagination not by simply referring to an external world but, as I argued earlier, by performing or bringing this world into being in the process of addressing it. Yet it is important to also remember that not all spectacles of suffering automatically nurture moral imagination. It is only the structure of the theatre that, in separating spectators from the spectacle of suffering so as to imaginatively re-engage the former with the moralizing potential of the latter, is capable of producing relationships of sympathetic identification with vulnerable others.

Taking its starting point on the theatre as a mechanism of sympathetic identification, the analysis of performativity explores, therefore, two dimensions of humanitarian performance, each of which cultivates a distinct orientation towards the spectacle of suffering. The first dimension focuses on our orientation towards the sufferer, or what we might call 'empathetic imagination', whereas the second focuses on our orientation towards the viewing public, or what we might call the 'reflexive imagination', which may lead to judgement upon the suffering (Marshall 1984: 594; Boltanski 1999: 24; 38–41). Even though these are inherently co-articulated dimensions of humanitarian performance, they need to be treated as distinct in the analytical process for the following reasons.

Empathetic imagination, in seeking to set up an affective relationship of identification between spectators and vulnerable others, raises the classical question of technological mediation, namely, whether the suffering of these others is a fact or whether it is a matter of media manipulation and, in so doing, renders *authenticity* a key analytical focus of the imaginary. The orientation towards empathy, in other words, urges the analysis towards the *strategies of authentication* by which the image and language of humanitarianism may turn suffering into a cause for our action. The contrast, for instance, between early appeals that rely on the realism of photojournalism and current NGO appeals that rely on a textually conscious aesthetic suggests that the paradox of authenticity is today resolved not by intensifying the empathetic claims of the spectacle of suffering but, precisely, by abandoning such claims and foregrounding instead the authenticity of the self.

At the same time, *reflexive imagination*, in seeking to establish a normative relationship between the spectator and the public we (supposedly) belong to, raises the question of *judgement* – of what the boundaries of this public are and whether or how they could be redrawn. The orientation towards other spectators, which is of course just as imaginary for the spectator as the encounter with the vulnerable other, draws therefore analytical attention to the *strategies of moralization* through which humanitarian performances constitute the spectator as a moral actor. Central to this process is the construal of the spectator's agency as encompassing not only the restricted community of 'proximal' sufferers but also the global South as part of our common, shared world – hence, the political significance of 'de/humanization' as a symbolic process of exclusion/inclusion that defines the permeable boundaries of western solidarity, discussed under 'Empire: The Bio-politics of Solidarity'. Changing strategies of moralization, it follows, indicate transformations in the performance of solidarity and, hence, in the self-perception of the West as a moral actor. To expand further on the example of appeals, the shift towards a non-realist representation of distant suffering may be indicative of a shift away from witnessing the pain of suffering and the emotions of indignation and empathy that come with it towards a minimal exposure to human vulnerability that privileges a self-oriented and fleeting sensibility of utilitarian altruism.

The performances of the imaginary, however, do not share the same performative logic across genres. Each genre is, instead, characterized by its own distinct performativity which, depending on the institutional relationships of each genre to the market and technology, generates its distinct strategies of authentication and moralization. The critical study of performativity requires, in this sense, a radically *interdisciplinary* approach that engages with each genre through an analytical framework specifically designed to shed light on the particularities of its own performances.

To this end, the four empirical chapters of this volume develop *four different analytical approaches*, each situating performativity within four distinct bodies of literature across the fields of visual and corporate communication, development studies, journalism studies, cultural studies and social theory. Whereas all chapters identify the strategies that the four performative genres of this study develop so as to address the paradoxes of the imaginary, each chapter provides a unique story about the historical controversies and transformations of solidarity as they occur in each genre.

The analysis of appeals, in chapter 3, for instance, develops the language of 'affective performativity', using insights from development studies and social semiotics, in order to show the increasing centrality of semiotic juxtaposition in contemporary appeals as a way to address the problem of compassion fatigue. Moving from documentary to increasingly brand-oriented styles, my analysis shows how these appeals render the problem of the reality of suffering irrelevant (authentication) and how, in so doing, they come to marginalize the humanity of the sufferer or the claim to solidarity in favour of a 'feel-good' online activism (moralization). The analysis of celebrity, in chapter 4, in contrast, draws on the literature of celebrity studies so as to develop the language of 'performativity as personification', which describes the mechanism by which celebrity performs solidarity in a dual sense, through the categories of 'persona', her or his performance as a public figure who authenticates suffering, and 'impersonation', her or his performance as a witness of suffering who seeks to moralize spectators into a cosmopolitan disposition. This analytical language demonstrates, in turn, how shifts in the authentication and moralization strategies of celebrity figures, from Audrey Hepburn to Angelina Jolie, reflect shifts in their proposals from an unconditional to a utilitarian form of solidarity.

The analysis of concerts, in chapter 5, makes use of popular culture studies to develop a language of 'performativity as charisma' and so to describe the ways in which rock star figures, such as Geldof and Bono, perform the role of the 'truth bearer' (authentication) so as to define the meaning of the Live Aid and Live 8 concerts from romantic, anti-establishment charity to pragmatic elite diplomacy (moralization). Finally, the analysis of news, in chapter 6, turns literature in journalism studies into a vocabulary of 'performativity as narrative' to tell the story of changes in the news (its authentication), which, in moving from expert to ordinary witnessing, suggests a broader shift towards a narcissistic discourse of solidarity in BBC's live blogs (moralization).

Taken together, these chapters come to tell a bigger story about the epistemic shift that marks the communication of solidarity today, from pity, and its universal moralities of salvation and revolution, to irony. In the spirit of a neoliberal ethics of pragmatism, my argument goes, ironic solidarity ceases to rely on the moral imperative to act on vulnerable others without asking back and asserts a new post-humanitarian morality that combines action on others with benefits for the self.

Conclusion: on the performances of the imaginary

I have here argued for the need to develop a novel approach to humanitarianism that can offer a nuanced account of solidarity in the age of global spectacle – an account that overcomes the pessimism of the critical school without ignoring the complexities involved in the mediation of solidarity. To this end, I proposed a theorization of the communicative structure of humanitarianism as a theatre of suffering, which capitalizes upon the spectacle of human vulnerability in order to move western publics into action.

Whereas this is a positive conception of the theatre, which appreciates the stage and the screen as crucial sites for our mundane habituation into solidary ways of feeling, thinking and acting on distant others, history reminds us that the theatre is simultaneously undermined by two paradoxes : the paradox of authenticity, inherent in the logic of the spectacle, and the paradox of agency, inherent in the power relations of humanitarianism. Instead of accepting negative accounts of humanitarianism, which tend to treat these paradoxes as static impasses that doom any call to solidarity to failure, however, my own account of the humanitarian imaginary treats these paradoxes as productive tensions that constitute solidarity within different public moralities, at different points in time.

If the conceptual value of the imaginary lies, therefore, in understanding humanitarianism as a communicative structure that cultivates our relationships to distant others through the age-long paradoxes of the theatre, its methodological value lies in enabling us to analyse this structure in terms of its performative practices. Even though they belong to distinct genres of the imaginary, what all these practices of the imaginary share is the unique moral power of the theatre to confront us with the compelling reality of suffering others but also, crucially, to provide us with the resources to judge whether and why this suffering may be a cause for our solidary action. My comparative focus on the key genres of the imaginary, spanning the past forty years, rests, in this sense, on the assumption that transformations in the performances of these genres can tell us an interesting story about the waning power of universal moralities and about the increasingly ironic ways in which we are invited to practise solidarity today. Let me start this story with a discussion of the genre of appeals.

3 Appeals

Introduction: the paradox of appeals

The paradoxes of the humanitarian imaginary are perhaps nowhere clearer than in the genre of appeals – a purely textual communicative practice, which engages with moral claims to common humanity in order to raise awareness around specific humanitarian agencies and their cause (deChaine 2005: 6–7). To do so, appeals have always struggled to settle the questions of how to visualize suffering, and how to inspire our feelings and actions on it, in ways that safeguard the legitimacy of their agencies in an increasingly competitive market. Yet, despite continuous efforts, the genre exists under a constant threat of delegitimization. From the early 'negative' imagery of emaciated children, denounced for dehumanizing the sufferer (Bethnall 1993), to the 'positive' imagery campaigns of smiling faces, accused of glossing over the misery of suffering (Lidchi 1997; Smillie 1995), to the more recent critiques of the 'commodification of solidarity' (Nash 2008), no style of representing human vulnerability seems to do justice to the moral claim of solidarity. Why is this so and what are the consequences of this perpetual threat to legitimacy for the morality of solidarity available in the genre of appeals today?

My approach to these styles of appealing takes them to be three distinct historical responses to the paradoxes of the humanitarian imaginary. In line with the methodological approach outlined in chapter 2, I focus, therefore, on the two dimensions of the imaginary, its historicity and its performativity. On the one hand, I discuss the historicity of appeals so as to show how the controversy over the genre's various imageries of suffering has followed the shifting dynamics of the humanitarian market towards increasingly entrepreneurial practices of communication. On the other hand, I focus on the 'affective performativity' of appeals, that is, on their strategic use of imagery and language with a view to generating emotion, so as to show how changes in the genre's authentication strategies, from photorealism to textual games, reflect further changes in its moralization strategies from emotional to self-reflexive proposals to action. This change, I argue, seeks to relegitimize the genre, by abandoning universal morality and grand emotion and by drawing, instead, on the new corporate and technological resources available in the humanitarian market today. As a consequence, I conclude, contemporary appeals become post-humanitarian: they privilege a self-oriented form of solidarity of short-term and low-intensity engagements with a cause, over an other-oriented solidarity of deeply felt, ideological commitments.

The crisis of the theatre of pity

Boltanski considers the legitimacy of humanitarian communication to be not simply a problem of appeals but, in line with my conception of the field as a social imaginary, also a problem in the very relationship between humanitarianism and politics. Specifically, he sees the constant struggle over legitimacy as a consequence of the tactical use of humanitarian argument in the service of political interest that often discredits the appeal to suffering as a universal moral cause (2000: 1–6; see also Mills 2005: 161–83). For my purposes, Boltanski's argument is helpful not only because of its critique of 'new humanitarianism', discussed in chapter 1, but primarily because of its analytical insight into the theatrical structure of humanitarian communication.

Contemporary politics, founded as it is on an Enlightenment discourse of the public good, he argues, draws its legitimacy not simply from its adherence to principles of democratic governance but also from its adherence to a universal conception of welfare towards vulnerable others; from the articulation of justice with pity. Whereas this emphasis on pity has enabled, partially but significantly, the alleviation of suffering among large populations in modern times, it has simultaneously established a dominant morality of action that relies on the theatrical presentation of suffering in public and on the concomitant language of grand emotions about this suffering – a reliance that, in Arendt's famous critique, subordinates politics to the 'social question'; it subordinates, that is, the long-term concern with establishing structures of justice to the urgent concern with doing something for those who suffer (Arendt 1963/1990: 59–114).

Boltanksi's diagnosis of contemporary humanitarianism in terms of a 'crisis of pity' can, in this sense, be understood as a crisis of this theatrical conception of politics, whereby the justification of action in the name of common humanity hides humanitarianism's own complicity with power behind emotion-saturated spectacles of suffering others – in line with the critique of empire. This is an imagery of sentimental gratitude that evokes appreciation for the benefactors who alleviate the suffering, in the solidarity of salvation, or an imagery of indignation or guilt that, as we saw in chapter 2, attributes responsibility to the perpetrators of suffering, in the solidarity of revolution (for these two topics of suffering, see Boltanski 1999: 35–54).

The inadequacy of this theatrical conception of the political, it follows, cannot be solely understood as an inadequacy of political performance as such, that is, as the failure of global institutions to address injustice or alleviate suffering. Indeed, despite sustained criticism of such institutions for strategic failures or tactical errors, the idea of humanitarianism remains strong today. This is so both in the arena of transnational governance, where there is a proliferation of INGOs monitoring policy implementation in developing contexts, and in the collective consciousness of the West, where humanitarian activism still plays a decisive role in nurturing moral imagination (Hale and Held 2011; deChaine 2005).

Instead, the inadequacy of this conception of the political can be understood as, at least partly, an inadequacy of the communicative structure of the theatre to evoke grand emotions (indignation and guilt or sympathy and gratitude) and, in so doing, to sustain a legitimate claim to solidarity within a deeply divided world. Boltanski's own formulation of the crisis of pity begins, indeed, from this diagnosis of the waning power of emotion as a justification for action today: 'Why is it so difficult nowadays to become indignant and to make accusations or, in another sense, to become emotional and feel sympathy – or at least to believe for any length of time, without falling into uncertainty, in the validity of one's own indignation or one's own sympathy?' (Boltanksi 2000: 12).

Taking my point of departure on this crucial question, I approach appeals as a communicative practice of the humanitarian imaginary that uses the language and imagery of suffering so as sustain its efficacy to produce emotion and to legitimize dispositions to action towards suffering others – what I call a practice of 'affective performativity'. My hypothesis is that this practice repeatedly fails to represent suffering as authentic, that is, to make a claim to truth that touches the West's heart without raising suspicions of manipulation (the critique of commodification) or without evoking the spectre of domination (the critique of empire) – and, consequently, continues to seek alternative ways to effectively habituate western publics into ways of feeling, thinking and acting about vulnerable others.

I begin this discussion in the section 'The Controversy around Appeals' where I outline the controversy over the power of 'negative' and 'positive' appeals to inspire solidarity. I then turn to an analytical discussion of the performativity of contemporary appeals (2006–8, by the UN World Food Programme, Amnesty International and Oxfam) and focus, on the one hand, upon their new authentication strategies, evident in an aesthetics of semiotic juxtaposition, and, on the other, upon their new moralization strategies, evident in a new reflexivity of humanitarian branding (section entitled 'The Reflexive Styles of Appealing'). I conclude with a discussion of the characteristics of this emerging style of appealing that, though not fully replacing the reflexive performativity of earlier styles, introduces a new, consumer-driven disposition to action – one that breaks with pity in favour of a potentially effective activism of effortless immediacy. In so doing, it comes to abandon the appeal to suffering as a universal moral cause and to challenge the relationship between humanitarianism and politics as we have known it so far (see 'Reflexive Appeals and Their Authenticity Effects').

The controversy around appeals

The historicity of appeals can be productively conceptualized as a controversy around their aesthetics of solidarity; around, that is, the different ways in which their imagery of suffering enacts paradigmatic forms of feeling and acting for the West. Two types of critique prevail in this controversy: a critique of the emotions of guilt and indignation, in the 'negative' aesthetics of early campaigns that portrayed sufferers as removed from the order of 'our' humanity, and a critique of the emotions of empathy and gratitude, in the aesthetics of 'positive' imagery that portrayed distant sufferers as people like 'us' (Lissner 1979; deChaine 2005; Dogra 2007). Each critique is associated with a specific historical moment of the humanitarian field and throws into relief the different emotional regimes and proposals of action that each moment puts forward. At the same time, both critiques focus on the power of the aesthetics of suffering to establish authenticity and inspire sensibilities to action and so point to the performativity of appeals as a key site for the study of this controversy.

Even though my discussion of historicity presupposes a view of appeals as performative, this view does not simultaneously presuppose that publics become what appeals intend them to become. Far from adopting a deterministic view, this performative perspective emphasizes instead the role of appeals as moral education – as a series of subtle proposals of how we should feel and act towards distant suffering which, as I argued in chapter 2, are introduced into our everyday life by mundane acts of mediation (television, internet or urban advertising) and shape our longer-term dispositions to action by way of 'habituation' (see also Chouliaraki 2008a: 831–47).

My discussion of 'negative' and 'positive' appeals, then, links up the critiques of the genre of appeals with insights into the public morality that this genre makes possible and legitimate to us at two distinct points in time. It is this discussion that sets the historical context against which I then analyse the emerging reflexive performativity of appeals in the humanitarian imaginary.

'Negative' appeals

Early examples of humanitarian appeals rely on a documentary aesthetics that authenticates suffering, by representing it in its plain reality. Contemporaneous with the emergence of the aid and development field, after decolonization, these appeals rely on what Edkins calls the 'medicalization of famine' (2000: 39). Departing from political understandings of famine as the outcome of historical processes of systemic inequality in the distribution of resources, characteristic of the solidarity of revolution, this medical conception of famine focused instead on immediate medical and nutritional support to enable new but poor states of the South to survive – in line with the solidarity of salvation. Given this western focus on survival, early appeals consequently sought to relieve the symptoms of famine, rather than addressing its causes, and focus, therefore, on the visible effects of starvation on the human body: 'Relief', as Edkins puts it, 'is aimed at preserving the life of the biological organism rather than restoring the means of livelihood in the community' (2000: 39).

The 1968 imagery in Figure 3.1, for instance, relies on raw realism to depict human bodies in an extreme state of starvation as 'ideal victims' (Hojer 2004). The image is a collective composition of children devoid of individualizing features – either biological, such as their age and sex, or social, such as their clothing. They are naked or half-naked, their self-abandoned nudity exposing emaciated body parts. Captured on camera, these body parts, shot from above as they are, become 'fetishized' (Hall 1997: 223–79): they do not reflect real human bodies with a life history but curiosities of the flesh that mobilize a pornographic spectatorial imagination between disgust and desire (Lissner 1979).

The authentication strategies of these appeals are 'victim oriented', that is, they focus on the distant sufferer as the object of our contemplation (Cohen 2001: 218). In so doing, they establish a social relationship anchored in the colonial gaze and premised on a maximal distance between this suffering other and the western spectator (Hall 1992/2001; Lidchi 1997). It is precisely this social relationship that Silverstone (2002: 283) refers to as the 'immorality of distance': a relationship whereby the figure of the spectator is fully sovereign in her/his agency over the sufferer – in terms of managing the technologies of recording, authoring the texts of appealing and generously engaging in charitable giving (Pinney 1992) – whereas the sufferer remains passive, unaware, quasi-human.

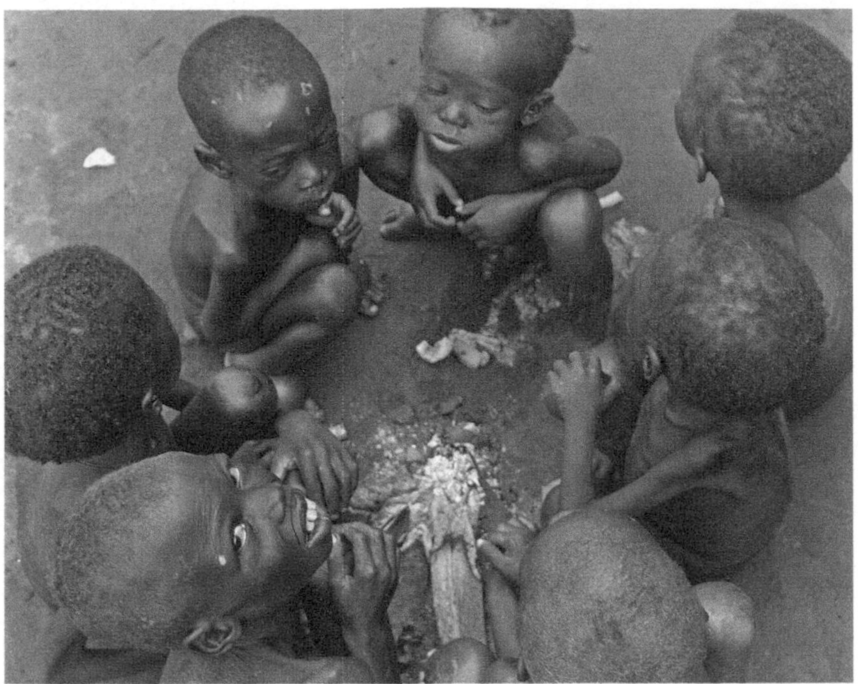

Figure 3.1 Famine in Biafra, 1968. Children suffering from hunger share food. 20 Sept. 1968, in the refugee camp of Opobo (FRANCOIS MAZURE/AFP/ Getty Images).

The immorality of distance that these 'negative' appeals enact is closely associated with an affective performativity of shame and indignation (adapted from Cohen 2001: 214). This performativity is primarily induced by the stark contrast between the bare life of these sufferers and the reality of the spectators' comfortable life – a contrast between, what Agamben calls *zoe*, physically deformed bodies in a state of animality, and *bios*, the civility of healthy bodies in western societies (1998). What this contrast, forcefully thrown into relief by the circulation of 'negative' imagery in western contexts of affluence and safety, sets in motion is the key moralizing trope of 'negative' appeals that relies on the logic of 'complicity' (Singer 1972/2008: 388–96; Wenar 2003/2008: 283–304).

On the one hand, the logic of complicity evokes the legacy of the colonial West and, with it, of the European responsibility in systematically disempowering distant others through imperial rule. This is a sense of historical complicity that figures in western consciousness as a sentiment of collective guilt (Flynn 1984: 51–69; le Sueur & Bourdieu 2001: 148–84). On the other hand, the logic of complicity renders the individual spectator a witness of the horrors of distant suffering and so makes our inaction towards suffering a personal failure to take responsibility for such horrors – a sense of everyday or banal complicity to distant suffering that taps into feelings of shame (Ahmed 2004).

The logic of complicity is, in this sense, not only a primary source of negative emotion but also of the moral agency of these appeals: failure to act, it implies, is failure to acknowledge our historical and personal participation in perpetuating human suffering. Guilt and shame, however, pivotal emotions though they may be in this type of imagery, do not exhaust the communicative repertoire of 'negative' appeals. In its most powerful manifestation, the logic of complicity transforms these emotions, often regarded as introverted modes of feeling towards suffering, into the more extrovert and assertive emotion of indignation. Here, the social relations of complicity can become political: they are externalized from the individual to society, as in the solidarity of revolution (Boltanksi 1999: 61–3). Consequently, the figure of the persecutor is objectified in the form of unequal structures of power and moral agency is linked to the imperative of social justice: *outrage into action* was Amnesty International's campaign slogan during the early 1990s.

The distinction between guilt and indignation is, no doubt, crucial in differentiating non-political from politicized forms of activism, with guilt encouraging more privatized, charity-oriented acts and indignation privileging public protest against injustice. The distinction granted, however, there is an inherent tension in all strategies of moralization that rely on the logic of complicity. By evoking guilt, shame or even indignation, critics argue, 'negative' appeals seek to turn grand emotions into action, by, at least partly, identifying the figure of the persecutor in the very audiences they address as potential benefactors – aren't we, as the critique of empire would put it, part of this western legacy, unwillingly but surely participating in the systemic inertia that reproduces the power relations between West and South? Guilt and indignation, in this sense, inform an ambivalent form of moral agency that both presupposes the western spectator's complicity in world poverty, collectively and individually, and at the same time enacts this complicity in the power relations that it seeks to expose and redress (Hattori 2003b: 164–5). The immorality of distance, which the 'negative' imagery establishes between those who watch and those who suffer, captures precisely this ambivalent moral agency that makes the West the benefactor of a world that it manages to symbolically annihilate.

The popular response to 'negative' imagery, known as compassion fatigue or the 'I've seen this before' syndrome (Moeller 1999: 2), may not directly draw on this theoretical critique of affective performativity, but it does reflect it in the form of two more pragmatic risks: the 'bystander' effect and the 'boomerang' effect. The former risk refers to people's indifference or reluctance to act on suffering as a reaction towards these flows of negative emotion that ultimately leave people feeling that there is nothing they can do or, as Cohen puts it, 'a sense of the situation so utterly hopeless and incomprehensible that we cannot bear to think about it' (2001: 194). The latter risk refers to people's indignation not towards the imagined evildoer but towards the guilt-tripping message of the 'negative' campaigns themselves – 'for bombarding you with material that only makes you feel miserable and guilty' (Cohen 2001: 214). Rather than encouraging a moral agency of solidarity, these risks ultimately undermine it.

'Negative' appeals, in summary, are defined by a performativity of guilt and indignation which claims authenticity through a realist imagery of suffering as 'bare life' and moralizes western publics through the logic of complicity, thereby risking compassion fatigue and apathy.

'Positive' appeals

A response to 'negative' appeals, 'positive' ones also rely on photorealistic strategies of authentication that represent the reality of suffering as it is. The difference is that these appeals reject the imagery of the sufferer as a victim and centre on the sufferer's agency and dignity.

Evident in the PLAN example (Figure 3.2), the two key characteristics of this style of appealing are: (i) the personalization of sufferers, which focuses on distinct individuals and portrays these individuals as actors (for example, as participating in development projects); and (ii) the singularization of donors, which addresses each one as a person who can make a concrete contribution to improve a sufferer's life (for example, through child sponsorship). It is now the presence of the benefactor, rather than the persecutor, which is instrumental in summoning up a new affective performativity of 'empathy, tender-heartedness and gratitude' in these appeals (adapted from Cohen 2001: 216–18).

Rather than complicity, the moralizing function of this affective performativity relies on 'sympathetic equilibrium', a communicative logic that orients the appeal towards a responsive balance of emotions between the distant sufferer and the spectator as potential benefactor (Boltanski 1999: 39). Specifically, the logic of the sympathetic equilibrium is established through the ways in which the imagery of suffering provides subtle evidence of the sufferer's gratitude for the (imagined) alleviation of her/his suffering by a benefactor and the benefactor's respective empathy towards the grateful sufferer.

It is, first, the personalization of the sufferer in the photos of smiling children, in the sentimental texts of child sponsorship or in the eyewitness

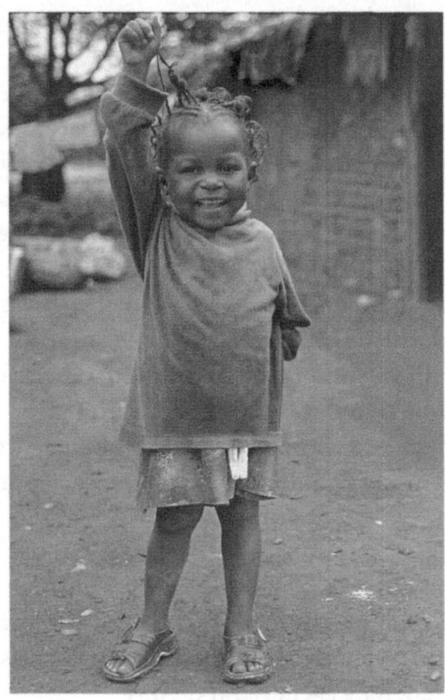

Figure 3.2 PLAN International Poster, 1993 (Plan/Adam Hinton).

accounts of aid workers that seeks to articulate this sense of fine-tuning between the donor and the receiver of aid. The use of bilateral emotion, here, not only empowers the sufferer, giving her a voice, but, in so doing, further animates the donor's 'modal imagination': our capacity to acknowledge in the suffering other a shared quality of humanity absent in 'negative' appeals. And it is, second, the singularization of the donor, as an individual who can make a difference in a practical way, that similarly seeks to empower audiences by showing us how our actions may lead to concrete and real change.

The moralization strategies of 'positive' appeals attempt, in this sense, to produce a new form of agency that avoids the evils of 'negative' appeals: people's sense of powerlessness towards distant suffering (the bystander effect) and people's resistance to the negativity of campaigns themselves (the boomerang effect). Importantly, however, these communicative practices are also closely linked to the new hegemony of interventionism in the humanitarian project, which, after the mid-1980s, went beyond aid to incorporate the demand for progress and to create frameworks for improved livelihood for vulnerable others. Imagery and the vision it informs are thus inseparable parts of this project; as the 1989 Commission for Images puts it, the problem of images and perceptions cannot be separated from the methodology of intervention.[1]

Yet, even if these spectacles manage to provide us with a more authentic understanding of the complexity of global divisions, they conceal crucial aspects of this complexity, which ultimately limit the capacity of the interventionist project to promote sustainable social change – the neoliberal instrumentalization of humanitarianism and the concomitant marketization of the field but also the 'new humanitarian wars' being some of these aspects (Hattori 2003a,b; Cottle & Nolan 2007).

It is the social relationship emerging out of spectacles of hope and self-determination, embedded as they are in the power relations of development, that Silverstone's 'immorality of identity' aptly describes (2007). Immorality here refers to the glossing over of the fundamental asymmetry between the two parties and to the assimilation of 'their' difference under 'our' norm. The immorality of sameness is, in this respect, a classic instance of what Bourdieu calls 'misrecognition', the euphemistic concealment of systemic power relations by the image of smiling children (1977: 183–97).

Central to the operation of misrecognition, in 'positive' appeals, is, as we saw, the moralization strategy of gratitude and fellow feeling. Dialectically linked to empathy, through the logic of the sympathetic equilibrium, the emotion of gratitude relies on the social logic of the gift between unequal parties – whereby the reception of a gift without the possibility of reciprocation, as is the case of development, binds the grateful receiver into a nexus of obligations and duties towards the generous donor. At the same time, the generosity and tender-heartedness of the West unite donors in a community of virtue that discovers in its own fellow feeling for distant others a narcissistic self-contentment (Hattori 2003b). Criticism against the 'positive' performativity of appeals centres precisely on this ambivalent moral agency that their imagery makes possible. Whilst it appears to empower distant sufferers through discourses of dignity and self-determination, 'positive' imagery simultaneously disempowers these sufferers by appropriating their otherness in western discourses of identity and agency.

The critique of the 'immorality of identity' at play, here, essentially addresses the ways that benevolent emotions operate as instruments of power, insofar as they render others the perpetual objects of 'our' generosity. Simultaneously, the critique reflects more pragmatic risks of misrecognition that feed into an increasing compassion fatigue for 'positive' styles of appealing, too. First, there is the risk of positive examples of 'aid in action' being misrecognized as fully addressing the problems of the developing world and, therefore, leading to inaction on the grounds of the argument that 'everything is already taken care of'; this is what we may call a misrecognition of the systemic relations of inequality (Small 1997: 581–93). Second, there is the risk that the plethora of smiling child faces may be misrecognized as children like 'ours', leading to inaction on the grounds of the argument that 'these are not really children in need'; this is a misrecognition of the social relations of difference and identity that positive imagery glosses over (Cohen 2001: 183–4). Rather than enabling action on vulnerable others, the misrecognition risks inherent in 'positive' appeals deepen the crisis of pity in that they introduce an element of suspicion into the spectacle of suffering – a 'how do I know this is real?' sensibility that cancels out the authenticity of photorealism and feeds back into the public suspicion of the media as manipulators of the imagery of suffering (Cohen & Seu 2002: 187–201).

'Positive' imagery, in summary, is defined by a performativity of benevolent emotion which claims authenticity by reference to a realist aesthetics of suffering and moralizes the West through the logic of sympathetic equilibrium and its emotions of empathy and tender-heartedness. Unable to resolve the problem of suspicion, however, 'positive' imagery runs similar risks of compassion fatigue as 'negative' imagery does.

The historical controversy around appeals throws into relief the theatrical paradoxes of the genre. Despite showing human vulnerability as it is, the authenticity of photorealism cannot, in fact, sustain its claims to the truth of suffering and, at the same time, despite their moralizing power, the grand emotions of indignation and empathy cannot sustain the legitimacy of their claims to solidarity.

By seeking, then, to confront us with the reality of distant suffering in two of its most authentic forms, shocking destitution and hopeful self-determination, the theatrical structure of appeals, nonetheless, seems suspended between two impossible public (im)moralities – the immorality of distance and the immorality of identity. The former animates the affective performativity of guilt and indignation to lead us into action but such negative emotions tie action to our own complicity in global injustice and run the risk of ultimate fatigue and apathy. The latter animates the emotional constellation of gratitude and tender-heartedness to persuade us to act, but such positive emotions tie action to a suspicious view of development as unreciprocated gift, which glosses over deep asymmetries of power and runs the risk of denying the very need for action on the grounds that it may be unnecessary or even unreal.

The reflexive styles of appealing

The genre of appeals reflects the paradoxes of humanitarian communication, as discussed in chapters 1 and 2. Its ongoing attempts to legitimacy occur in this contradictory field, where the reality of suffering appears through different norms of realism and activates different regimes of emotion without, however, managing to transcend its contradictions – without managing to construe suffering as the cause of authentic emotion and action 'for any length of time', to recall Boltanski's quote.

It is in the light of this inherent instability that I now turn to examine the emergence of a style of appealing which coexists with the previous two styles but departs from them in terms of both its performative properties: its aesthetic quality, which relies on authentication strategies that now problematize rather than reproduce photorealistic accuracy, and in terms of its agency, which relies on moralization strategies that break with the registers of pity as motivations for action (guilt and indignation, empathy and gratitude). This emergent style can be characterized as 'reflexive' in that, unlike the previous two, it does not seek to legitimize claims to solidarity by resolving the paradoxes of appeals but, in contrast, by rendering these paradoxes the very object of our contemplation and reflection.

The reflexive style, I argue, makes possible a new disposition of solidarity that disengages action on suffering from grand emotions whilst it invites us to rely on our own judgement as to whether such action is possible or desirable. Drawing on recent examples from the United Nation's World Food Programme ('No Food Diet' appeal, 2006), Amnesty International ('Bullet. The Execution', 2006) and Oxfam ('Be Humankind', 2008), I discuss each appeal in terms of its aesthetic quality and moral agency.

Aesthetic quality: Reflexive performativity

The aesthetic feature that cuts across all three appeals is semiotic juxtaposition, that is, the contrast between different elements of each appeal's meaning-making system (Jewitt & Kress 2003). Specifically, each text is constituted by particular forms of juxtaposition between (i) verbal and visual modes, in the WFP 'No Food Diet' appeal, (ii) visual form and visual content in Amnesty International's 'Bullet. The Execution' and (iii) textual and physical space-time in Oxfam's 'Be Humankind'.

The 'No Food Diet' WFP appeal (similar WFP imagery appears in Figure 3.3) relies on the contrast between language and image. On the visual plane, the dominant imagery is that of an African family, with a focus on the

Figure 3.3 World Food Programme, 2006 (WFP/Marcelo Spina).

mother who makes food and puts her children to bed. The sequence evokes an aura of 'universal' everyday domesticity that is further enhanced by the reassuringly intimate tone of the voice-over that recites a recipe – the 'No Food Diet'. As the title of the appeal suggests, however, the content of the talk provides a different framing for the visual: the recipe refers to the old trick of fooling children to sleep in the expectation of a dinner that is never to come. The voice-over continues by contrasting the effectiveness of our familiar 'Atkins Diet' with the 'No Food Diet' and concludes with 'guess what . . . it is so effective that 25,000 people on the no food diet die every day.' At this point, the visual shifts to African people looking frontally at the camera; the familiar aura of domesticity has now given way to the more traditional imagery of an arranged line of silent figures to be contemplated. The last frame is the WFP web address with a subtle invitation to donate embedded in it: www.wfp.org/donate.

The juxtaposition between language and image, which is central to the appeal, works effectively to situate a western diet discourse in the context of African famine and, in so doing, it manages to throw into relief another contrast between a lifestyle of scarcity and a lifestyle of abundance. The rhetorical effect of this contrast is a Bakhtinian 'tragic irony', a sense of the absurdity of our cultural habits 'echoed' in the appeal's two voices:

Figure 3.4 Bullet: The Execution (Amnesty International, 2008).

theirs and ours (Pateman 1989: 203–16). Unlike the realism of 'negative' appeals, this ironic 'double-voicedness' does not work to remind us of the radical otherness of the African poor, but operates as a strategy of 'cultural estrangement' – reminding us of the otherness of our own cultural habits as they are placed against the background of their struggle for daily survival.[2]

'The Bullet. The Execution' Amnesty appeal relies on a different juxtaposition between image form and content. At the level of form, the appeal consists of a three-dimensional animation technique which simulates a prisoner's execution. Three formal properties are important: *colour*, dark and subdued, *rhythm*, slow motion, and *design*, an exaggerated realism that focuses on the detail of human figures, such as body posture, muscle movement, gaze, but also on the detail of objects, such as the jerking of the gun, the gun fire, the vector of the bullet shooting through. The combined effect of these formal properties is hyper-reality, a perfected sense of the real that can only be fictional (Baudrillard 1988: 43–4).

At the level of content, the story is about the rescuing of a prisoner's life through the paper shield of petition sheets signed by Amnesty supporters. As we follow the bullet moving slowly towards the prisoner's body, petition papers start flying through and hover in space between the bullet and the body. They are being ripped by the bullet but ultimately succeed in protecting the body – then there is an extreme close-up of the prisoner's eye and the sigh of his relief. The claim 'Your petitions are more powerful than you think,' followed by Amnesty's e-address (www. AmnestyInternational.fr), is the only linguistic text of the appeal. There is a sense of extreme intensity in

Figure 3.5 Be Humankind (Oxfam, 2008).

Figure 3.6 Be Humankind (Oxfam, 2008).

this 'silent' sequence, which endows the piece with an ecstatic sense of temporality, where *time stands still* and a *minute seems to last a lifetime* (Barker 2002: 75) – a temporality that we often associate with the visual genres of adventure fiction (Chouliaraki 2006: 97–115).

Finally, the 'Be Humankind' Oxfam appeal relies on yet another form of juxtaposition: chronotopic estrangement (Holquist and Kliger 2005: 613–36). This Bakhtinian term refers to the manipulation of the categories of space and time, whereby the imagery of the most familiar spaces of our everyday life, such as the street, the local shop or the square, are defamiliarized and presented as objects of our contemplation. The appeal introduces the imperative to act on vulnerable others through a graphically animated story of a senior citizen who, indifferent as she initially appears to be towards the mediated spectacles of suffering available in the streets of her home town, ultimately realizes the consequences of her indifference for her own life and joins fellow citizens in her town square to confront the 'monster of injustice'. As they all 'speak out' against the monster, a phantasmagoria of fireworks wrapping up the planet concludes the appeal. The only linguistic text of the campaign is the 'Be Humankind' slogan, accompanied by the Oxfam brand and contact details (text number and website address). Chronotopic estrangement takes place, here, through an aesthetics of graphic animation which, in presenting a person like 'us' in a cartoonesque manner, fictionalizes the context of 'our' everyday living and enables us to reflect on the consequences of our denial.

In so far as these appeals still rely on the authenticating force of the imagery of suffering to construct the humanitarian cause, they do not drop claims to truth in their communicative practices. They do, however, shift away from photorealism as a vehicle of authentic witnessing, evident in the 'negative' and 'positive' appeals, and move towards self-conscious textualities as yet another aesthetic choice through which suffering can be staged. This occurs through various forms of semiotic juxtaposition that invite a contemplative relationship to distant suffering as the new content of already familiar popular genres and remind us that we are now confronted not with the facts of suffering but with acts of representation.

Moral agency: fleeting commitment

This rupture with the aesthetic quality of earlier appeals simultaneously implies a further rupture with the moralization strategies of those appeals whereby one thing, the photorealism of suffering, is assumed to be translated into another, action on suffering. What informs this rupture is the assumption that emotional connectivity based on authentic suffering is no longer a prerequisite for motivating solidarity; seeing suffering does not lead to acting on suffering (Cohen & Seu 2002: 200–2). Which are, then, the properties of moral agency in these self-consciously aestheticized appeals? I focus on two: the technologization of action and the de-emotionalization of the cause.

Technologization of action

In line with processes of technologization, as described in chapter 1, a key feature of the new appeals is the simplicity of their proposals to action:

click your mouse. The call to action figures modestly as a *slash/donate* in the WFP web address (www.wfp.org/donate) or simply as a reference to Amnesty's address (e.g., www. AmnestyInternational.fr). The use of technology here significantly simplifies the spectator/user's mode of engagement with the humanitarian cause: all we need to do is to click under the 'sign petitions' or 'make donations' links. There are two dimensions to this simplification.

The first dimension of simplification has to do with the use of the internet as the dominant vehicle for public action on distant suffering. Speed and on-the-spot intervention, both features of online activism celebrated as catalysts for a new democratic politics (Bennett 2003), are here instrumental in addressing the key problem of the humanitarian sensibility mentioned earlier: the non-sustainability of grand emotions towards a humanitarian cause *for any length of time*. The simplification of action, in this sense, is not only an inevitable but also a desirable dimension of technologized humanitarian communication. At the same time, however, unlike forms of public action that require collective and sustained practices of activism, this no-time engagement with technology suggests that expectations of effortless immediacy, the most prominent element of contemporary consumer culture, are increasingly populating the moral imagination of humanitarianism. What emerges, as a result, may be a form of 'cool' activism that, following McGuigan's definition of 'cool capitalism' as a lifestyle of effortless immediacy and instant gratification, seeks to seduce its publics 'by the delights of high tech and "cool" commodities, promising to satisfy their every desire, especially if they are different and vaguely rebellious in tone' (2009: 124).

The second dimension of simplification has to do with the absence of any justification of action towards suffering – any hint of the question as to why action may be important. As opposed to the other two styles of appealing that promote their message by drawing on universal moralities, that is, by evoking either the West's complicity to world poverty or the recognition rights of vulnerable others, emergent appeals abandon universal morality altogether.

What they communicate instead is the organizational brand itself: the WFP and AI web addresses constitute, indeed, the only linguistic text of the appeals. Responding to the risks of emotion-oriented appeals that tell the public what they should feel (risks of cynicism, fatigue and suspicion), this style relies instead on signalling the strong 'brand equity' of these organizations, that is, their solid image and international reputation, in order to promote their cause (Arvidsson 2006; Slim 2003).[3] Insofar as they strategically replace moralistic exhortation with brand recognition, thereby moving from an explicit marketing of suffering as a cause towards an implicit investment on the identity of the humanitarian agency itself, this emergent style is inspired by practices of corporate branding (Vestergaard 2008). Regarded as the most effective form of corporate persuasion, branding works through ellipsis: it is not the verbalization of argument but the 'aura' of the brand that sustains the relationship between product and consumer (Arviddson 2006: 73–94).

In this spirit, the branding of suffering abandons visual realism, grand emotion and the question of why in order to tap into the readily available assets of historical organizations, such as WFP or Amnesty, and to allow consumption-savvy publics themselves to infer the appeals' associations of solidarity as the sovereign creators of brand meaning. An important consequence of this highly technologized and brand-driven style of communication is the transformation of the affective performativity of suffering in those reflexive appeals.

The de-emotionalization of the cause

All three appeals inevitably articulate certain affective dispositions towards suffering, since without emotion no appeal to action could be legitimate. These dispositions rely on the traditional affective regimes of humanitarian communication, namely guilt, shame and indignation or empathy and gratitude. They do so, however, in ways that evoke these regimes not as immediate emotions that may inspire action but rather as objects of contemplation to be reflected upon.

The 'No Food Diet' appeal relies on ironic estrangement, a textual trope characterized by a high degree of self-consciousness, that sets western concerns about weight control against the drama of survival in Africa – echoing perhaps Bob Geldof's quote, 'it is absurd that people die of want in a world of surplus' (Geldof in Youngs 2005). Rather than relying on the contemplation of the other, brought close through the imagery of the sufferer, this appeal relies on the contemplation of the self through imagery that creates a distance from our own taken-for-granted habits in a world of abundance. This ironic self-reflexivity conveys a sense of suppressed guilt that gently hints at the affective regime of 'negative' appeals in the final sequences of African people gazing at the camera; these, however, do not seek to shock us by exposing the extremities of the human condition, as these African people are not portrayed in a state of 'bare life', only to give us perhaps a glimpse of the absurdity of injustice at the heart of our conditions of existence.

'The Bullet. The Execution' appeal relies on the sublimation of the moment of execution, where the battle of good versus evil, reflected in the minute face details of the prisoner and the executioner, works to evoke a suppressed reference to heroic sacrifice: the spectator's noble power to do good, to save the life of a conscience prisoner. Again, this is not the heroism of indignant denunciation that has, in the past, so powerfully inspired movements of international solidarity against tyrannical regimes. It is rather a dispassionate emotional regime of estrangement, where the act of saving a life is coded into the aesthetics of digital gaming and the proposal to action is disconnected from political discourse, containing a minimal message of empowerment: *your petitions are more powerful than you think*.

Finally, the 'Be Humankind' appeal uses narrative estrangement to interrupt the naturalized assumptions about where we are and how we orient ourselves to the world, by use of cartoon animation that makes possible two further reversals: the visualization of an intangible concept, injustice, and the invisibility of physical bodies, the suffering others. The visualization of injustice as a monster disappearing into a firework inscribes the question of injustice in a simplistic celebration of the 'us'/good vs 'it'/evil struggle, foreclosing the meaning of justice itself, whereas the invisibility of suffering others (except in the doubly mediated form of 'news on suffering' within the appeal) addresses compassion fatigue by avoiding the sufferer and focusing instead on the lifestyle of the western actor. Narrative estrangement may, in this way, invite us to reflexively engage with ourselves as a way into the disposition of 'humankindness', but simultaneously maximizes the distance between 'us' and vulnerable others, and renders their existence irrelevant to the justification of 'becoming humankind'.

In summary, the move from the affective performativity of grand emotions to the reflexive performativities of ironic estrangement demonstrates a radical shift in the authentication strategies of the genre of appeals and, consequently, in the proposals of solidarity that they seek to legitimize. These proposals, I have argued, refract grand emotions into what we may call 'low intensity' affective regimes that insinuate the classic constellations of emotion towards suffering but do not quite inspire or enact them. Guilt, self-sacrifice and commited activism reappear not as parts of a grand narrative of solidarity but as decontextualized fragments of such narratives that render the psychological world of the spectator a potential terrain for estrangement and self-reflection. What I wish to do in the final part of this section, therefore, is to reflect on the nature of this new moral agency, in 'The Post-Humanitarian Public', as well as on the enactment of solidarity today, in 'Solidarity or Narcissism?'

Reflexive appeals and their authenticity effects

Approaching appeals in terms of their affective performativity has thrown into relief the communicative practices by which authenticity has been produced in the humanitarian imaginary in the course of the past 45 years. Operating on a theatrical conception of politics as pity, which privileges the spectacle of vulnerability as a source of emotion for and action on distant sufferers, appeals have long relied upon this affective performativity to present suffering as authentic and to evoke emotions of guilt and indignation or tender-heartedness and empathy as motivations for action on it.

What the shift from an affective to a reflexive performativity signals, in this sense, is not simply a shift from a realist to a textually conscious aesthetics of suffering, but a fundamental shift in the very communicative structure of the imaginary away from the theatre, which establishes the encounter between 'us' and 'them' as necessary for habituating the West into dispositions of solidarity, and towards a 'mirror' structure where, in the absence of suffering and its justification, we are confronted with our own image as a resource for making sense of solidarity. What are the implications of this receding theatricality of the imaginary? It is, I conclude, the emergence of a post-humanitarian public – a public that embodies a new morality of solidarity, suspended between technological activism and self-indulgent narcissism.

The post-humanitarian public

It is the public disposition of low intensity emotions and a technological imagination of instant gratification and no justification that I call post-humanitarian. What the term refers to is the ways in which emotion becomes increasingly detached from the contexts in which it is produced, that is to say, from the domain of immediate subjective experience (and its aesthetics of realism), and is inserted into contexts of technological communication where it becomes the object of self-conscious reflection and regulation. Whereas still dependent on realistic imagery (of the poor, the wounded or the about-to-die), the key feature of post-humanitarianism lies precisely in loosening up this 'necessary' link between seeing suffering and feeling for the sufferer and, so, in decoupling emotion for the sufferer from acting on the cause of suffering. At the heart of this communicative structure lies, in this sense, a particular form of subjectivity that Mestrovic calls 'post-emotional' – 'the post-emotional individual', he says, 'takes cues from . . . the media and cyberspace as to when he or she should rationally choose to exhibit a vicarious indignation, niceness or other pre-packaged emotions' – emotions, Mestrovic continues, that are 'easy to slip on and off' and, therefore, remain 'detached from genuine moral commitment and or meaningful social action' (1997: xi–xii).

Central to the orientation towards a '*vicarious*' affectivity is the particularization of the morality of solidarity, where suffering becomes disembedded from the morality of common humanity, capable of inspiring grand emotion and long-term commitment, and relies instead on solidarity as a personalized request to act online, which is 'easy to slip on and off'. It is this contrast between the universalisms of earlier appeals and the particularisms of the new that renders post-humanitarianism vulnerable to critiques of commodification. In requiring little emotional involvement, minimal time and no long-term commitment, its solidarity has been accused of promoting a corporate brand rather than speaking of justice (Mestrovic 1997; Cohen 2001).

What this commodification critique of post-humanitarianism ignores, however, is that previous styles of appealing were also informed by a similar tension between politics and the market – between awareness-raising and fund-raising (Lissner 1979). Indeed, the dominant conception of the political, introduced earlier, that connects the legitimacy of public action with the production of emotion is not itself devoid of economic interest. Rather, both 'negative' and 'positive' appeals are situated squarely within a market logic of persuasion, insofar as they also seek to communicate emotion for their own ends. The privileging of either negative or positive emotion is, at once, an articulation of political passion in the service of solidarity and a strategy of the market that legitimizes the organizational brand.

The difference then between the affective performativity of early humanitarianism of the 1970s–1990s and post-humanitarianism lies essentially in the principle that each style of appealing uses to secure its legitimacy: moral universalism in the former and reflexive particularism in the latter. The particularization of the humanitarian cause in today's appeals should be seen, in this light, as a market response to the universalization of the cause in the emotion-oriented ones. In portraying sufferers as powerless victims or as dignified agents, these campaigns intend to produce either a universal morality of justice, through 'negative' emotions that ultimately dehumanize the sufferer, or a universal morality of empathy, through positive emotions that eventually appropriate the sufferer in a world like 'ours'. Neither of these two forms of universalism, as we saw, ultimately manages to sustain a legitimate claim to public action on suffering.

From this perspective, rather than claiming that the post-humanitarian style commodifies appeals, it would be more productive to claim that it shifts the terms on which the commodification of appealing occurs today. Whereas earlier appeals assume that emotions and their universal claims operate in a moral economy of abundance, an economy where everyone can, in principle, feel for and act on distant suffering in an unrestricted manner, post-humanitarian appeals assume instead that emotions operate in an economy of scarcity 'where the emotional wealth of one agent necessarily comes at the expense of another' (Gross 2006: 79).

It is precisely the recognition of this tension between the proliferation of moralizing claims, prescriptive and perhaps inauthentic as they are, and the public's bounded ability to feel and act on distant others, which lies at the heart of INGO branding and its post-humanitarian publics. By foregrounding the act of communication rather than emotional affiliation towards suffering, this style acknowledges that compassion fatigue lies not so much in the excess of human suffering that transcends our individual capacity to feel for or act on it, but rather in the excess of universal moral claims around which we are called to organize our feelings and action towards suffering.

Solidarity or narcissism?

To come full circle to the question of legitimacy in the humanitarian imaginary, I propose to understand post-humanitarianism as a specific response to the crisis of pity – one that seeks to reclaim the legitimacy of appeals by recourse to the market practice of branding that technologizes and particularizes the premises for action on suffering, rendering such action irrelevant to the moralities that have traditionally informed public agency on suffering in the first place.

As a consequence, post-humanitarianism offers an alternative vision of public agency – one whose political implications are deeply ambivalent. In activating low-intensity emotions, this style proposes a model of action that 'cleanses' the communication of solidarity of sentimentalist argument and introduces self-reflection as a new justification for solidarity. In so doing, post-humanitarianism further foregrounds the power of personal rather than collective action in making a difference to the lives of vulnerable others. What this form of agency asserts, in particular, is the capacity of consumer culture to expand the domain of politics towards mundane tactics of subversion, such as playful estrangement, through various tropes of semiotic juxtaposition. In this way, post-humanitarianism challenges traditional forms of agency, where solidarity requires the subordination of the self to a higher cause, and privileges the pleasures of the self as a more effective way of making a difference to distant others (Hartley 2010: 233–48).

At the same time, however, in capitalizing on our personal resources without offering a justification for action, the post-humanitarian sensibility runs the risk of perpetuating the narcissism of the West: a cultural disposition that returns distant suffering to the domain of individual experience and so renders the emotions of the self the measure of our understanding of the sufferings of the world at large (Sennett 1974: 324; Illouz 2007: 36–9). By projecting a 'mirror' structure in the hope that distance from ourselves may inspire us to act on distant others, post-humanitarianism ultimately forgets that the moral education of the humanitarian imaginary is about pushing us beyond our comfort zone so as to grapple with the questions of who the 'human' is and why it is important to act on its cause; it is, in other words, about realizing that solidarity may after all be more relevant and effective when orientated towards those whose needs have been historically and systemically neglected, rather than to others like 'us'.

Post-humanitarian appeals may, thus, be mobilizing a momentary activism but do so at the expense of cultivating a deeper understanding of why humanitarian action is important – thereby also failing to operate as agents of moral education. As a consequence, rather than challenging the historical patterns of injustice inherent in the moral economy of scarcity, which this emergent style has so accurately diagnosed, these appeals may be reinforcing it. Out of care to renew the legitimacy of humanitarian calls to action, post-humanitarian appeals may be feeding back into a dominant western culture, where the over-emotionalization of 'our' own suffering goes hand in hand with the de-emotionalization of the suffering of distant others.

Conclusion: the ambivalence of 'cool' activism

This chapter followed the trajectory of appeals which have traditionally sought to legitimize their claims to solidarity by relying upon the spectacle of suffering as a source of emotion and action. Whilst appeals had provisionally addressed the theatrical paradoxes of humanitarianism by resorting to photorealistic imagery as proof of the authenticity of suffering and to the emotions of pity, guilt and tender-heartedness, as motivations for solidarity, they have not managed to resolve these paradoxes once and for all.

The contemporary moment addresses this (inevitable) failure by abandoning the theatrical structure of the imaginary in favour of a reflexive engagement with the self. Even though this distance from the self, inherent in the reflexive performativity of appeals, can be seen as a welcome acknowledgement of public fatigue with the universalisms of common humanity, it simultaneously introduces into the morality of solidarity the logic of corporate branding. This is an ambivalent logic that seduces us into a 'cool' activism whilst keeping us in a comfort zone that offers neither justifications as to why we should act on the suffering of others nor the opportunity to confront the humanity of those others. Whilst, therefore, reflexive performativity entails both the promise of a new solidarity and the risks of narcissism, as long as our relation to others is only accomplished through an imagination *of ourselves*, solidarity can never become a matter of commitment and justification. It will always remain just a vague and self-complacent prompt to 'be humankind'.

4 Celebrity

Introduction: the celebrity as expert performer

If appeals address the paradoxes of the humanitarian imaginary by resorting to self-reflexive performances of solidarity, the genre of celebrity uses a different repertoire of communicative resources that, nonetheless, address these paradoxes to similar effect. Today, I argue, celebrity produces post-humanitarian publics, too. This has not always been the case, however, and the current chapter tells the story of this transformation, situating celebrity advocacy in a historical trajectory of controversy and change within the imaginary.

Celebrity has engaged with the moral imperative to alleviate suffering since the nineteenth century. But celebrity humanitarianism, which places Hollywood icons and rock stars at the forefront of the humanitarian project, is 'barely a generation old' (de Waal 2008). Within this short timespan, celebrity has shifted from a 'powerless' elite (Alberoni 1962/2006) to become the official communication strategy of the United Nations and global INGOs, as well as the source of major private initiatives (Bishop and Green 2008). Such developments have not only elevated celebrity to a powerful elite (Marshall 1997) but also contributed to transforming the governance of poverty as well as the premises of public action in the West (A. F. Cooper 2007; Cmiel 1999).

These transformations towards the empowerment of celebrity in global politics have been theorized as emanating in: (i) the decline of public trust in bureaucratic governance institutions (Marks & Fischer 2002); (ii) the expansion of the fields of social marketing and show business into politics (Nash 2008; Littler 2008); and (iii) the shifting policy priorities in humanitarian institutions towards corporate models of communication (A. F. Cooper 2007; West & Orman 2002). Building on these perspectives, my argument nevertheless does not aspire to explain the rise of celebrity humanitarianism but to understand the implications of this transformation for the humanitarian imaginary as a force of moralization for western publics.

To this end, I take my point of departure on the strategies of authenticity that celebrity employs, namely her or his unique expertise to perform moral discourse in ways that massively touch our hearts and minds. Such expertise, I argue, brings into focus the inherent theatricality of humanitarianism as an arrangement of separation between those who watch at a distance and those who act on the spot upon human suffering. Even though celebrity may be an ideal performer in this theatrical arrangement, I caution against two emerging properties of celebrity humanitarianism: first, the intensification of the relationship between humanitarian politics and commercial moralism that displaces public action in favour of personal diplomacy, in line with the new spirit of entrepreneurial capitalism (Boltanski & Chiapello 2005), and second, the hyper-emotionalization of the moral relationships of humanitarianism that displaces a focus on suffering and its causes onto a focus on celebrity and her or his publics, in line with a post-humanitarian sensibility. What these emerging properties throw into relief, I conclude, is a major limitation of contemporary humanitarianism: its over-reliance on the authenticity of celebrity, which breaks down the function of the theatre as moral education and may ultimately reproduce a narcissistic solidarity obsessed with our own emotions rather than oriented towards action on suffering others.

Theatre, celebrity, authenticity

> 'As I have a bit of visibility, I can use that to go on television, or do an interview, or raise funds, or go to hundreds of galas. . . . That's sort of a bonus now which I can use for children'
>
> Audrey Hepburn, Christian Science Monitor interview, 5 October 1992

Celebrity as a theatrical figure

By describing her role as a UNICEF Goodwill Ambassador in terms of raising the visibility of suffering, Hepburn captures an important dimension of humanitarianism: its dependence on spectacle. Rather than criticizing this style of communication as a 'commodification' of suffering, on which more below, the point I wish to emphasize is that this relationship between humanitarianism and spectacle is characteristic of a theatrical conception of politics as pity. Born out of the moral universalism of the Enlightenment, let us recall, this conception of politics as pity has established the imperative to act on vulnerable others as the dominant moral order of modernity (Taylor 2002; Rifkin 2009). This is an order that, whilst it is unable to engage western publics in direct action upon distant suffering, it mundanely uses the spectacle of suffering so as to habituate these publics into this moral imperative and sustain a disposition of solidarity beyond the West. Acting simultaneously as a form of moral education and a means of political legitimization of the global world order, as I have argued in chapter 1, this arrangement of separation between those who watch and those who suffer becomes, therefore, crucial in the theatrical performance of humanitarianism. This is because the theatre uses images and stories about action so as to enable us to imagine ourselves as citizens of the world – by speaking out (through protest or petition) and by paying (through donation) in the name of a moral cause.

In this light, celebrity is a crucial dimension of the theatrical structure of humanitarianism, insofar as it introduces into its imaginary a new communicative figure – a figure who commands the necessary symbolic capital to articulate personal dispositions of acting and feeling as exemplary public dispositions at given historical moments (Dyer 1986). Claims such as Audrey Hepburn's 'The world, I have discovered, is full of kind people' and 'I think every human being is filled with compassion . . .,'[1] or Angelina Jolie's 'I don't believe I feel differently from other people. I think we all want justice and equality, a chance for a life with meaning,'[2] illustrate how celebrity manages to communicate aspirational performances of solidarity for all to share. Rather than providing didactic exhortations of the 'you should help the poor' type, such quotes 'impersonate', instead, specific public dispositions of care and responsibility (King 2006: 246–7): through references to an undefinable 'everybody', that is to say, they already presuppose these moral dispositions as already existing virtues not only of celebrity itself but also of her or his publics – hence the 'aspirational' nature of the performance.

Far from a matter of linguistic claims only, the impersonation of altruism is a complex process that depends both on the management of the public image of celebrity, beyond her or his humanitarian missions, and on her or his expertise in conveying the message of suffering as a moving moral plea. This process points to the fact that, in seeking to shape dispositions of solidarity for the many, aspirational performance also articulates the voice of the institutions that are delegated to act on suffering, notably the United Nations (Alleyne 2005), and the voice of those who suffer at a distance (Magubane 2008).

This 'multi-vocality' renders celebrity a complex communicative figure in the humanitarian imaginary that, on the one hand, reflects and reproduces the political arrangement of separation between watching and acting on distant suffering and, on the other hand, tries to overcome this arrangement by bringing the social relationships of humanitarianism between organizations, sufferers and publics together within particular aspirational performances.

A recent articulation of such aspirational performance can be found in the communication strategy of the United Nations towards the attainment of the Millenium goals, as formulated by then-UN Secretary-General, Kofi Annan:

> You are here because you want those people to know more about the hardship of others, and because you want to encourage them to do something about it . . . Whenever you put your name to a message, you raise awareness far and wide, among policymakers and among millions of people who elect them. . . . Our chances of breaking through the barrier of indifference are vastly improved when we have people like you in our corner and for our cause. (UN Press Release SG/SM/7595; 23 October 2000)

This formulation reflects the theatrical arrangement of separation between the acting celebrity and their watching publics, 'policymakers' and 'millions of people', whilst also thematizing the impersonation of solidarity, that is, the articulation of aspirational discourse, a crucial function of humanitarianism: 'you want those people to know more' and 'encourage them to do something about it'. Implicit here is a conception of the theatre as moral education, that is, a space of performance that produces exemplary dispositions of emotion and action on distant others for publics to identify with (Williams 1973: 225). Instrumental in this pedagogical conception of humanitarianism is the expertise of celebrity not only to impersonate such disposition for her or his publics, but, in so doing, to also amplify the voices of suffering, coded into the formulations ' the hardship of others', and that of the United Nations, 'our chances . . . vastly improved'.

Celebrity and authenticity

The logic of the theatre, however, is not simply a logic of moral education but, as we know, also of the market. It is by way of association, by putting a famous 'name to a message' and by having 'people like you in our corner', that the performance of humanitarian discourse can amplify the power of the organization – to 'improve the chances' of the United Nations. It is this logic of associational representation that introduces a commercial dimension to the communicative practice of celebrity, insofar as the meaning transfer from celebrity to 'message' simultaneously reflects a transfer of exchange value from the former to the latter. Whereas the high exchange value of celebrity derives from the symbolic power that celebrity possesses in the global culture industry, particularly Hollywood entertainment, its capacity to convert this into a legitimate humanitarian message, for instance, 'save the starving children in Somalia' relies on the corporate strategy of branding – a strategy that operates by setting up symbolic relationships of equivalence between unequal 'goods' with a view to capitalizing on the existing 'aura' of one commodity in order to promote another (Arvidsson 2006; Rojek 2001 for the commodification of celebrity).

This use of market strategies in favour of noble causes has nowadays become common practice in the field of humanitarianism because, as Annan puts it, such strategies are capable of reaching publics 'far and wide'. Such meaning transfer, however, simultaneously raises doubts over celebrity humanitarianism ('is this yet another spectacle set up for the benefit of those who act it out?') and places the paradox for authenticity at the heart their aspirational performance. Caught between a pervasive suspicion about the power relations of humanitarianism, on the one hand, and a celebration of the power of celebrity, on the other, the question of authenticity in celebrity humanitarianism currently remains under-researched: 'Despite the increasing visibility of celebrity humanitarianism,' as Yrjölä puts it, 'no research on their representations and truth-claims has been done' (2009: 1).

It is this historical controversy around the authenticity of celebrity that I explore in the first part of this chapter. Authenticity is here best explored, I argue, through an analysis of celebrity as a communicative practice that brings the offstage performance of celebrity (or the 'persona') as an altruist together with her or his onstage performance of the voices of suffering as a message for action (or her 'personification'; King 1985/2006: 230–5; 244–6). This communicative practice draws attention to the fact that the authenticity of celebrity, rather than being reflected in the truthfulness of her or his claims, produces such truthfulness in the course of performing aspirational dispositions of solidarity. Shifts in the communicative strategies of authentication, it follows, further imply transformations in the moral relationships of humanitarianism that this structure articulates. My aim, therefore, in exploring the authenticity of celebrity is to identify these transformations since the appearance of celebrity humanitarianism 'a generation ago', and reflect on their implications for the moralization of western publics.

After reviewing the theoretical controversy around celebrity humanitarianism, which premature normativity, I argue, forecloses the study of significant shifts in the field ('The Celebrity Controversy'), I introduce my analytical approach to the study of authenticity in humanitarian celebrity ('The Performativity of Celebrity Humanitarianism'). Evidence from the performance of UNICEF Ambassador Audrey Hepburn (1988–1993) and UNHCR Ambassador Angelina Jolie (2001–10), spanning the lifetime of celebrity humanitarianism, demonstrates significant variation in the authentication strategies of celebrity across these two key 'moments' ('"Moments" of Humanitarian Performance'). In the light of these variations, I reflect on the transformations that celebrity may have contributed to bringing about in the economic and political relationships of humanitarianism ('Celebrity and Its Authenticity Effects') and conclude with remarks on the limitations of the theatrical practice of celebrity to moralize the West along the lines of cosmopolitan solidarity ('Conclusion: Towards a Utilitarian Altruism').

The celebrity controversy

The historical controversy around the role of celebrity humanitarianism in public life falls within two competing discourses: the sceptical and the optimistic.

The sceptical discourse

The sceptical discourse bifurcates in two types of argument, an empirical and a theoretical one, both of which consider celebrity humanitarianism as an inauthentic expression of aspirational performance.

The *empirical argument* describes the rise of celebrity humanitarianism as a new type of transnational agency, which functions as compensation for the political shortcomings of institutions such as the UN or major INGOs (A. F. Cooper 2007). Two risks are associated with celebrity as a communicative 'cover-up' for the inadequacy of existing structures of governance.

The first risk is about celebrity concealing the fact that complex political realities may necessitate complex solutions. In the absence of greater sophistication in humanitarian policies, celebrity promotes an easy message of effortless efficiency and carries the logic of a 'quick fix': 'development buzz has to keep its message simple, driven by the needs of slogans, images and anger. Unfortunately, although the plight of the bottom million lends itself to simple moralizing, the answers do not' (Collier 2007: 4). The second risk is that celebrity, as the most popular voice on a humanitarian cause, may stifle the plurality of alternative voices, managing to 'defuse, drain or even suffocate more radical forms of protest and political mobilization' (A. F. Cooper 2007: 13; Nash 2008). Whereas the first risk touches on the relationship between celebrity and the institutions it comes to represent, the second raises questions about celebrity and the public it seeks to inform.

Both forms of scepticism, different points of departure as they may have, point to the lack of legitimate representation as a problem in celebrity humanitarianism. Insofar as he or she condenses the representation of the multiple figures of pity in one single individual, celebrity raises suspicion as to whether he or she is entitled to genuinely represent those he or she claims to speak for and, thus, tends to intensify rather than resolve the problem of delegation: 'celebrities lack a mandate to be active in global politics. . . . These stars are not democratically elected to public office . . . Their legitimacy is derived from their personal credibility' (Dieter & Kumar 2008: 262).

The *theoretical argument* situates the scepticism of the empirical argument in a critique of empire, denouncing humanitarianism as an arrangement of power that reproduces the systemic inequality between those who are active and those who remain passive in the space of pity. There are, again, two sides to this argument. The first situates celebrity humanitarianism in a neocolonial framework of the 'white man's [*sic*] burden': images of beautiful westerners in stark contrast to the African poor perpetuate historical relationships of power between missionaries and indigenous locals – the latter, now as much as then, subject to the civilizing project of the former (Magubane 2008). Extending this orientalist discourse, celebrity humanitarianism today not only rests on assumptions of passivity on the part of local populations, but further glamorizes the idea of a western sovereign subject who acts in the name of those unable to represent themselves. In so doing, celebrity seeks to conceal a scandalous contradiction: by appearing to care for the 'wretched of the earth' whilst enjoying the privilege of rare wealth, it glosses over the ongoing complicity of the West in a global system of injustice that reproduces the dependence of the 'bottom million' through acts of development charity (Littler 2008).

The second side to the theoretical argument situates celebrity advocacy within a critique of the spectacle. Here, celebrity embodies the false promise of commodified individualism as a force of social change – the illusion of a single person fighting against structures of injustice (Marks and Fischer 2002). A version of the early 'cult of personality' critique of mass society, this argument debunks humanitarian celebrity as yet another false promise of the ideology of hyper-individualism that subordinates political agonism to the 'heroism' of the acting few. More than a manifestation of the decline of public collectivities (Boorstin 1961), the commodification argument further regards celebrity humanitarianism as evidence of the 'ecstatic communication' of show business, where suffering turns into fleeting spectacle without moral content (Littler 2008).

In summary, by bringing together a suspicion of the theatre as empire, exemplified in a new orientalism that sustains relations of subordination between an acting West and the suffering 'rest', with a suspicion of the spectacle, exemplified in the replacement of an acting body politic by a 'corporate' body, the theoretical critique of humanitarianism regards celebrity as sham humanitarianism. This accusation of inauthenticity, however, seems to me to conflate the power relations of humanitarianism, which celebrity is inevitably embedded in, with the distinct communicative practice of celebrity as a historically specific figure of power in the theatre of pity. Whereas celebrity inevitably participates in the systemic paradox of the humanitarian imaginary, I suggest that we move away from the conceptual fallacy of the sceptical discourse, namely to prematurely denounce as inauthentic all benevolent appearances of celebrity (the fallacy of the 'destruction of illusion'; Sayer 2009). We need to focus instead on celebrity as a performative site that enables the emergence of various strategies of authenticity at different points in time. It is by examining authenticity as a historical and, therefore, ever-changing claim to the truth of suffering, rather than altogether denying its truth as sham, that we can identify variations of solidarity in the historical course of the humanitarian imaginary.

The positive discourse

The positive discourse avoids the sceptical fallacy in that it takes a positive approach to the authenticity of celebrity, but, as we shall see, it suffers itself from a different kind of fallacy. There is a predominantly empirical argument in the positive discourse, albeit with significant theoretical underpinnings.

This argument welcomes celebrity humanitarianism as a strategy of re-enchantment for humanitarian agencies, whose reputation has been tarnished or outdated: 'these individuals', as West and Orman put it, 'have a fame that transcends public service and a reputation for personal integrity. This allows them to succeed politically in ways that are unavailable to more conventional kinds of politics' (2003 in 't Hart & Tindall 2009: 5). Central to the re-enchantment argument is a conception of fame as an intangible good with a high exchange value not only in show business but also in the political sphere. Taking this point further, the argument has it that celebrity not only re-enchants humanitarian organizations but politics itself, insofar as celebrities cease to act only as mediators of others and become public leaders that can set the humanitarian agenda (Bishop & Green 2008: 198–200). Drawing on a case study of the Bono–Geldof double act during the 2005 G8 summit (of which more in chapter 5), A. F. Cooper argues that, provided they combine the right tactics with clear objectives, 'celebrities have considerable opportunities not only to formulate but to sell their initiatives, targeting not only to the public but to selective state leaders' (2007: 7).

The other side of this empirical argument is that celebrity amplifies the voice of distant sufferers on the world stage ('t Hart & Tindall 2009: 6). Celebrities' competitive advantage vis-à-vis humanitarian organizations lies in the fact that celebrity personalizes the voice of the sufferer, combining what Cooper calls 'an assertive individualism characteristic of the West with an appreciation of universal or cosmopolitan values' (A. F. Cooper 2007: 5). Whereas, as we saw, celebrity remains open to the critique of orientalist hypocrisy, a celebrity's capacity to draw on discourses of 'shared history' with suffering, in the case of Oprah's African roots, and 'mutual recognition', in the case of Bono's Irish origins, shows that they can use their privilege to emphasize their common humanity with distant sufferers and, thereby, to maximize the force of their appeal in the West (Magubane 2008).

Rather than problematizing the 'multi-vocality' of celebrity as illegitimate, these arguments welcome celebrity as a communicative practice that successfully articulates the many voices of humanitarianism: the first, as we saw, focuses on the re-enchantment effect that celebrity bears both in rebranding organizations and in changing the terms of action in the sphere of politics; the second touches on the beneficiaries of action, emphasizing the role of celebrity as a mediator of the voices of suffering.

Whereas, as Yrjölä (2009) observes, there is no theoretical framework that contextualizes this positive argument in an existing body of literature, I argue that this argument is informed by a positive theory of the spectacle as the site of moral education (Marshall 1984) – a morality that, as I argued in chapter 2, takes the power relations of colonialism for granted whilst relying on the market to foster new forms of solidarity between West and the global South. Central to this conception of the spectacle is an instrumental view of celebrity as an economic entity, namely a commodity with transferable symbolic capital (Kurzman et al. 2007: 360).

On the one hand, the brand value of celebrity legitimizes her or his function as a source of collective moralization – captured in Kofi Annan's quote on the UN earlier, 'whenever you put your name to a message, you raise awareness . . . among millions of people.' This view of the brand, let us recall, has an implicit pedagogical dimension insofar as the moralizing work of celebrity occurs here through aspirational performance that engages public sensibilities at the level of imagination: 'When they speak genuinely, and from their own experiences, stars . . . speak from a place that politicians almost never approach: the inside of their audience's imagination' (Marks

& Fischer 2002: 387, quoting Browstein). On the other hand, the brand value of celebrity legitimizes its entry into elite politics on the grounds that the morality of solidarity needs to be complemented by a pragmatic ethos of 'getting-things-done': 'in a perfect world', Buston (Buston in Vallely 2009) says, 'we would have a democracy in which everyone is perfectly informed, everyone's voice is heard and public policy reflected the collective best interest . . . but the world isn't like that. It is a world of media moguls, corporate lobbyists and powerful interest groups . . . what we are doing [with celebrity] is redress[ing] that balance.'[3]

Far from approaching celebrity with suspicion, this instrumental view of the spectacle renders the question of inauthenticity irrelevant to the humanitarian imaginary. Displaced neither onto the structures of colonialism nor the market, the authenticity of solidarity is now seen as residing in the intentions of celebrity – as a question of truthfulness – that can be held in check by the same mechanism that promotes it, namely the 'relentless public scrutiny' of the media (Cowen 2000: 170).

In a manner antithetical to the sceptical discourse, the positive discourse nonetheless similarly conflates two things that need to be kept apart: the interiority of celebrity as a moral being committed to the truth and the communicative practice of celebrity as part of the social relationships of the humanitarian imaginary that transcend individual intention. Whereas celebrity inevitably operates as a singular moral self, expressing her or his interiority in various ways, I suggest that we move away from the conceptual fallacy of the positive argument, namely to seek authenticity in the 'truth' of the individual (a fallacy of essentialism; Yrjölä 2009) and to focus on how authenticity itself comes to be produced in the course of the celebrity's aspirational performances of humanitarianism.

In summary, the literature on humanitarian celebrity engages with the question of authenticity but does not problematize it as an object of analysis. The sceptical argument challenges the authenticity of celebrity as a moral performer on the grounds that celebrity is linked to the historical power relations of humanitarianism, empire and the spectacle. The positive argument considers celebrity a truthful performance of morality on the grounds that the power relations of humanitarianism constitute a positive economy – an economy of both commercial efficiency and moral education. Torn between sceptical and positive discourses, whilst leaving the concept of authenticity itself intact, the controversy around celebrity humanitarianism cannot but remain inconclusive at the level of theoretical argument. I, therefore, now move towards an analytical framework for the study of authenticity in the performativity of celebrity before I proceed with an analysis of two key 'moments' of celebrity humanitarianism, reflected in the historical figures of Audrey Hepburn and Angelina Jolie.

The performativity of celebrity humanitarianism

Impersonation, the aspirational performance that posits the imperative to act on vulnerable others as an already existing disposition of western publics, is conditional upon two further dimensions of the performativity of celebrity: on the one hand, the expertise of celebrity to manage her or his public image, or 'persona', and, on the other, her or his expertise to communicate the voice of distant suffering as an urgent message that moves us all, or 'personification' (King 1985/2006: 230–5; 244–6). Without these forms of expertise, the impersonations of celebrity as a figure of solidarity would be considered as 'out of face', failing to touch and persuade her or his publics (Rojek 2001: 17).

Rather than generated at the will of celebrity, however, such expertise should be seen as the manifestation of communicative norms that, at least partly, regulate the individual performance of celebrity (Dyer 1979: 4; Marshall 1997: xiii). The concept of performativity, let us recall, refers to this normative dimension of performance as the 'reiteration of norms which precede, constrain and exceed the performer and in that sense cannot be taken as the fabrication of the performer's "will" or "choice"' (Butler 1993: 234). The performativity of celebrity then draws attention to the dialectic between a repertoire of communicative strategies that 'exceeds the performer' and thus tends to regulate the range of their individual performance, and each single performance of the celebrity, which demonstrates a necessary variation and may subvert these normative strategies in the very act of reproducing them.

The view of acting as performativity, which acknowledges the transformative force of individualized acts of performance within a matrix of normative relationships of power, finds particular resonance in the figure of celebrity. This is so insofar as the celebrities of Hollywood cinematography, what Dyer calls 'the stars' (1979), are indeed characterized both by intense articulations of individuality and by the fact that such individuality is universalized as a representation of the potential of any individual.

The concept of *persona* captures this dialectic by defining celebrity as a specific form of public self that articulates universal discourses, such as a discourse of human vulnerability and everyday ordinariness, with aesthetic choices of unique individuality, such as rare talent or beautiful looks, that establish the celebrity as a figure both intimate and distinguished in our public culture (Rojek 2001). In the context of humanitarianism, this tension of the persona must provisionally stabilize towards discourses that construe the offstage celebrity self as sharing our common humanity. It is this dimension of humanity that renders celebrity an authentic vehicle for the impersonation of a solidary disposition. For, without the 'humanization' strategies that manage to domesticate their extraordinariness (either by de-celebritizing or by hyper-celebritizing their persona) and to build up their moral self as an example for all (by 'living out' a particular ethos of solidarity), the celebrity would always remain in the shadow of inauthenticity. The *strategies of humanization* at work in the personae of Audrey Hepburn or Angelina Jolie constitute, therefore, the first part of my analytical discussion.

What further complicates the moral agency of celebrity, however, is that the persona, who he or she is offstage, cannot be separated from who that celebrity is onstage, as a theatrical performer. Further theorizing the celebrity of stardom, which both Hepburn and Jolie embody, King talks about the celebrity self precisely in terms of this fusion between their persona and their acting. Such fusion, he argues, ultimately leads to 'displacing emphasis for what an actor can do *qua* actor onto what the actor *qua* person or biographical entity is' (2006: 245, emphasis in the original).

The concept of *personification* comes to refer precisely to this capacity of celebrity to continue performing his or her own persona, as an offstage (or 'real') character, at the moment that she acts out a theatrical character on stage. Resting on the assumption that 'there is an unmediated existential connection' between the celebrity's self in extra-theatrical circumstances and the character she enacts on stage, personification manages, nonetheless, to intensify rather than obliterate the distance between celebrity as persona and celebrity as performer (King 1985/2006: 245). This is because, insofar as the celebrity draws on her repertoire of expert techniques to personify a character and yet remains recognizable as who she 'is', she keeps a constant tension between displaying the expertise of the performer, calculated and repeatable as it is, and expressing her own private interiority – 'being herself'. This kind of 'auratic distance' (Marshall 1997: 187) between who the celebrity 'is' and what role she enacts, which lies at the heart of the 'elusive' or magical nature of the star, is also instrumental in the theatricality of humanitarianism. It is this distance that also enables celebrity to articulate their ('real') persona into his or her own aspirational performance – to personify, that is, the voice of suffering others as the authentic articulation of her own emotional interiority.

Indeed, the personification of humanitarian discourse takes place through first-hand accounts of human misfortune that the celebrity formulates as her personal testimony from the zones of suffering, balancing accurate description with the evocation of genuine emotion. It is only accounts of suffering which keep this balance between description and emotion that manage to authenticate the voices of suffering and invite the spectator to identify with the sufferer (Boltanski 1999). Personification, in this sense, refers to the authentication of the voice of the sufferer, who cannot speak of her/his misfortune, refracted as this is through the celebrity's own performance of emotion about the sufferer's experience. The second part of my analytical discussion turns, therefore, towards the celebrity's personification of suffering and looks into her *strategies of witnessing* as moral discourse that demands an urgent response.

It is the performance of celebrity, articulating her/his public image as a 'real' self with the acting out of her or his emotion of suffering as if it were the celebrity's own, that lies at the centre of both the sceptical and positive arguments on the authenticity of celebrity humanitarianism. Whereas these positions were earlier discussed in the context of a historical controversy, a theoretical discourse that remains forever dilemmatic, I now turn to the authenticity of celebrity as the object of empirical analysis.

'Moments' of humanitarian performance

Audrey Hepburn and Angelina Jolie are the two Hollywood celebrities with the strongest humanitarian profiles in the history of the United Nations: the former as UNICEF Ambassador, 1988–1993, and the latter as UNHCR Ambassador, 2001 to the present. My choice of these two figures, both global mega-stars at different times, is guided by a principle of difference-in-similarity. This makes it possible to focus on their shared quality as celebrities whilst, at the same time, enabling a focus on variation along the temporal trajectory of celebrity humanitarianism – Hepburn its emergence and Jolie its peak. The biographical grounds for such variation granted, for my purposes, the point of variation is to identify historical transformations in celebrity humanitarianism and its conceptions of solidarity.[4]

My examination of Audrey Hepburn and Angelina Jolie focuses, in turn, on (i) their *persona*, which refers to the strategies of humanization that seek to domesticate the extraordinariness of celebrity and construe an authentic public self compatible with the ethos of solidarity, and (ii) their *personification*, which refers to the strategies of witnessing each celebrity uses in order to authenticate the suffering of others as her own personal testimony of their misfortune.

Figure 4.1 Audrey Hepburn – actress and UNICEF Goodwill Ambassador (UNICEF/ John Isaac).

Audrey Hepburn

Hepburn reached iconic status as a consequence of her performances in movie classics, such as *Roman Holiday* (1953), *Breakfast at Tiffany's* (1961) and My *Fair Lady* (1964), which established her as a legendary figure in Hollywood glamour and made her one of the three first actresses in US show business to receive a fee of $1 million. At the same time, she is publicly anchored in the realm of the ordinary, first, through her memories of the German occupation in Holland, including the famine and disease she endured as a child, and, second, through her choice of motherhood over Hollywood – she abandoned the latter in the early seventies to raise her two children away from the spotlight. These personal experiences informed her decision to accept the position of the UNICEF Goodwill Ambassador in May 1989, which she remained fully dedicated to until her death in January 1993.

Hepburn's persona: de-celebritization and unconditional altruism

Two strategies seek to authenticate Hepburn's persona as the carrier of a common humanity: the *de-celebritization* of her persona, taking a distance from all forms of social distinction, and the *ethicalization* of her persona, systematically projecting an ethos of unconditional altruism.[5]

The first strategy of humanization seeks to distance Hepburn's humanitarian persona from any sphere of expertise, such as film acting or global politics, that would construe Hepburn as a public figure of distinction. This strategy involves references to 'celebrity' as a 'remnant' from her years in the film industry, as well as a re-imaging of her previous glamorously youthful self into the simple, yet elegant, presence of the middle-aged activist on mission in Ethiopia, Sudan, Bangladesh or Pakistan. The strategy also involves Hepburn's systematic distantiation from the political sphere, insisting that humanitarianism is about an immediate response to the urgent needs of suffering: 'Politics has nothing to do with one helping a dying child. Survival, that's what it's about.'[6] This discourse of Good Samaritanism juxtaposes an ethics of compassion to a politics of power: 'perhaps with time, instead of there being a politicization of humanitarian aid, there will be a humanization of politics',[7] and comes to consolidate the de-celebritization of Hepburn's persona, insofar as it displaces expertise onto others, whilst foregrounding Hepburn's humanity as the most important reason for her UNICEF work: 'It would be nice to be an expert on education, economics, politics, religions, traditions and cultures. I'm none of those. But I am a mother and I will travel' (UNICEF webpage).

The reference to 'I am a mother and I will travel' introduces Hepburn's second strategy of humanization: the ethicalization of her persona through a discourse of solidarity as the natural disposition of motherly care. 'It's automatic', she says of her humanitarian commitment, 'if a child falls you pick it up. It's that simple. There is no great merit to it.'[8] The theme of childhood vulnerability also emerges in the context of Hepburn's own experience in post-World War II Europe: 'I can testify to what UNICEF means to children, because I was among those who received food and medical relief right after World War II.'[9] By occupying the position of the sufferer, Hepburn not only construes her UNICEF work as an act of gratitude but, importantly, acknowledges suffering as a universal condition that touches us all, thereby further disarticulating solidarity from her celebrity status: 'I never led what people think is this glamorous life,' she objects to a CBS journalist, commenting on her life shift from glamour to humanitarianism. 'I have always been me. I've always been aware of what goes on in the world . . . and I've always known, you know, that I was privileged and many were not.'[10] This moral orientation to the world despite her celebrity status ('I have always been me. I've always been aware . . . I've always known') emphatically reiterates Hepburn's solidarity as a lifelong inclination to care for others that, grounded as it is on an awareness of her privilege, sets no conditions and requires no rewards: 'The human obligation is to help children who are suffering. The rest is luxury.'[11]

Insofar as humanitarianism relies on the ethos of celebrity to function as an exemplary disposition for her publics, it is evident that, as well as authenticating Hepburn's persona, this strategy simultaneously impersonates an aspirational disposition for all to identify with. Unconditional solidarity, in this sense, seeks to engage western publics with the moral disposition to act on vulnerable others without anticipating reciprocation. Whereas de-celebritization authenticates Hepburn's persona by removing her from a context of intense particularity (Hollywood stardom), ethicalization authenticates her UNICEF role as the natural extension of an ethos of motherly care and moralizes western publics along the lines of an unconditional solidarity.

Hepburn's personification: the dispassionate witness

Personification involves the celebrity giving voice to 'those who cannot speak for themselves', as Hepburn puts it, through strategies of witnessing. Grounded as they are on the 'I' of the narrator, these strategies enable Hepburn to authenticate the suffering of distant others by articulating their vulnerability through her own emotionality.

Here is Hepburn's first-hand description of the death of a child in Somalia:

> A.H.: This boy was sitting with just a bit of cloth around him, rail thin, I mean, really just bones and eyes and absolutely struggling for breath . . . I was suffering so for him because I did have asthma as a child . . . and all the things that come with first degrees of malnourishment . . . – and I just felt I wish I could breathe for him but he literally sort of just lay down while I was there and was gone.
>
> *Interviewer*: Died?
>
> A.H.: Mm hmm . . .
>
> *Interviewer*: In front of you?
>
> A.H.: Yes.[12]

Two features of this account are characteristic of witnessing. First, there is the detailed description of the boy's physical condition as evidence of the reality of his suffering ('cloth around him', 'rail thin', 'just bones and eyes', 'struggling for breath') and, second, the elliptical, almost suggestive, reference to the moment of his death (prompted by the interviewer rather than volunteered by Hepburn: 'was gone', 'Mm . . . hmm', 'Yes'), which points to the 'unspeakability' of witnessing death. Whereas the former, detailed description, refers to witnessing as testimony of the historical world of events and therefore bears the credibility of a fact, the latter, unspeakability of death, points to witnessing as 'bearing witness' of the horrors of human suffering and therefore endows the testimony of death with the moral gravity necessary to denounce it (Peters 2009). Taken together, these two functions of witnessing personify a discourse, whereby Hepburn's own individuality becomes the magnifying lens through which the suffering of a single child turns into an object of western attention – notice the repeated use of the 'I' in the extract: 'I was suffering so for him . . .', 'I did have asthma . . .', 'I just felt I wish I could breathe for him . . .'[13]

In describing the death of a child as a fact whilst struggling to put words to it, such narratives of witnessing further place the calculated management of emotion at the centre of Hepburn's humanitarian performance. Referring to her communication with western publics, she says 'It's important to me to make them feel what I feel. . . . Emotion – the ability to communicate emotion – that has to be a gift. I don't contribute anything else. I don't have great knowledge, great expertise.'[14] Emotion emerges, then, both as an object of professional reflexivity ('It is important to me to make them feel . . .') and as spontaneous feeling ('what I feel'), showing how the personifying capacity of the actress functions as a carrier of aspirational performance. This professional 'acting out' of one's personal emotions is construed as the actress's single key contribution to the humanitarian project ('I don't contribute anything else'), further throwing into relief the centrality of acting as personification in the theatrical space of the imaginary.

What such personification of emotion involves, as we saw, is the disciplined disposition of the dispassionate witness – a disposition that organizes Hepburn's performance around the cautious verbalization of emotion: 'I have a broken heart. I feel desperate. I can't stand the idea that two million people are in imminent danger of starving to death, many of them children . . .'[15] This management of emotion in the face of suffering, communicating a strong yet dignified sense of moral righteousness, is a unique form of expertise available to Hepburn precisely because of her training as an actress: 'She [Hepburn] knew how a sentiment had to be boiled down into a phrase, a "sound-bite". She was able to deliver it with all the force of her art.'[16]

In summary, Hepburn's humanitarianism eclipses celebrity from her persona and promotes an unconditional solidarity that capitalizes on her acting expertise to give voice to those who suffer.

Angelina Jolie

Even though Jolie's star status is partly due to highly acclaimed performances in *Gia* (1998, Emmy and Golden Globe Awards), *Girl, Interrupted* (1999, Academy Award) and *Changeling* (2008, nominated for BAFTA and Academy Awards), she acquired international fame as a sex symbol for appearances in films such as *Lara Croft: Tomb Raider* (2001) and *Mr. and Mrs. Smith* (2005). By 2009, she was considered both the most beautiful and the highest-paid female celebrity in Hollywood, with an annual income of £27 million.[17] At the same time, there is a human element that grounds Jolie's persona in the realm of the 'ordinary'. This is construed primarily through accounts of her troubled childhood as an isolated girl of divorced parents with self-destructive tendencies. It is also construed, similarly to Hepburn, through her commitment to domestic life as a mother of six children; life after motherhood, she says, has transformed her into a peaceful person: 'When I look at myself, I just see somebody at peace, and I see a mom. Something else comes out of you when you become a parent . . . you start to see more character in your face' (28 November 2008).[18] Jolie was appointed UNHCR Goodwill Ambassador in 2001 at the age of 26 and remains one of the most active and influential celebrities in the field.

Jolie's persona: hyper-celebrity and utilitarian altruism

Two strategies of humanization seek to address the tension in Jolie's humanitarian persona between a universal discourse of motherhood, inviting identification with western publics, and a discourse of intense particularity, including glamorous looks and legendary wealth, setting her apart as an object of popular fantasy. Unlike Hepburn's, however, Jolie's strategies construe a different persona, which rests on *hyper-celebritization*, an intensification of her celebrity persona (rather than distancing the celebrity past from the humanitarian present) and on a process of *ethicalization* that promotes a utilitarian solidarity (rather than the unconditional solidarity of motherly care).

The first strategy, hyper-celebritization, brings into focus Jolie's excessive visibility across spheres of life – private, professional and humanitarian. Unlike Hepburn, whose private life was relatively insulated from the public, Jolie's domestic choices, including partners, pregnancies and adoptions, are part and parcel of her persona – often encouraged by her own intimate interviews on her children and her love life. Similarly, Jolie aims for maximum visibility in the uses of her professional and economic capital to the service

Figure 4.2 Angelina Jolie – actress and UNHCR Goodwill Ambassador (AFP/Getty Images).

of humanitarianism. Unlike Hepburn, who kept a distance from her acting career, Jolie systematically appears in films that address human rights issues, such as *Beyond Borders* (2003) and *A Mighty Heart* (2007), as well as in documentaries that feature humanitarian emergencies.[19] At the same time, she donates one third of her annual income to various humanitarian causes and has further established her own foundation, the Jolie–Pitt foundation (2006), which offers substantial support to NGOs and local development initiatives. This financial network works in tandem with Jolie's broader advocacy agenda that has pursued specific refugee-related issues, such as 'No Peace Without Justice' and 'Partnership for Children of Conflict' – both of which engage global political elites, such as the US Congress, the World Economic Forum, the European Commission and the US Council for Foreign Relations. By capitalizing on this 'extraordinary ordinariness', Jolie establishes herself as both an 'ordinary mum', whose toy shopping trips make the 'gossip news', and a political actor in the global scene, whose private initiatives have turned her into an icon of the humanitarian world.[20]

The second strategy of humanization brings into focus Jolie's altruistic ethos. Whereas, like Hepburn, Jolie's ethos of care also relies on her experience of motherhood, the ethicalization of her persona draws upon a discourse of utilitarian solidarity. Instead of a natural inclination, Jolie's engagement with suffering others is construed as part of a trajectory towards personal self-fulfilment: 'I never felt satisfied. I never felt calm . . . But I think that's something that comes with finding responsibility, finding some use, finding some sense of purpose.'[21] As a moment of self-enlightenment, humanitarianism is, therefore, more than a professional commitment to an organization; it is a conscious lifestyle choice that permeates all aspects of her existence: 'I am forever changed', she claims, speaking about her first encounter with suffering children in Cambodia. 'The question is not how I could live as I did before, but how I could not live as I do now.'[22] This lifestyle commitment is evident in the construal of her family, consisting of three adopted and three biological children, not only as a site of private emotion but, importantly, of cosmopolitan education: 'I look at Shiloh [biological daughter] – because, obviously, physically, she is the one that looks like Brad and I when we were little – and say, "If these were our brothers and sisters, how much would we have known by the time we were six that it took into our thirties and forties to figure out"'? It is this value of the others as a source of knowledge for oneself that introduces an element of utilitarian solidarity in Jolie's persona – further reflected in her construal of adoption as an enhancement of her personal life, a 'gift', rather than as an act of unreciprocated giving: 'it is not a humanitarian thing, because I don't see it as a sacrifice, it's a gift.'[23]

Hyper-celebritization consolidates the authenticity of Jolie's persona in terms of an extraordinary ordinariness, the projection of a 'saturated' self that fully lives out her aspirational discourse (Littler 2008), whereas ethicalization impersonates a disposition of solidarity that foregrounds the desires of the self as a motive for doing good to others.

Jolie's personification: the passionate witness

Similarly to Hepburn, the 'I' of the witness lies at the centre of Jolie's testimonies of suffering. Her witnessing strategy, however, differs from Hepburn's in that it relies not on dispassionate but on dramatically emotional accounts of human misfortune.

In a formal intervention at a Clinton Global Initiative conference on 'education for children in conflict', Jolie anchored her argument on the story of a young girl, whose intelligence and resilience saved her and her baby sister from the assassins of their family and brought them to the safety of a refugee camp – it was the camp's educational programme, Jolie's point was, that made a difference in the girl's life, as she struggled to get over the trauma of losing her family.[24] Rather than a dispassionate delivery, the speech was an emotional occasion with Jolie visibly fighting to hold back her tears as she spoke of her encounter with the girl. Similarly, in a National Geographic documentary on West African refugees, she bursts into tears on camera as she follows their impossible trip to safety, whereas in an Oprah Winfrey interview, she pauses to resume control of her emotions as she talks about the hardships of refugee life in Cambodia; as she explains elsewhere, 'Maybe because my son's adopted, I see him as those children. They're just like my son. And he's from one of those countries.'[25]

Unlike Hepburn's controlled disposition of the professional witness, Jolie's personification of suffering appears to fuse factual description with the spontaneous expression of emotion that, in bearing witness to the horror of suffering, cannot be contained as a professional object of reflection. Providing a self-description that emphasizes control rather than spontaneity as a personality trait, 'I'm very careful with my emotions, and I don't let them run free. If I'm upset, it's usually for a very good, very deep reason', says Jolie, implicitly acknowledging the deep impact that the experience of suffering bears on her emotions. In summary, grounded in the realm of intimate relationships ('I see him as those children. They're just like my son'), Jolie's personification of suffering emerges not as the product of a calculated management of emotion but as the authentic manifestation of her moral interiority and a natural consequence of her 'saturated' humanitarian persona.

Celebrity and its authenticity effects

Approaching celebrity as performance has thrown into relief the communicative practice by which authenticity is produced in the theatrical space of pity. Authenticity emerges in the performance of the celebrity persona as a moral self, through strategies of celebritization and ethicalization, combined with the performance of emotion towards suffering, through strategies of witnessing.

In this final section, I explore two crucial effects of the management of authenticity in celebrity humanitarianism. Taking my analysis of two exemplary celebrity figures as two key 'moments' of humanitarianism, I treat these authenticity effects as the manifestation of transformations in the social relationships of the humanitarian imaginary.

Under 'Entrepreneurial Moralism', I address the shifting relationship between celebrity and the organizational milieu of humanitarianism, namely the United Nations. Expanding on the critique of the spectacle, I argue that such a shift reconfigures the relationship between humanitarianism and the market along the lines of what Boltanski and Chiapello call 'the new spirit of capitalism' (2005). Under 'Post-humanitarianism', I elaborate on a shift in the relationship between celebrity and western publics. Expanding on the critique of empire, I argue that such a shift reconfigures the relationship between humanitarianism and politics by displacing the relationship between spectator and sufferer onto a 'confessional' relationship between celebrity and his or her publics. In the conclusion, 'Towards a Utilitarian Altruism', I reflect on the limitations of contemporary celebrity as a force of moralization for the West.

Entrepreneurial moralism

Even if the authentication of aspirational performance draws upon elements of an ordinary individuality, it is ultimately the extraordinary qualities of celebrity in terms of beauty, wealth and talent that fascinate public imagination. Whereas the critique of the spectacle has focused on the ways in which such extraordinary qualities tend to displace the complex realities of development and downplay the responsibility of global institutions in the governance of poverty, it has not drawn enough attention to potentially significant transformations in the market practices of the humanitarian imaginary itself. Let us revisit the analytical insights that may point to such a transformation.

Hepburn's persona, as we saw, relies on a process of de-celebritization that downplays her stardom in favour of a non-expert but highly visible mediating role between those who suffer and those who watch at a distance. This persona can be characterized as 'ambassadorial', in line with the homonymous UN position, insofar as she speaks on behalf of a broader humanitarian project and capitalizes on the celebrity brand to maximize the public communication of her message. As a 'well-known member of an established movement', Hepburn's ambassadorial persona employs her professional expertise to maximize the visibility of suffering and to represent the 'larger public consciousness' that she participates in (Marks & Fischer 2002: 378). Harshly criticized for 'just sharing impressions of poverty' rather than raising the political questions of suffering, as Malloch Brown[26] put it, alluding to figures like her, the ambassadorial style subordinates the celebrity's own voice to that of its institution. Hepburn's brand may be capitalizing on the entertainment industry to promote the humanitarian message, yet her persona serves UNICEF's agenda, submitting her own professional brand to the brand of the United Nations. De-celebritization, in this sense, manages precisely this subordination of her stardom to the organization.

By contrast, Jolie's persona relies on a process of hyper-celebritization that capitalizes on all spheres of her life so as not to simply mediate voices but to catalyse action. This is so both on the political level, where she engages in the inner circles of elite lobbying (e.g., Davos), and on the financial level, where she is in charge of her own foundation. This persona can thus be characterized as 'entrepreneurial', reflecting the autonomous creativity and assertive individualism of a new capitalist spirit that, dedicated as it may be to the humanitarian project, ultimately stands above, rather than within, the communitarian duty to a larger collectivity – more on this in chapter 5 on 'Concerts' (and see also Boltanski & Chiapello 2005). In so doing, not only does Jolie explicitly rely on her own Hollywood mega-brand to maximize the UNHCR brand, but further mobilizes her personal capital, economic and symbolic, to develop an independent network of relationships in order to promote a broader humanitarian agenda. What emerges is not a relationship of brand subordination, as in Hepburn's ambassadorial persona, but of an equal brand partnership between Jolie and the UN, which has powerful re-enchantment effects for both parties (Yanacopulos 2005).

This transformation from an ambassadorial to an entrepreneurial persona points to the emergence of a tighter link between celebrity and the private use of economic capital in the space of humanitarianism – what Bishop and Green call 'philanthro-capitalism' (2008). Whereas the humanitarian ethos of capitalism is no news, reflecting the constitutive link between theatrical spectacle and commercial moralism in the humanitarian imaginary, discussed in chapter 1, philanthro-capitalism signals a novel manifestation of this relationship – one that could be seen as functioning to consolidate the power relations of humanitarianism through what Boltanski and Chiapello call the incorporation of critique into the global order of capitalism: 'In obliging capitalism to justify itself, critique compels it to strengthen the mechanisms of justice it contains, and to refer to certain kinds of common good in whose service it claims to be placed' (2005: 42). It is to the critique of humanitarianism as philanthropy without justice, which Hepburn's Good Samaritanism is representative of, that this hyper-politicization of celebrity comes to respond to today. It does so by legitimizing the public morality of solidarity not only by way of circulating stories and images of suffering, but also by acting as a sovereign player in the humanitarian scene.

Two consequences follow from this 'entrepreneurialization' of the celebrity persona. The first consequence is what Cmiel calls a move from a participatory to a 'post-populist' style of humanitarian politics (1999). Even though public attention remains important, hence the celebrity role of 'raising awareness far and wide' in Annan's words, the idea of 'post-populism' reflects a historical shift away from mass mobilization and towards a reliance on massive private donations and on 'third-party' politics, where 'a human rights organization could now help a victim in Asia, for example, by influencing a "third party", the government of the United States' (1999: 1242). Insofar as it forms part of an elite 'group of well-informed activists winning entrée to the corridors of power' (Cmiel 1999: 1242), celebrity is a catalytic force in marking the shift from grass-roots to 'third-party' interventions – what A. F. Cooper calls 'celebrity diplomacy' (2007). Whereas this move raises important questions regarding the expertise of celebrity to go beyond aspirational and engage with political discourse (de Waal 2008; Dieter & Kumar 2008), for my purposes the question is how this hyper-politicization of humanitarianism in the name of 'getting things done' may be linked to the moral dispositions of solidarity.

The second, therefore, consequence of the 'entrepreneurialization' of the celebrity persona that I focus on is the move from an unconditional solidarity, à la Hepburn, to a utilitarian altruism – expressed, for example, in Jolie's lifestyle and professional choices not as disinterested acts but as rewarding projects of the self. Rather than reflecting inherent personality traits (though this may also be), these are normative discourses that, let us recall, 'exceed the performance' of each celebrity and inform the construal of her aspirational discourse. As a manifestation of public morality, therefore, utilitarian solidarity should be seen as reflecting and legitimizing the 'spirit' of entrepreneurial capitalism – a form of ethics that, in the post-populist context of receding collectivities of solidarity, relies upon the calculation of mutual utilities and throws into relief the consequentialist ethics that lie at the centre of its assertive individualism – a view that I develop fully in chapter 7 in terms of an 'ironic solidarity'.

Indeed, even though the egoism of altruism is an old and well-known philosophical debate (Williams 1973), it is this explicit articulation of the self-interested basis of solidarity as a mode of justification for action that constitutes an emerging property of the humanitarian imaginary, rendering our encounters with distant suffering increasingly post-humanitarian.

Post-humanitarianism

Heartbreaking stories, such as those of Hepburn's dying boy, turn distant suffering, usually just a number in western news, into a cause for concern for all. Yet the magnification of the last moments of the African child becomes a story of moral urgency at a cost: it may be the truth of the boy's suffering that is the object of narration but it is Hepburn's emotion that becomes the object of identification with these publics. Whereas the critique of empire accuses personification for re-installing colonial power at the heart of the humanitarian imaginary, whereby the voice of the sufferer remains subordinate to the western imaginary of the celebrity, my focus is rather how shifts in the personification of aspirational performance may also imply shifts in our ethical relationship to distant suffering.

Hepburn's personification style, let us recall, is that of the dispassionate witness who communicates emotion through the eloquent use of language rather than visible signs of emotionality. This style can be characterized as 'ceremonial' insofar as it authenticates the unspeakability of suffering through the mastery of acting rituals, such as the proper use of elocution, rhythm and pause – Hepburn's 'art of the profession' (Marks and Fischer 2002, for this use of 'ceremonial'). In contrast, Jolie's style is that of the passionate witness who communicates emotion not only through skilful language use but, primarily, through the body. This style of personification can be characterized as 'confessional' insofar as it authenticates the unspeakability of suffering by going beyond words to a corporeal expressivity – Jolie speaking with a broken voice or bursting into tears.

This shift from a ceremonial to a confessional style of personification is, I propose, indicative of a mutation in the communicative practice of celebrity from what Sennett calls sincerity, 'the suppression of the personal in the service of the performance of the self as defined by social position and social role' to that of authenticity, 'the open expression of private feelings' (Sennett 1978 in King 2008: 116). Whereas both practices point to a modernist conception of the self, where the emotion of aspirational performance is authentic only when it comes from a 'genuine' individuality (King 2008; Marshall 1984), the move towards confession suggests that the process of authentication has today become hyper-emotionalized: instead of subordinating the expression of personal feelings to the service of a public role, as in Hepburn's 'restrained' witnessing on behalf of UNICEF, confession relies on the uncontrollability of emotion, as in Jolie's tearful witness.

Far from suggesting that all contemporary celebrity is emotional, the confessional captures, rather, a pervasive orientation of contemporary publicness towards practices of self-disclosure as the performance of authenticity – what King calls 'para-confession' (2008).[27] Whereas King draws attention to the 'pre-scripted' nature of the para-confession as a technique for the presentation of the celebrity persona, what concerns me is the tendency of para-confession to subsume the emotions of suffering into the psychological realm of the persona and, thereby, to blur the boundaries between the condition of the sufferer and the tearful celebrity.

It is this blurring of the boundaries that points to the post-humanitarian nature of confessional discourse, insofar as such blurring destabilizes the theatricality of personification: the performance of the voice of suffering *as if* it were the celebrity's own. By eliding this crucial as-if, confession collapses the voice of the sufferer, invisible, distant and unnamed, with the voice of the celebrity, visible, 'intimate' and world famous, and displaces the affective relationship between spectator and sufferer onto a relationship of 'reflexive sympathy' between spectator and celebrity as the most 'authentic' figure of pity (Eagleton 2009: 65). Independently of whether such relationship may entail cynicism (rejecting the authenticity of celebrity) or admiration (accepting such authenticity), post-humanitarianism brings into focus the function of confessional celebrity as a medium of self-recognition – where the aspirational performance of solidarity gravitates around the interiority of her emotion and, consequently, around those who reflexively mirror themselves in her – instead of other-recognition, where aspirational discourse involves us with images and stories that orient us towards suffering others.

Rather than questioning the authenticity of confessional witnessing, then, what I wish to draw attention to is the potential of 'unmediated' emotion, articulated as it is by contemporary humanitarian celebrity to intensify rather than bridge the gap between distant suffering, continuous and inescapable for those who endure it, and the confessional celebrity, whose emotion is ultimately discontinuous and temporary – only part of a complex persona, subsequently pictured at an awards gala or a film premiere.

This gap suggests that, even though the communicative practice of celebrity may enchant western publics as spectators of the drama of suffering, it may not be able to provide these publics with a more enduring orientation to action. This is because, in proposing a 'feel for the celebrity's feelings for the feelings of the sufferer' disposition, this communicative practice runs the risk of inspiring talk about the celebrity herself and so of inserting aspirational performance into registers of ineffective speech, 'a flow of chatter about everything and nothing in which, consequently, nothing particularly matters' – rather than into registers of effective speech, what Boltanski (1999: 185) calls the 'intentional attitudes such as I will, I believe, I think'. Even if only 'in the form of a whisper', effective speech is instrumental for the public morality of the humanitarian imaginary because it construes suffering as the object of potential commitment and entails a promise to engage – a disposition to action that sustains the 'public connection' amongst spectators as citizens of the world.[28]

In summary, post-humanitarianism is a public disposition to action that relies on the utilities of the self whilst, at the same time, it hyper-emotionalizes, without challenging, the power relations of humanitarianism. In a manner similar to appeals, despite their different performative practices, the post-humanitarianism of celebrity articulates human suffering as a cause for solidarity, by intensifying connectivity with people like 'us' but without engaging us with the condition of suffering others: 'when most people think of the UN now they think of Angelina Jolie on a crusade, not the work that goes on in the field . . . celebrity is at the heart of every UNICEF campaign and the association is being sold incredibly cheap.'[29]

Conclusion: towards a utilitarian altruism

My engagement with celebrity as a communicative figure that articulates aspirational performances of solidarity sought to analyse the humanitarian imaginary as a politics of pity based on a theatrical conception of action: the circulation of images and stories about suffering that propose dispositions of emotion and action to the West.

Whereas the critique of celebrity humanitarianism challenges celebrity as spectacle that produces inauthentic aspirational performance, my analysis of two key 'moments' of celebrity humanitarianism, Hepburn's late eighties and Jolie's contemporary 'moment', demonstrates that there is significant variation in celebrity claims to authenticity – each bearing distinct implications as to the dispositions of solidarity it proposes to the West.

Hepburn's ambassadorial/ceremonial version of humanitarianism proposes an apolitical version of pity as salvation whilst communicating emotion through a 'theatrical' delivery of testimonies on suffering. Jolie's entrepreneurial/confessional style, which can be seen as developing in dialectical relationship to the ambassadorial, hyper-politicizes humanitarianism as a form of 'celebrity diplomacy' whilst communicating emotion by speaking 'from the heart'. Even though, compared to the ambassadorial style, Jolie's own generous entrepreneurialism steps up celebrity impact in relief and development donations, the confessional style may not actually work as a force of moralization for the West. Insofar as its communicative structure prioritizes the 'authentic' emotions of celebrity and, through 'reflexive sympathy', our own emotions towards her, it may be encouraging the narcissistic disposition of voyeuristic solidarity rather than a disposition of commitment to the humanitarian cause.

This disposition can be juxtaposed with the authenticity of sincerity, exemplified in Hepburn's 'feel for my descriptions of what those who suffer feel', which disarticulates celebrity from her emotion and prioritizes instead the communication of the cause. Crucial to the communicative practice of sincerity, I argue, is the preservation of the theatricality of pity. Sincerity, in this sense, makes explicit use of the subjectivity of the celebrity as acting a role so as to 'teach spectators ways of ceasing to be spectators and become actors of collective practice' (Rancière 2009: 8), without claiming that what the celebrity does is what the celebrity is or feels. It is, let us recall, the tension inherent in the personification of emotions between the 'I' of the persona and the 'me' of the role, sustained in Hepburn's de-celebritization but collapsed in Jolie's hyper-celebritization, that differentiates sincerity from authenticity as modalities of aspirational discourse within the humanitarian imaginary (see Williams 1973 for a discussion of a similar contrast in terms of the egoism–altruism distinction).

Whereas this subtle but crucial 'as-if' of the theatre could make a difference between humanitarianism as narcissistic introspection or as moral education, the historical development of the theatre of pity from apolitical salvation to entrepreneurial moralism, poses a more pertinent question: to what extent is the very use of celebrity as an authentic voice a morally appropriate and politically adequate choice for the communication of solidarity? I return to this question in my Conclusion, but, for now, the many authenticities of celebrity point to something important. Rather than criticizing celebrity humanitarianism for lacking authenticity, as the pessimistic argument tends to do, authenticity compels us to ask just how the imaginary might, if at all, move beyond the truth of emotions and support more radical imaginations of solidarity – imaginations that may manage to reclaim justice as the new imperative of action on human suffering. One of the genres of the humanitarian imaginary that come closer to articulating this demand for justice is the genre of concerts, particularly the 2005 Live 8 series of rock events around the world, and it is to this genre that I now turn.

5 Concerts

Introduction: rock as ritual ceremonies

The Live 8 concerts, ten rock mega-events simultaneously broadcast around the world, focused global attention on the 2005 G8 meeting at Gleneagles and, in so doing, put pressure on powerful governments to end third world debt and establish new fair trade rules. Designed as a follow-up to Live Aid, the 1985 dual concerts that raised unprecedented funds for the Ethiopian famine, Live 8 was also organized by the mastermind of its legendary predecessor, Bob Geldof, this time teaming up with U2 lead singer Bono. In his capacity as a leading humanitarian activist, Geldof was quoted evaluating the outcomes of the Gleneagles summit as follows: 'On aid, 10 out of 10; on debt, 8 out of 10; on trade . . . It is quite clear that this summit, uniquely, decided that enforced liberalization must no longer take place . . . Mission accomplished, frankly.'[1]

It is this authority of a rock celebrity to announce the chronic and complex problem of global poverty as a 'mission accomplished', neatly amenable to an evaluation of a ten-point scale, that today informs both the public fascination with the increasing power of rock culture to intervene in the political process and the scepticism that surrounds the role of such culture in catalysing a new cosmopolitanism. It is this ambivalence between celebration and scepticism, inherent in the rock performances of solidarity throughout the past twenty-five years, which I explore in this chapter.

I argue that the concerts of Live Aid and Live 8 are crucial performances of the humanitarian imaginary, insofar as they use the global appeal of rock to disseminate and legitimize the moral imperative of solidarity – the imperative to act on vulnerable others without the anticipation of reciprocation. The power of these events to articulate aspirational performances of solidarity lies in their quality as 'media events' – globally staged events, which use rock music as a form of 'ceremonial politics' so as to bring people together around a cause (Dayan and Katz 1992: viii). Even though media events have been criticized for aestheticizing politics, in that they privilege spectacle over argument, from my perspective, the ceremonial politics of rock concerts simultaneously throws into relief the profound theatricality of the humanitarian imaginary as a site of moral education: 'such events', as

Dayan and Katz put it, 'portray an idealized version of society, reminding society of what it aspires to be rather than what it is' (1992: ix).

Taking my starting point in this productive tension between the aesthetics and ethics of solidarity, at the heart of humanitarian imaginary, I provide an account of the Live Aid and Live 8 media events as two of the most significant moments of ceremonial humanitarianism. My argument is that, in performing solidarity, this humanitarianism relies upon the aesthetics of what Dayan and Katz call the 'conquest': a communicative script of 'rare events, both in occurrence and in effectiveness', which uses the presence of charismatic figures, or 'heroes of a new sort', in order to enchant publics and set a new paradigm of action (1992: 26). In the case of rock concerts, charisma is embodied by figures of the music star-system, Geldof and Bono, who, by uniquely combining romanticist self-expression and commercial entrepreneurship, manage to authenticate rock culture as an aspirational performance of solidarity in the global public scene.

The moralizing impact of such performance lies, here, in the capacity of its media events to produce the West as an imaginary 'we' – a collectivity that perceives itself as an actor upon vulnerable others beyond its immediate reach. The moral subject of ceremonial humanitarianism, it follows, is not a pre-existing public that waits dormant to be called into action. This moral subject is instead itself an effect of ceremonial humanitarianism, emerging out of the ritualized performances of rock culture and using its specific strategies of communication in order 'to sustain and/or mobilize collective sentiments and solidarities' (Cottle 2006a: 415). The ritual function of media events is, in this sense, performative: it mobilizes the discursive resources of language and image in order to construct the boundaries of political community in ways that may either confirm our existing sense of belonging or extend this sense to encompass the zone of distant suffering.[2]

Performativity is, therefore, again my key analytical perspective on ceremonial humanitarianism. Whereas the performativity of authenticity refers to the discursive strategies that authenticate the charisma of rock stars, the performativity of community focuses on the moralizing strategies of rock events as they seek to turn distant suffering into a cause of solidarity. In light of this dual focus, the chapter explores historical change in ceremonial humanitarianism by comparing Live Aid with Live 8.

I begin with the intense controversy around ceremonial humanitarianism, which is torn by the tension between celebrating community, inherent in the logic of media events as rituals, and denouncing commodification, co-nascent with media events as spectacles ('Aid Concerts: Communitas or Cynicism?'). Arguing that this controversy reproduces the impasses of theoretical discourse, with each side simply confirming its own normative position, I propose instead an analytical approach to ceremonial humanitarianism that suspends theoretical argument so as to explore the communicative practices through which the paradoxes of humanitarianism are provisionally resolved in specific media events, in the 1985–2005 time frame ('An Analytics of Ceremonial Performativity'). Subsequent sections focus, therefore, on the distinct authentication and moralization strategies used at these two different 'moments' in order to show that, whereas changes in these concerts' claims to authenticity reflect an increasing disenchantment towards ceremonial humanitarianism as spectacle, changes in their moral claims reflect a move away from the universal morality of salvation towards a pragmatic morality of celebrity diplomacy and towards what I have already defined as post-humanitarian activism – an activism that combines doing good with the pleasures of new media consumerism ('The Authenticity Effects of Ceremonial Humanitarianism').

Even though, as in the case study of Angelina Jolie, the post-humanitarian character of contemporary rock concerts also appears to emphatically utilize a vocabulary of justice, this vocabulary is, in fact, subordinated to a vocabulary of authenticity – it foregrounds, that is, the pleasures of the western self rather than engaging with distant others. This, I conclude, has to do with the fact that, even though both historical 'moments' appear to depend upon mediated spectacle, Live 8 is undermining the theatricality of the event and, in so doing, tends to turn its moral message into narcissistic self-expression. Ultimately, then, it is the western community of consumerist rock fandom that ceremonial post-humanitarianism brings about, rather than a cosmopolitan community of solidarity that engages with claims to justice ('The authenticity effects of ceremonial humanitarianism').

Aid concerts: communitas or cynicism?[3]

The debate around solidarity-related rock concerts reflects a deep ambivalence at the heart of ceremonial humanitarianism – the ambivalence between its integrative force, celebrated for constituting communities of solidarity, and its commodification effects, criticized for depoliticizing solidarity. Central to this ambivalence, as I show below, are, the competing conceptions of authenticity that inform the debate on ceremonial humanitarianism. Whereas the positive argument emphasizes the power of rock concerts to mobilize a global economy of genuine commitment that can make a real difference to vulnerable others, the sceptical argument draws attention to the profound inauthenticity of media events such as Live Aid and Live 8 in that they commercialize, rather than enhance, commitments to solidarity and reproduce, rather than challenge, colonial stereotypes of vulnerable others.

The authenticity debate is not unique to the genre of rock concerts. It is, as we know, co-nascent with the theatrical structure of the humanitarian imaginary itself and reflects a broader historical ambiguity as to whether the 'truths' of theatrical spectacle act as forms of moral education or as vehicles of moral corruption. This debate, however, takes on specific characteristics when it comes to the media events of ceremonial humanitarianism. My own exploration of these characteristics rests on the assumption that any assessment of the moralizing role of such humanitarianism should go beyond a general discussion on authenticity and, instead, comparatively analyse the historically specific performances through which each humanitarian genre produces its own distinct claims to authenticity and solidarity. Before I move on to this analysis, however, let me first engage with the theoretical debate, commencing with the positive argument.

The *positive argument* postulates that the emergence of solidarity-related concerts, initiated by Live Aid in 1985 and followed by a broad range of other similar events,[4] signals the power of popular culture to appropriate and galvanize political causes in ways that potentially reconfigure consumers into active citizens of the world. There are two distinct, yet interrelated, sides to this argument: the first sees solidarity-related concerts as catalysts of a cosmopolitan community whilst the second sees them as making a real difference in the lives of vulnerable others.

The first argument, the creation of a cosmopolitan public, is regarded as a direct consequence of the integrative function of media events. Evidenced in the more-than-two-billion spectatorship that each of the two events attracted (see below, p. 118), the rock concert is the media event, par excellence, to achieve 'social integration of the highest order' (Dayan and Katz 1992: 15). Live Aid and Live 8 operate, in this account, as music rituals that cut across national divisions and connect people around the globe under the noble banner of the humanitarian cause – 'the event's principal success,' says Bennett of Live Aid, 'was that it was able *to focus, however briefly, people's attention on a world problem* by utilizing a key element of their leisure and lifestyle' (A. Bennett 2001: 2, emphasis added).

Central to this possibility of cosmopolitan connectivity are two distinct processes: the culture of rock itself, which articulates a universal sensibility of protest and resistance in its ritual performances (Auslander 1998), and its technologies of mediation, which enable this universal sensibility to break through the spatio-temporal restrictions of specific concert venues and enchant audiences around the world (Compton and Comor 2007). These two conditions of possibility, the cultural and the technological, open up a potentially global symbolic space where rock culture becomes explicitly invested with moral meaning as the authentic expression of public commitment towards vulnerable others: 'Having watched 10 hours of the Live Aid bash at Wembley,' as the *Guardian*'s Terry Coleman put it, 'you have to be a bit amazed at the sheer, sweet, innocent, hopeful, impossible altruism of the whole idea, and of the thousands of people in that stadium. Christian missionaries are long out of fashion, but I believe some of these people have that same hope of a perfect world.'[5]

A crucial feature of this kind of 'sheer, sweet, innocent' commitment is that, rather than being rationally expressed, it is performed through an economy of affect organized around 'the audience's close and intimate relationship to the pop star' (Marshall 2006: 205). Commenting on the remarkable politicizing effect of Live Aid, for instance, Garofalo confirms that 'by the end of the 1980s, there was scarcely a progressive social issue that had not become the theme for a fundraising concert or the subject of a popular song or both – environmental issues, homelessness, child abuse, racism, and AIDS, to name a few' (2005: 326). Even though such politicization may not necessarily end up in cosmopolitanizing audiences, the point here is that ceremonial humanitarianism does entail the potential to mobilize genuine planetary compassion – what Jenkins calls 'the global consciousness of pop cosmopolitanism' (2006: 156).

The second positive argument, the power of rock concerts to make a difference in the global South, relates to the power of what Compton and Comor call the 'integrated spectacle' of ceremonial humanitarianism (2007). Rather than the integration of publics into cosmopolitan communities, 'integrated spectacle' refers instead to the strategic alliance between the rock star system with the political and the economic fields – an alliance that pushes humanitarian politics into public visibility and turns rock stars into influential players of global decision making (A. F. Cooper 2007). In this account, Geldof or Bono and the G8 leaders do not operate in oppositional fields but, on the contrary, interact in ways that not only increase the accountability of traditional politicians but, importantly, may enable these rock stars to contribute to shaping the politics of development (Bishop and Green 2008): 'you must engage with the [political] process as it is,' Geldof says, describing the practice of celebrity diplomacy, 'not as you imagine it to be, or as you would wish it to be, or even as you think it should be – but as it is. You must engage with the power and the persons and institutions and methods that wield that power' (*Guardian*, 28 December 2005).

This pragmatic approach to politics is driven by celebrity figures who, in Cooper's description of Live 8, 'are both transformative and results oriented, in that they combine a critical sensibility on social justice issues *with a desire to fix things on an instrumental basis*' (A. F. Cooper 2007: 5, emphasis added). The insistence on 'fixing things' on the ground, rather than reiterating empty words, lies at the heart of the positive argument on solidarity-related rock concerts as the authentic manifestation of humanitarianism. What such practical ethos reflects is an anti-bureaucratic culture that challenges the old-style politics of 'hollow promises', in Geldof's words, and orients it towards real and immediate change whilst, simultaneously, yielding a series of mutual benefits to both the rock industry and political elites. Against accusations of the former as being co-opted to the latter, Geldof's response points, again, to the moral argument of real effects: 'Yeah but people are *alive* . . . what price criticism when the end result of a bunch of people in the studio is without doubt the end result of millions of people being helped to stay alive?" (*Rolling Stone*, 5 December 1985 quoted in Hague, Street and Savigny 2008: 12, emphasis in the original).

Taken together, the vision of genuine cosmopolitan commitment and the promise for real impact point to the centrality of authenticity in the positive argument of ceremonial humanitarianism. On the one hand, the affective economy of rock culture appears to be a catalyst in galvanizing the West into a genuinely committed and fully present subject of solidarity whereas, on the other, the integrated spectacle of rock and politics speaks to a pragmatic conception of political agency as authentic, in the sense of making a real difference to the lives of those who need it.

The *critical argument*, in contrast, views the rise of ceremonial humanitarianism with suspicion. Rock concerts, this argument has it, do not signal the power of popular culture to galvanize publics into political subjects in new ways, but, in fact, signal the power of consumer culture to reduce humanitarian causes into depoliticized commodities, devoid of political and historical content. There are, again, two main sides to this argument: the first sees solidarity-related concerts as catalysts of consumerist communities of fandom (the critique of the spectacle) whilst the second sees them as a co-option to hegemonic agendas that corrupt, rather than promote, humanitarian politics (the critique of empire).

The consumerist publics of rock concerts emerge, in this account, out of a radical commodification of the field of humanitarianism, which turns human suffering into spectacle and subordinates the humanitarian cause to the charismatic performance of the rock star. Part of a broader discourse of suspicion towards the culture industry and its alienating effects, this view originates in the Frankfurt School account of popular culture as an illusion of individual expression that, in reality, seduces public agency in practices of passive or 'regressive listening' (Adorno 1938/1991: 270). The contemporary critique of the spectacle, however, updates this early critique in two ways. First, it points to the function of global rock in sustaining and legitimizing colonial continuities in its iconographies of distant suffering. Rather than construing a truly cosmopolitan community, critics say, ceremonial humanitarianism perpetuates a deeply unequal world order that rests on the cultural division between a civilized 'us' and an inferior 'other' – what the 2001 VSO report calls the 'Live Aid Legacy': 'The stereotypes of extreme deprivation and poverty, together with powerful images of Western aid, add up to a strong sense of Africa . . . as the helpless victim, deserving and requiring Western aid in order to survive' (2002: 4).

Second, the commodification critique points to the intimate links between solidarity-related concerts and the market, postulating that, rather than the radicalism of rock culture, Live Aid and Live 8 are, in fact, driven by a market spirit of instrumental efficiency, which subordinates systemic questions of power to the logic of immediate effects – 'getting things done' rather than addressing the complexities of development (Hague, Street and Savigny 2008). A key consequence of this subordination of politics to the market is the reconfiguration of concert audiences into masses of fans, whose participation in such events is confined to practices like 'texting and watching, leaving active involvement to the elite' (Crouch 2004: 49). Having little to do with the enactment of global citizenship, this consumerist participation operates, instead, as 'a theatre of legitimation for the neoliberal agenda, a stage-managed simulation of democracy "at work"' (Biccum 2007: 1112).

The first critical argument of ceremonial humanitarianism is, therefore, about disclosing the inauthenticity of 'pop cosmopolitanism' as a deficient form of collective identity, which both denies the legitimacy of the distant sufferer, through its 'othering' iconographies, and reduces western publics to consuming fans by commodifying their participation in its media events.

The second critical argument of ceremonial humanitarianism moves from disclosing the inauthenticity of cosmopolitan *publics* towards denouncing the political *agents* of rock concerts as an equally inauthentic expression of western hegemony. In contradistinction to the positive argument, the integration of rock music with the market is now regarded as responsible not for the success but for the failure of humanitarianism to provide a radical response to the causes of poverty. Particularly prominent in the case of Live 8, which is accused of surrendering to the seduction of celebrity spectacle, this denunciation of co-option is nonetheless already present in Live Aid – the first exercise of 'marketing' for a good cause: 'What Live Aid represented', argue Hague, Street and Savigny, 'was the one value that Geldof attributed to music: the capacity to draw crowds and to make money'

(Hague, Street and Savigny 2008: 10). At the heart of this critique of inauthenticity lies a view of ceremonial humanitarianism as a form of political legitimization that no longer relies on collective activism but operates, instead, at the level of elite personalities, including rock stars, who decide behind closed doors. The cultural politics of celebrity may, in this sense, inject traditional structures of global governance with the new symbolic capital of rock charisma, but does not, ultimately, manage to democratize the field of humanitarianism. Insofar as it functions within this 'post-democratic' framework, humanitarianism runs the risk of 'merely putting a happy face on organization[s] that have serious shortcomings in how they promote themselves and how they conduct international relations' (Alleyne 2005: 183).

Inauthenticity, then, turns out to be a central theme of the critical argument, insofar as it challenges the capacity of ceremonial humanitarianism both to construe a cosmopolitan public and to democratize global politics. Whereas the critique of the spectacle throws into relief the 'othering' effects of the spectacle and the consumerist constitution of western publics, the critique of empire illustrates the hegemonic role that celebrity plays in perpetuating, rather than challenging, the power relationships of development.

In summary, the literature on ceremonial humanitarianism centres around the concept of authenticity in order to either celebrate or criticize the role that rock concerts play in catalysing collectivities and in legitimizing solidarity. The positive argument considers the cultural politics of rock concerts as an affective economy capable of conjuring up genuine commitment, whilst the cynical argument challenges the authenticity of rock concerts as moral discourse, on the grounds that it is ultimately linked to the power structures of humanitarianism: spectacle and empire.

Even though each argument makes a convincing case within its own premises, the debate as a whole remains inconclusive, in that it is ultimately exhausted in perpetuating two relatively plausible yet radically incompatible assertions. Rather than attempting to take an a priori position in this debate, at the risk of further reproducing its theoretical impasses, I, therefore, propose that we now provisionally suspend theoretical argument and turn towards empirical analysis. This analytical procedure, I suggest, should not take authenticity for granted, asking whether ceremonial performances of humanitarianism are genuine or not, but should come to problematize the concept of authenticity itself as a necessary truth-claim of all theatrical performance, which does not pre-exist its communicative practices but is, instead, constructed through these very practices at specific historical 'moments'.

By turning authenticity from a criterion of assessment of the moral power of ceremonial humanitarianism into an object of analysis of the production of this power, it is now possible to move towards a hermeneutic framework that explains how rock concerts produce meaning about solidarity and thereby privilege certain forms of community over others. Following this analytical framework, I then discuss the two key 'moments' of ceremonial humanitarianism, Live Aid and Live 8.

An analytics of ceremonial performativity: Live Aid and Live 8

The performance of solidarity through the aesthetics of rock concerts is the object of what we may call an 'analytics' of ceremonial performativity. The concept of analytics, taken from Foucault's Aristotelian distinction between theoretical and analytical argument on the nature of power, draws attention to the fact that the rock concert, as a practice of humanitarianism, is an instrument of power, not because it imposes a homogeneous ideology of solidarity, but because it subtly regulates the social relationships between performers and spectators through the normative discourses that it makes available to them (Chouliaraki 2006). From this perspective, the focus on the visual, aural and linguistic aspects of the rock concert is not simply about describing the aesthetics of 'conquest', the key script of this media event, but it is about identifying how this aesthetics produces truth about solidarity and how, in so doing, it shapes the moral conduct of its spectators in terms of who they should care about and why.

The analytics of ceremonial humanitarianism consists, it follows, of a dual focus on the performative aspects of the rock concert: the *performance* of humanitarianism, which analyses the aesthetic choices of language, image and sound through which these concerts are produced as forms of 'authentic' commitment to their cause, and its *performativity*, which identifies the discursive effects of these choices in constituting western spectators as the moral subject of solidarity.

This analytical language, inspired by Butler's (1993) post-structuralist theory of meaning, avoids deterministic conceptions of performativity that overestimate the role of discursive power in fully regulating subjects and emphasizes instead the productive tension between performativity and performance. Whereas performativity, as I mentioned in chapters 2 and 4, refers to the normative dimensions of ceremonial humanitarianism, that is, to the 'reiteration of norms which precede, constrain and exceed the[ir] performer and in that sense cannot be taken as the fabrication of the performer's "will" or "choice"' (Butler 1993: 234), performance refers to the unique mobilization of these norms in specific ceremonial events and therefore entails the possibility of variation that may subvert the norms in the very act of reproducing them. It is precisely this productive tension that makes possible the historical comparison between Live Aid and Live 8, as the assumption of the analytics is that exploring the changing aesthetics of performance allows us to illustrate transformations in performativity – the norms of its moral discourse.

Even though *the performative* is also central to the logic of celebrity, ceremonial humanitarianism belongs to a distinct communicative practice which is not organized around the individualist figure of the film star, as with Audrey Hepburn or Angelina Jolie, but around the collectivist figure of the rock hero. Collectivism here suggests that this figure functions as a 'truth bearer', that is, as the legitimate representative of a distinct music culture with its own public rituals and is, therefore, responsible for uniquely articulating, as much as routinely reproducing, its own aspirational performance for its audiences (Eyerman and Jamison 1998: 24). Equally theatrical as the Hollywood celebrity may be, then, ceremonial humanitarianism mobilizes a different logic of theatricality and requires a different analytical language to describe how its key figures may perform solidarity.

This analytical language, I propose, begins with the acknowledgement that the rock concert is an economy of affect, which regulates audiences by transforming pleasures into a range of moral and political commitments: 'the most common relationship to popular culture', as Grossberg puts it, 'is determined by the cultural production of pleasures' so as to produce 'mattering maps . . . maps which direct our investments in and into the world . . . as potential locations for our self-identifications' (2006: 584–5).

Central to this moral economy of affect is the performance of *charisma*, a form of public authority that, according to Weber (1978), regulates social integration by relying on emotions of admiration and attachment – 'on devotion to the exceptional sanctity, heroism or exemplary character of an individual person, and of the normative patterns or order revealed or ordained by him' (in Kronman 1983: 67). The religious overtones of this original definition of charisma granted, charisma has today come to encompass secular forms of authority that, nonetheless, retain an emphasis on the affective or irrational dimensions through which power can be exercised. A case in point is the 'conquest', the communicative script of rare media events that, as I have argued, are driven precisely by 'dashing, daring heroes acting singlehandedly against all odds' (Dayan and Katz 1992: 31).

If Live Aid can be defined as a conquest, then, this is not only because it has been a unique moment of broadcasting, hailed as 'a turning point' in the mediation of fund-raising for a cause (Edkins 2000: 106), but crucially also because, together with Live 8, it is associated with the extraordinary agency of singular individuals – Geldof and Bono. Charisma, in this context, does not refer to a God-given authority that these individuals are naturally endowed with, but to this communicatively construed possibility for action that mobilizes affect so as to represent such action as unique, extraordinary and 'against all odds' (Dayan and Katz 1992). In this sense, secular charisma is not only about the individual agency of the rock star but is further implicated in the formation of a collective 'we', as the heroic figures of rock call up a public body of spectators 'to witness [their] almost impossible undertaking' (Dayan and Katz 1992: 31). It is precisely this magic of witnessing charisma through technologies of mediation that turns the spectators of Live Aid/Live 8 into enchanted publics, able 'to transcend national frontiers and . . . to be both national and international' (Hall and Jacques 1989: 11).

Enchantment, in this context, refers then to the affective power of charismatic performance that brings global audiences together under a single collective identity, 'by sharing feelings and thoughts . . ., by joining a "community" of other fans who share common interests' (Jenkins 2006: 41). Whilst the act of witnessing can be construed as a 'regressive' activity of seduction, à la Adorno, witnessing as enchantment can also be seen as empowering in that it enables a massive community of rock fans to use their alignment with the charismatic star so as to express their collective will 'as one'. Rather than prematurely aligning with either of these two potentials for agency, the regressive or the empowering, I prefer to treat enchantment as a discursive effect of ceremonial humanitarianism that may change over time.

Charisma, the extraordinary agency of rock stars, and *enchantment*, the magic connectivity that construes the West as a witness of this charisma, are the two analytical categories that explore how authenticity is performed in ceremonial humanitarianism; how, that is, rock concerts communicate their cause as genuine in its intentions or real in its effects, so as to maximize what Grossberg calls our 'strength of investment' to this cause (2006: 585).

These communicative strategies, however, do not operate in a vacuum but come to authenticate historically specific performances of solidarity towards vulnerable others. Reflected in the language and images of suffering that frame each rock concert, in promotional campaigns, artists' speeches, screen projections or survivor testimonies, it is this performance of solidarity that ultimately turns the spectatorship of the concert into a moralizing experience. What the performance of solidarity enables here is, again, an act of witnessing, albeit this time not simply of the music event per se, as Dayan and Katz put it, but also of the spectacle of distant suffering – an act of witnessing that now defines what Grossberg calls the 'nature of concern' that gathers rock publics together (2006: 585).

It is the *dual act of witnessing* the vulnerability of others within an enchanted performance of rock that comes to constitute the global spectatorship of Live Aid and Live 8 as an ambivalent collectivity – a potentially cosmopolitan public and, at the same time, a commodified group of music fans. Suspended between rock fandom and moral commitment, this ambivalent performativity of ceremonial humanitarianism lies at the heart of my analysis of these concerts' moralizing strategies. In line with the argument that today's humanitarianism is subject to processes of instrumentalization and technologization, my hypothesis is that changes in the aesthetic properties of the rock concert, from the 1985 Live Aid to the 2005 Live 8, may simultaneously reconfigure the moral agency of audiences towards more entrepreneurial practices of fandom. The extent to which such practices may be empowering or not is, as I have noted, not a theoretical but an empirical question to be addressed, at least partially, in the course of analysing the specific performative practices of concerts.

In conclusion, following the dual focus of the analytics, my discussion consists of two dimensions of the rock concert as a moral economy of affect. The first dimension focuses on the *authentication strategies* of each rock concert. Aiming to show how two key aesthetic choices of each concert construct the event as authentic and, thereby, intensify its fans' commitment to the cause, this analysis addresses (i) the *performance of charisma*, which constitutes the figure of the humanitarian rock star as 'hero', and (ii) the *evocation of enchantment*, which constitutes concert fans as witnessing publics through the technological effects of omnipresence and liveness. The second dimension of the economy of affect focuses on the *moralizing strategies* by which the aesthetic choices of each concert propose specific dispositions of solidarity to their publics. The single most important category here is the *witnessing of suffering*, which refers to the ways in which human vulnerability enters the rock concert as a cause for collective commitment. Let me start with the analysis of Live Aid.

Live Aid

The Live Aid concert, part of the 'Feed the World' campaign, took place on 15 July 1985 with a spectacular line-up of rock stars performing songs for charity, including Status Quo, Queen, Dire Straits, David Bowie, Phil Collins, U2, and George Michael, performing the Bob Geldof/ Midge Ure song 'Do They Know It's Christmas?', at two world locations

Figure 5.1 Live Aid, 1985 (Getty Images).

simultaneously – the Wembley Stadium, London, and the JFK Stadium, Philadelphia. Described as the 'Woodstock of the Eighties', Live Aid was put together by Bob Geldof, then singer of the Boomtown Rats punk/rock group, with a view to donating money for famine relief in Ethiopia.[6] A sixteen-hour long marathon, this double concert raised £30 million in donations and £120 million in subsequent merchandise, whilst it attracted more than 72,000 and 90,000 spectators in the Wembley and JFK stadia respectively. Moreover, making use of satellite television in 150 countries, the event was a watershed moment in terms of configuring a global spectatorship – the number of television viewers is estimated at 1.9 billion, one of the biggest-ever audiences of a media event.[7] How did this concert manage to establish its cause, Feed the World, as authentic and to persuade a massive global audience to participate in it? It was, I argue, a combination of rock *charisma*, as expressed primarily by Bob Geldof, and popular *enchantment* in the face of its unprecedented, planetary-scale connectivity and, of course, its legendary live performances.

The performance of Live Aid

The charisma of rock romanticism

Live Aid materialized as a response to Geldof watching a compelling BBC news piece on famine in the Ethiopian Korem camp, on 23 October

1984.[8] Described by him as 'humanity laid bare', the piece urged Geldof to act by using the resource he best knew, music: 'So I thought, what can I do? I have a platform. I can write tunes but the Rats are not having hits. It's embarrassing . . . it was clear I had to gather some people together.'[9] Geldof's single-handed initiative and its subsequent success already points to his charisma – an extraordinary form of agency that used the music industry in order to call up a community of solidarity. Despite their prima facie incompatibility, I argue that the romanticism of solidarity and the commercialism of the industry are constitutive elements of Geldof's charisma, which both equally define the character of Live Aid as a historical moment of ceremonial humanitarianism.

A key feature of rock culture, romanticism construes rock as the signifier of a true, primordial self against societal constraints – a music that is 'truly expressive of the artists' souls and psyches, and consistently politically and culturally oppositional' (Auslander 1998: 5). Aligned with a broader romanticist movement, rock figures in this discourse as a music culture that glorifies the will of the individual in its heroic, because asymmetrical, opposition against structures of power. Romanticism is, in this sense, a key marker of authenticity that enables rock to style itself as part of the popular history of social protest and mass mobilization: 'Everything I've done,' says Geldof, 'has been through the lens of music, the opportunity it gave me to articulate that, FUCK OFF, THINGS DON'T HAVE TO BE LIKE THIS. . . . And that all comes from being 11 years old and listening to John and Paul and Mick and Bob and Pete' (capitals in the original).[10]

Both elements of romanticism, self-expressivity and the anti-establishment sensibility, are evident in Geldof's words, 'everything I've done has been through the lens of music', emphasizing his non-institutionalized education through the sounds of rebel musicians – 'that all comes from being 11 years old and listening to John and Paul. . .'. Geldof's charismatic agency emerges here as a natural disposition to live unconventionally, using rock as a means of spontaneous opposition to the status quo – a disposition that is further authenticated, here and elsewhere, by his consistent use of offensive language, 'fuck off, things don't have to be like this', but also the artist's characteristically angry and untidy public image, unchanged for the past 25 years.

Yet Geldof's charisma is not purely romanticist. It is simultaneously informed by a rival discourse of commercialism which construes rock music as a signifier of 'big money' and is reflected in Geldof's rationale for recruiting the biggest rock stars for Live Aid: 'the more multimillion-record selling acts the better, because people will watch their favourites and contribute' (1986: 264). Closely associated with this commercialist discourse is the logic of 'getting things done', which informs, as we saw, the practice of Live Aid as primarily a fund-raising enterprise. Evident in Geldof's dramatic albeit controversial call, 'Give us your fucking money', to the BBC audience halfway through the concert, this anti-establishment instrumentalism combines elements of both discourses, romanticism and commercialism, in a hybrid form of agency that uses a 'no-nonsense' script to both challenge and exploit the system to its own benefit.

Geldof's charisma lies, in this sense, not only in his unconventional agency but in the strategic articulation of this agency with an aggressive instrumentality. A deeply individualistic disposition, his rock charisma can, thus, be best summed up as an anti-corporatism through corporate means: 'I want money', as he once put it, 'because it will buy me individual freedom . . . this society constrains me, it inhibits me, I don't like it, I really just want out of this society and the only way I can see it is to have more money than anyone else, to give me choices, options . . .'[11]

Reflecting this corporate anti-corporatism, the Live Aid fund-raising strategy turned indeed away from politics and 'the hollow promises offered by old-style politicians' (Hall and Jacques 1989: 11), and relied instead on unmediated giving that minimized, for instance, artists' copyright costs in favour of direct donations and corporate sponsorships: 'the idea was: no recordings, no films, no videos, just 15 minutes of your hits, then goodbye.'[12] This practice had a long-term effect on the humanitarian field, in that it favoured a 'transaction model of public engagement' that emphasized 'the power of giving and little else' and, as we shall see, marginalized the politics of famine in Ethiopia.[13]

The enchantment of technology

'There was something totally unique', Status Quo's lead singer said, describing the event, 'and I am not sure I've ever felt it since.'[14] It is precisely this indescribable quality of uniqueness that can be defined as enchantment – a 'condition of exhilaration' that involves 'an active engagement with objects of sensory experience . . . a state of interactive fascination' (J. Bennett 2001: 5). Whilst the term originally refers to the function of religious rituals to galvanize communities of faith, enchantment is today associated with celebrity culture, insofar as 'celebrity and fan cultures provide a forum for modern and secular forms of worship and idolatry' (Hjarvard 2008: 2). Two dimensions of the enchantment of Live Aid are relevant to my discussion: *omnipresence*, the sense of witnessing *with* others and *liveness*, the sense of witnessing what is happening *right now*.

Omnipresence was made possible by the then cutting-edge satellite infrastructure that enhanced the awareness of collective witnessing for transatlantic audiences throughout the sixteen-hour broadcast of the event. This infrastructure was provided by major regional broadcasters,[15] but concert timings were also arranged so as to guarantee that performances were synchronized across time zones so that both sides of the Atlantic could follow each other's acts. Uniquely in the history of rock concerts, Phil Collins further performed in both venues, by flying across on Concorde, but the equally ambitious idea of a coordinated transatlantic performance by Mick Jagger and David Bowie, in Wembley and JFK stadia respectively, had to be abandoned for technical reasons.

Moreover, verbal references to the unprecedented global character of Live Aid included the opening salute by BBC presenter, Richard Skinner, 'It's 12 noon in London, 7 a.m. in Philadelphia, and around the world it's time for Live Aid', the first act to perform in Wembley, tellingly Status Quo's 'Rockin' All Over the World', as well as frequent references to the numbers of people watching, such as the closing act of 'Do They Know It's Christmas?', where Geldof's comment on technical difficulties – 'if we are to cock it up, we might as well cock it up with *two billion people watching*' – provoked intense applause from the stadium's audience.

If electronic simultaneity is a ritual that returns us to the tribal experience of collective listening, then Live Aid's omnipresence managed to constitute its audiences as a planetary community connected by the shared experience of rock – in the words of a participant: 'I watched the whole Wembley show and stayed up to watch the Philadelphia show as I wanted to see if Phil Collins had made it across the Atlantic in time. Nothing will ever top the original Live Aid show at Wembley!'[16] Yet, even if satellite technically reinvents spectatorship as an experience of global resonance, the catalyst for the tribalization of the concert, its ritual integration into communities of affect, lies in its sense of liveness.

Performed by the most significant stars of the industry and supported by one of the biggest technical apparata of sound production ever set up, Live Aid has been hailed as simply the greatest music spectacle of all time: 'I remember Status Quo coming on', a participant recalls the 'feeling' of the London concert, 'and the noise of the crowd cheering getting louder and louder so you could hardly hear the music start, then the unmistakeable sound of "Rockin' All Over the World" and I felt like the whole country was cheering.'[17] Central to the experience of enchantment as a sense of 'interactive fascination' is precisely this live sound of the Status Quo song, 'the unmistakeable sound of "Rockin' All Over the World"', which not only set off a sensory experience of togetherness within the stadium, 'the noise of the crowd . . . louder and louder', but ultimately expanded beyond it – 'the whole country was cheering.' Talking about this very moment, Status

Quo's lead singer similarly recalls an extraordinary emotional resonance, which blurred the boundary between him as a performer and his fans: 'we were playing to a crowd who were really part of it – they hadn't paid out just to turn up, they were part of the event.'[18]

Enchantment emerges here out of a music ritual that not only connects across space but, as the very name of Live Aid suggests, also integrates in time. Live is that magic moment of simultaneous witnessing, which, as Dayan and Katz put it, 'suspends disbelief, represses cynicism and enters a "subjunctive" mode of culture' (1992: 141). It is precisely in evoking this utopian being-together that liveness is further regarded as the strongest guarantee for the authenticity of rock music. In contrast to sound recordings, as Grossberg argues, 'it was here – in its visual presentation – that rock often most explicitly manifested its resistance to the dominant culture, but also its sympathies with the business of entertainment' (1993: 204).

Even though this awareness of collective power as resistance is certainly part of the humanitarian imaginary of solidarity, Grossberg's reference to 'the business of entertainment' simultaneously draws attention to the ambivalence of the live spectacle not only as enchantment but also as commodification. Voicing a deep suspicion towards ceremonial humanitarianism, this argument, let us recall, approaches Live Aid as yet another instance of the alienation of morality by the market. The question, then, remains as to how these two strategies of authentication, charisma and enchantment, managed to produce Live Aid's moral commitment to solidarity. It is to this question that I now turn.

The performativity of Live Aid

No other instance best captures the moralization strategy of Live Aid than the BBC news imagery of famine and death in Korem, projected on the Wembley and JFK screens: 'a close-up baby – a tiny body but a large head, and its mouth open in a silent cry', Edkins begins her description of the most compelling scene of the screening, 'It is held close to its mother's face. She shields it with the cloth that drapes them both, drawing it to her, and looks down. The infant's silent anguish, eyes closed, mouth wide, screaming, continues' (Edkins 2000: 107). The immediate impact of this imagery was reflected in the significant increase in the donations rate following the screening, yet its deeper impact lies in introducing the witnessing of human suffering as the most important affective force of the concert.

The sublimation of suffering

Witnessing Korem touches our emotions, yet it does not offer us the practical means to act upon it: 'we are', as Edkins puts it, 'watching, helpless to prevent, yet implicated' (2000: 115). The ceremonial humanitarianism of Live Aid is, I argue, an attempt to overcome the problem of action in the face of unbearable suffering by 'sublimating' Korem. A key symbolic trope through which distant suffering has historically been domesticated in the West, 'sublimation' focuses on the staging of human misfortune as a spectacle to be contemplated upon in all its magnitude yet in an aestheticized manner that ultimately protects the spectator from its full affective impact (Boltanski 1999).

Two features of Live Aid make this possible: the insertion of the Korem visuals within the broader aesthetic apparatus of the concert and the simultaneous call for charity. A series of haunting images of human vulnerability, the Korem visuals were introduced by David Bowie and used as background to The Cars' performance of 'Drive'. Not only was there no verbal framing of the images, and hence no explanatory narrative of the scene, but the song lyrics themselves severed the scene from its historical context and inserted it in the literary world of an eloquent, albeit generic, melancholy: 'Who's gonna tell you when it's too late, who's gonna tell you things aren't so great, you can't go on thinking nothing's wrong, who's gonna drive you home tonight?'. The repetition of 'Who's gonna . . .' and the multiple references to 'You can't go on thinking nothing's wrong' may hint at the romanticist discourse of opposition to the status quo, yet the visuals themselves represent human vulnerability as colonial 'bare life'. They foreground and thereby objectify the corporeal aspects of famine (emaciated body, elongated face, silent cry), and, in so doing, they ignore the victims as historical subjects who act under immense constraints, economic and political (Edkins 2000).

Sublimation is, in this sense, the symbolic effect of a double move, whereby the spectacle of Korem both provides testimony to human misfortune in its most abject form, through camera close-ups on the suffering body, and protects its spectators from trauma by removing such spectacle from the realm of historical life through The Cars' stage performance and lyrics. Yet, even if sublime suffering subordinates the horror of human vulnerability to the tribal comfort of rock performance, it can only retain its moral legitimacy if it abandons such a purely aesthetic contemplation and 'rapidly pass[es] through other topics on which it briefly touches' (Boltanski 1999: 129). It is Geldof's regular pleas, 'Don't go to the pub tonight. Please stay in and give us your money. There are people dying now,'[19] that put forward the demand for action as a complementary trope of representation in Live Aid.

What has today pejoratively become the 'legacy of Live Aid' (VSO Report 2002), then, refers precisely to the normative implications of sublime suffering as an object of our benevolent giving, which de-historicizes the context of non-western suffering, 'others' its subjects as corporeal beings devoid of dignity and continues to reproduce the power relationships between the developed West and the subordinate South.

The universal morality of aid

The Live Aid legacy is informed by a normative morality whose imperative is 'to save lives in the immediate future without waiting for a political analysis' (Edkins 2000: 120). A politicized rationale for the systemic contradictions underpinning the Ethiopian starvation is present in this morality, as for instance in Geldof's statement that 'We were seeing something palpably unnecessary, a crime in my view. Thirty million people are dying. Meanwhile in Europe we're spending tax to grow food we don't need' (4 January 2011). The emphasis, however, does not fall on a vocabulary of justice that views famine as the outcome of political relations of global injustice and local conflict, but on a morality of salvation that views famine as an immediate threat to life per se and, hence, as immune to political argument: 'I could do anything to make this work', as Geldof put it, 'because the one luxury of this particular exercise was the certainty that anything you did was morally justified' (1986: 224).

Anchored in the sublimated corporeality of starvation, this morality is universal not only in that it evokes the human body as evidence of its moral superiority, but also in that it supresses alternative moral claims, including a claim to justice, so as to present itself as the only legitimate morality of humanitarianism. It is precisely this universality, whereby 'no one could argue with the fact that "we" all opposed famine' (Hague, Street and Savigny 2008: 18), that has become the object of harsh criticism of Live Aid. Common humanity, critics say, obscures the conditions of violence and poverty responsible for famine in the first place, whilst the politics of donation substitutes a more radical response to suffering that challenges these historical conditions and promises a fairer world (Edkins 2000). Rather than universal, they continue, the solidarity of Live Aid is a specific, depoliticizing response to the Korem catastrophe that has defined the ways in which the West has since conceptualized Africa and the political question of development – or, as the VSO Report concludes, 'sixteen years on, Live Aid, Band Aid and the Ethiopian famine still have a powerful hold on our views of the developing world' (2002: 5). How has Live 8 changed the representational practices of suffering and norms of solidarity, twenty years after its predecessor?

Figure 5.2 Live 8 Concert, 2005 (Eric Vandeville/Gamma-Rapho/Getty Images).

Live 8

Coinciding with the twentieth anniversary of Live Aid, the Live 8 concerts took place in the G8 states, South Africa and Edinburgh, on 2 July 2005, just before the 6–8 July G8 Summit. Led by Geldof and Bono, these concerts were framed by a political agenda and took place in collaboration with a major NGO coalition, the Global Call to Action Against Poverty, named Make Poverty History, in the UK and the ONE campaign in the USA. Unlike Live Aid, therefore, Live 8 was not simply about donations but about public petitions and policy change and, to this end, it engaged major public figures such as Kofi Annan and Bill Gates (in the London concerts), and Nelson Mandela (in South Africa). The events involved more than one thousand musicians and were broadcast on 182 television networks and about 2,000 radio networks. They also capitalized on convergence technology, which purportedly brought audience figures up to an unprecedented 5.5 billion worldwide – though the number has not been confirmed.[20]

The performance of Live 8

The professionalization of charisma

Unlike Live Aid, which was spontaneously initiated by Geldof's impulse upon seeing Korem, Live 8 emerged out of a calculated double act between two professional celebrity diplomats: Geldof, by now an experienced global player, and Bono, a skilful lobbyist throughout the Millennium Development Goals (MDG) initiative. Whilst Geldof enacted his well-established 'provocative anti-diplomat' self, Bono relied on his 'charming and persuasive manner' to play a savvy diplomatic game (A. F. Cooper 2007: 8–11).

Both versions of charisma, Geldof's and Bono's, were professionalized in that they had little to do with Live Aid's angry dismissal of elites and instead enacted an informed and realistic approach to global governance – one that saw its success as depending upon a struggle from within, rather than outside, the core of political elites. Despite its oppositional style in Geldof's brand statement, 'If any of them [G8 leaders] won't come to our party, and believe me, we'll have a hell of a party, they can fuck off',[21] Live 8 is therefore dominated by an ethos of professionalism that gravitated upon Bono's diplomatic skills and policy-making knowledge (Traub 2005). Far from an untrained visionary, Bono emerged in the year-long run-up to Live 8 as, indeed, one of the most competent figures of public advocacy, whose tactical intelligence turned him into, what Cooper calls, a 'master manipulator' of global politics (A. F. Cooper 2007: 7).

Perennial to this professional ethos is the demand for justice, as is evident in Bono's opening lines at Live 8: 'This is our chance to stand up for what's right. We're not looking for charity. We're looking for justice. We can't fix every problem, but the ones we can, we must.' Departing from Live Aid's charity message, Bono's salute to Live 8 crowds not only emphasizes an orientation to 'what is right' and to 'justice', but also reflects a pragmatic approach to politics: 'we can't fix every problem but the ones we can, we must.' Organized around the tripartite agenda of increased aid, debt annulation and fair trade, this demand for justice is not, therefore, simply an exercise in popular protest but part of a broader strategy of public lobbying associated, as I mentioned, with the MDG (starting in 2004 and culminating at Gleneagles, 2005): 'Eight of the most powerful men on earth are meeting on a golf course in Scotland,' Bono continues, 'There's a lot at stake. We have a message for them: this is your moment, too. Make history, by making poverty history.'

Whilst 'Make Poverty History' was a strategic choice of language that, unlike Live Aid's depoliticized message, sought to problematize poverty as part of the historical relationships of global injustice, the campaign was also promoted as a strong philanthro-capitalist brand that heavily relied on the financing and technological structures of the corporate sector (Biccum 2007). Unlike Live Aid, then, Live 8 now consists not only of a star-studded line-up, but of the totality of promotion practices of the Global Call to

Action Against Poverty coalition that defined the meaning of the concert, such as celebrity-led ONE 'click' advertising trailers, the mass selling of the 'Make Poverty History' wristbands, the media promotion of free online broadcast and, importantly, the use of celebrity politicians as supporters of the concert – Bono's comparison of the Blair–Brown Labour pair as the 'Lennon and McCartney of politics' is, for instance, telling of the ethos of Live 8 as an 'integrated spectacle.'[22]

There was, in summary, a new performance of charisma in Live 8 which favoured pragmatism over romanticism, replacing the plea to save lives with concrete policy changes, and enhanced corporatism by framing Live 8 within a broader field of promotional strategies of solidarity that culminated in, but exceeded, the concert itself. Instead of the anti-corporate corporatism of Live Aid, Live 8 was a politically efficacious instance of show business that, despite not being a fund-raising event, managed to generate a surplus of $16 million for the non-profit sector.[23]

Disenchanted enchantment

Even though Live 8 was authenticated by the double charisma of its two rock stars in a new brand of professionalized activism, this very integration of humanitarianism with politics and the market is, simultaneously, responsible for associating Live 8 with a 'disenchanted' form of enchantment – a tribal affect of commitment that is, nonetheless, acutely aware of its own limitations as a performance of solidarity. This is evident in both dimensions of Live 8's enchantment: omnipresence and liveness.

First, despite the large numbers that Live 8 drew to the screens as well as on the ground, the 20-year-long history of solidarity concerts since Live Aid had managed to demystify the enchantment of a global 'get-together': 'Two decades of charity records, concerts and celebrity endorsements', as the *Guardian* put it, 'have undoubtedly dulled the impact of even the stellar lineup that Geldof has assembled.'[24] At the same time, digital spectatorship, that is, the shift from television to mobile screens, had since also transformed the experience of omnipresence into a more individualized and fragmented act of watching (Deuze 2006), partially, at least, fracturing the global resonance around a cause into a more versatile but also solitary participatory activity: 'that romantic resonance wasn't there,' as Geldof put it. 'Live Aid had the "give me your fuckin' money" moment. And Bowie introducing the famine film . . . ,' he continues, 'Live 8 though . . . people never really got their head around the fact that all I needed was for you to be . . . there.'[25]

This lack of 'romantic resonance' in Live 8 was also related to key commercial and political choices that defined the character of the event as contradictory: on the one hand, claiming omnipresence whilst excluding the voices of African artists and, on the other, seeking to stage a massive live protest, yet allowing the powerful to affect the agenda.

Building upon the existing corporatism of Live Aid, Live 8's argument put forward a strong case for engaging only with 'the biggest selling artists in the world, nationally and internationally. For all their great musicianship,' as Geldof argued, 'African acts do not sell many records. People wouldn't watch. Networks wouldn't take the concert.'[26] It is this intense focus on the marketability of the event that eventually set the dominant framework for understanding Live 8 as mega-business, attracting top media players, such as Reuters AOL music.com, Time Warner and CNN, and so acting as the key benefactor not only of the global South but, importantly, also of the then-emerging digital market: 'As a piece of digital broadcasting history,' Biccum says, 'Live 8 helped to put AOL on the broadcasting map . . . winning AOL tens of thousands of new customers for its new service. In addition, Live 8 became a success story for the freedom of choice available for consumption in the free market economy, made possible via new technologies.' (2007: 1121). The exclusion of artists from Africa, on the grounds that the concert's success depended on the brands of western music industry, and the huge benefits that this industry enjoyed from Live 8, seriously undermined enchantment around the cause of 'development for justice'.

At the same time, while Live 8 did offer the magic of live performance, the Edinburgh concert having been concluded 'with magnificent incongruity, by James Brown himself, driving the crowd insane with "I Got You (I Feel Good)"' (Traub 2005),[27] there is evidence that the authenticity of liveness was further undermined by the political agenda imposed by G8 leaders: 'We hear', Monbiot claimed in the *Guardian,* 'that Bob Geldof has told artists not to criticize George Bush from the stage. I would have thought that that quite limits their scope.'[28] Echoing a broader scepticism about the tight embrace between humanitarianism and the political establishment, which was also expressed by a number of coalition NGOs, this is the argument of co-option, where Live 8 is not seen as a challenge to dominant policies that have led to current global divisions but as a legitimization of these policies that can bring no real change.

In response to Bono's voluntarist call to Live 8 crowds to 'gang up on them [G8 leaders]', as 'they are nervous and want to do the right thing,'[29] critics, therefore, juxtapose the argument that powerful states would never concede to changes in international trade which would ultimately impact upon their own well-being. Referring to this double-bind as a 'structural deficit' of the campaign, Nash convincingly argues that, 'it was naïve to expect existing international institutions to use the power they have to give away some of those advantages to poor, weak states,' arguing that such a benign expectation 'shows a deficient understanding of the social relations between rich and poor' (2008: 177).

Disenchanted enchantment captures, in summary, the collective consciousness of an audience that may still be attracted by the solidarity calls of the rock industry, yet is fully aware of the systemic limitations that dictate the terms of this solidarity. Characterized by a political pragmatism, which not only abandoned the romanticism of Live Aid whilst intensifying its commercialism, but further tightened the link between show business and the global elites, Live 8 is an exemplary illustration of contemporary media events that, as Dayan puts it, can 'still mobilize huge audiences but they have lost a large part of their enchantment. Bureaucratically managed, they are an exploited resource within a political economy of collective attention. Their magic is dissipating. They have become strategic venues' (2008: 396).

The performativity of Live 8

Unlike Live Aid's witnessing moment, the Korem imagery, Live 8 refrained from screening visuals of human vulnerability. It is this absence of figures of suffering, not only on the concert stage but also in the broader iconography of the Make Poverty History and the ONE appeals, that defines Live 8's performances of solidarity in terms of a strategic, rather than universal, morality.

The absence of suffering

Even though verbal references to suffering in Africa were present, as in Bono's opening line, '3,000 Africans, mostly children, die every day of a mosquito bite. We can fix that . . . 9,000, people dying every day of a preventable, treatable disease like AIDS . . . We can help them,' Live 8 contained no visualization of human vulnerability. Its only imagery of suffering was the replay of the BBC Korem footage, with the original 'Drive' soundtrack, ending with the still image of an unconscious girl in her father's arms. Rather than an act of witnessing, in the manner of Live Aid, however, this imagery was now contextualized as an act of memory: 'See this little girl,' said Geldof, 'she had 20 minutes to live but because we did that, last week she did her agricultural degree . . . I wanted to show you when we started this long, long walk to justice I want to show you just in case you forgot why we did this film.'[30]

A high emotional point of the London concert, the stage appearance of the Korem survivor, Birhan Woldu, worked as a 'liminal' moment through which the ritual of Live 8 most forcefully reaffirmed itself as a sustained community of benefactors – merging, extraordinarily, the reality of suffering with its vision of making a difference to produce what Dayan and Katz call 'a "subjunctive" mode of culture' (1992: 141). Whereas privileging a beautiful, healthy and smiling survivor over images of abject suffering resonated both with the aesthetic logic of the concert, in that it amplified enchantment (Birhan Woldu remained onstage, dancing to Madonna's 'Like a Prayer'), and with its social logic, in that it spoke to the 'making a real difference' ethos of Live 8, this absence of suffering should also be situated within the representational logic of contemporary humanitarianism which, as we saw in chapter 3, tends to eliminate the spectacle of suffering from public visibility.

Evident in the communicative practices of the Make Poverty History and ONE campaigns, this shift is characterized first, by the replacement of the iconography of 'bare life' with the clean and glamorous imagery of Hollywood celebrity (Nash 2008), and second, by giving voice to a survivor who can be assimilated in 'our' community as one of 'us' (Woldu was introduced as a recent graduate of a nursing college who was about to start her first job). Both communicative choices reflexively respond to critiques of Live Aid as a practice of empire, either by eliding the vulnerable other (in the ONE campaign) or by humanizing her presence (in the concert itself). Yet, at the same time, they also point to a crucial shift in the performativity of humanitarianism away from other- and towards self-oriented representations of vulnerability – a shift to post-humanitarianism that I return to later. For now, let us turn to the aspirational performance of solidarity that this absence of suffering legitimizes in Live 8.

The strategic morality of entrepreneurship

Contrary to Live Aid's focus on saving lives, Live 8 is informed by the imperative to redress inequalities that perpetuate the loss of life in the first place: 'The demands', as Nash put it, 'were for the restructuring of international institutions and socio-economic relations, not for Northerners as individuals to give money directly to those suffering the effects of injustice' (2008: 169). It is to this end that Live 8 worked on a pragmatic rationale of action, which prioritized lobbying with the powerful rather than pressuring from below: 'Sometimes', as Bono put it, 'instead of climbing over the barricades, you've got to walk around them, and sometimes you discover that the real enemy is not what you think it is.'[31] What I call strategic morality, then, refers precisely to this calculated rearticulation of a vocabulary of justice with political and economic power, whereby elites are preferable to 'barricades' and the powerful West becomes an ally rather than an 'enemy' of social change, with a view to maximizing the diplomatic benefits of global politics.

This is not a vocabulary that aspires to be politically efficacious in substantially redressing global inequalities, however – for instance, through shifting the terms of international trade. In fact, as numerous critics have pointed out, little has changed since the Gleneagles Summit. Five years on, a major humanitarian disaster was imminent again in the Ethiopian, Sudanese, Kenyan borderlands because, as Vallely put it, the G8 Summit promises, including the more recent ones made in L'Aquila 2009, had not been delivered: 'Without it [the West's commitment]', he continues, 'the destructive cycle will not be broken which forces hungry pastoralists to sell their means of production – livestock – as part of a short-term survival strategy. If famine is poised to stalk the dry lands of Africa again, it will not be nature that is to blame, but the warlords of Africa and the complacency of the rich West' (Vallely 2011).

Instead of real change, then, Live 8's vocabulary of justice associated political efficacy with the ceremonial communication of justice in slogans like 'Make Poverty History', whilst the political process itself conceded to measures on fair trade only on the basis of certain 'conditionalities': 'the things that poor countries must do in order to qualify for that debt relief, which are as onerous, as burdensome as the debt itself is.'[32]

Despite, then, reflexively moving beyond Live Aid's morality of salvation, the morality of Live 8 not only suffered from a structural deficit, in its failure to grasp the complicity of the West in perpetuating injustice, but also educated its ceremonial publics into a light-touch, entrepreneurial activism of signing online, wearing a wristband or watching an online stream of their favourite band. Termed as the 'media deficit' of Live 8 (Nash 2008: 178), this orientation towards a massive 'feel-good' ritual relied on the strategy of 'flattering the powerful in order to get them to stay the sword, and to be a little bit kinder, and to offer a little more tea and sympathy',[33] at the cost of marginalizing critical debate on the implications of debt cancellation and fair trade on western states themselves. What does, then, the trajectory from Live Aid to Live 8 tell us about the changing dispositions of solidarity available to western publics today?

The authenticity effects of ceremonial humanitarianism

Approaching the rock concert as a genre of ceremonial performativity has thrown into relief yet another key communicative practice by which solidarity is performed in the theatrical space of humanitarianism. Solidarity, I argue, emerges in the performance of the rock concert as an act of authentic commitment to a cause, accomplished through strategies of charisma and enchantment that, in turn, enable publics to witness the suffering of distant others.

In this final section, I explore two crucial transformations of the performativity of this humanitarianism in the past twenty years. Under 'Pragmatic Solidarity', I address the changing relationship between ceremonial events and the organizational milieu of humanitarianism. Expanding on the critique of the spectacle, I argue that this shift rearticulates the relationship between humanitarianism and the market towards an entrepreneurial corporatism – what I have earlier referred to as, 'the new spirit of capitalism' (Boltanski & Chiapello 2005). Under 'The Post-humanitarian Public', I elaborate on a shift in the relationship between ceremonial humanitarianism and Western publics. Expanding on the critique of empire, I argue that this shift transforms the relationship between humanitarianism and politics, by replacing the unsettling encounter with vulnerable others, in Live Aid's Korem imagery, with voices of self-expression – our own or our favourite celebrities'.

Pragmatic solidarity

Two transformations define the solidarity of ceremonial humanitarianism today: the shift from a romanticist corporatism to an *entrepreneurial corporatism*, which intensifies the market links between the music-media industry complex and the humanitarian field; and the shift from a universal discourse of morality, which defines the concert as a humanitarian affair, towards a *strategic discourse of morality*, which defines the concert as part of a professionalized politics of development.

Associated with the aesthetics of charisma, the transformation of solidarity towards entrepreneurial corporatism reflects not only the ways in which the Live 8 concert set in motion a global spectacle with rock mega-brands, as indeed Live Aid had similarly done, but crucially the ways in which, this time uniquely, it embedded this spectacle in a broader corporate agenda. Unlike the simpler concert-related donations structure of Live Aid, Live 8 developed, as Biccum says, a complex, fund-raising mechanism that relied both on the professionalization of the NGO-media relationship and the tighter links between NGOs and their private sponsors (2007). Emerging under conditions of intense global competition in the aid and development market, she continues, the Global Call to Action Against Poverty coalition 'was financed in part by a US$ 3 million grant from the Bill and Melinda Gates Foundation. It received endorsements from Brad Pitt and Bono, as well as Evangelical Christian leaders such as Pat Robertson and Rick Warren' (2007: 1112). This entrepreneurial corporatism can be seen as yet another benign instance of philanthro-capitalism that draws private capital into development investments with benefits of renewed legitimacy, not only for the corporate and the humanitarian fields but also for charismatic celebrities themselves. Yet, there are risks.

Resonating with Marks and Fischer's claim that 'the impact of celebrity activists is felt not in the content of their message, but in the form of their political participation and the public's response to it' (2002: 393), the charismatic leadership of the Live 8 rock stars managed, indeed, to generate public consent for a post-populist model of global governance that marginalizes the voices of civil society, including the heterogeneous NGOs of the MPH coalition, in favour of the dominant will of elite politics: 'MPH', as Payne put it, 'had become unduly influenced by celebrities and had positioned itself too close to Blair and Brown and the like.' At the same time, he quotes the director of the Focus on Global South NGO in arguing that the MPH leadership 'chose not to radicalize [Gleneagles]. "Let's work with the G8", and a rather mellow atmosphere, while other mobilizations have been more confrontational' (2006: 8). The consequence of this pragmatic politics of solidarity, as I showed, is that stark disparities remain, with small and/or poorer countries struggling to make any impact at all with the WTOs infamous "green rooms" whilst 'all the major players – G8 and G20 alike – press their core national interests in private' (Payne 2006: 21).

If entrepreneurial corporatism points to the risks of the symbiosis of humanitarianism with capital, the shift from universal to strategic morality points to a new symbiotic relationship of humanitarianism with politics (Payne 2006). It is, here, that the replacement of the urgency to save lives with the 'mellow' consent of Live 8 signals the emergence of a pragmatic solidarity – a solidarity that understands development as good governance, offering conditional debt relief, yet leaving intact the dominant financial regime that regulates the relationship between the West and the global South (Fine 2009; Schuurman 2009). The G8 version of development has, in fact, been accused of imposing a neoliberal hegemony in the field of humanitarianism, whereby free market rules now define the politics of development without addressing structural transformations and the creation of a new international economic order: 'Gleneagles', as Payne puts it,

> presented the best public face that could be put on the raw power of the G8 countries, but it could not conceal some harsher continuing realities: that countries in need of aid are still, in essence, supplicants at the top table, that the HIPCS remain closely supervised by the IFM and the World Bank, and that the policies of rich countries are rarely driven for long by notions of generosity. (2006: 18)

Strategic morality, in this sense, effectively blocks broader deliberation about the meaning of solidarity not just as anti-poverty policy-making but also as a critique of capitalism – a deliberation that would have involved a challenge to, rather than convergence with, the Gleneagles agenda. The techno-spectacle of Live 8 contributed to this moral deficit in that, by drawing on the compelling authenticity of enchantment as a unique moment of collective commitment, it removed development questions from the 'sphere of legitimate controversy', where critical debate is routinely practised, and placed it within an exceptional 'sphere of consensus' that precluded as illegitimate any views that challenged its common sense orthodoxy (Dayan 2009: 29). Yet, even if Live 8's pragmatic solidarity could, at best, somewhat improve but never change the social inequalities of human vulnerability, the concert's primary purpose was nonetheless to galvanize a collective consciousness of cosmopolitanism among its vast audiences – to create, as Nash put it, 'new relationships between individuals and groups' (2008: 168). How far did it manage to achieve this?

The post-humanitarian public

Whilst Live Aid moved beyond a communitarian consciousness through the performance of sublimated suffering, Live 8 relied on a different communicative practice that maximized the use of new technologies yet excluded the suffering other from public visibility. It is this dual practice, I argue, echoing my analysis of appeals, that construes Live 8 publics as post-humanitarian publics – publics whose orientation towards vulnerable others is articulated through a technologized economy of pleasure oriented towards the self.

The first key feature of this performativity is the mediation of solidarity through a network of market technologies as diverse as digital screens, online petitions, plastic wristbands and A-list celebrity appeals. Such technological proliferation, as we know, facilitates humanitarianism's claim to authenticity, that is, its quest for a genuinely committed West that can make a real difference to the lives of vulnerable others. The use of technologies has, indeed, intensified public commitment, as shown both in the massive engagement with the live streaming of the concerts (an estimated total of three billion viewers), and in participation in the online petition (a total of twenty-six million signatures).

The massive reach of e-mobilization and ethical consumption granted, what such practices simultaneously point to is, what I have earlier theorized as, the 'technologization' of solidarity – the enactment of solidarity through various technologies of connectivity, such as e-petitions or the 'Make Poverty History' wristbands, that combine the act of doing good to others with the instant gratification of feeling good for oneself. Rather than criticizing such practices for simply commodifying solidarity, as for instance McGuigan's association of such practices with 'cool' capitalism does (in my analysis of appeals in chapter 3), technologization points instead to the ambivalence of ceremonial humanitarianism, insofar as it manages to thin out the moral content of solidarity by gathering massive momentum, in its name: 'Wearing wristbands', as a citizen reflecting on Live 8 succinctly puts it, 'is a way for people to express support for a cause without actually doing anything. The ubiquitous wearing of meaningless wristbands does more than diminish a sense of genuine urgency about the real issues.'[34] The ambivalence of ceremonialism, in this sense, has perhaps less to do with technologization per se and more to do with the broader logic of celebrity culture, which the solidarity of instant gratification is embedded within – a logic of charisma and enchantment that lies at the heart of rock concerts.

A crucial feature of this solidarity, then, and this brings me to the second key transformation in Live 8's performativity, is the visual priority of celebrity over the vulnerable other. Evident of a new reflexivity as this choice may be, the marginalization of vulnerability in Live 8 eliminates the space within which a moral encounter between us and the distant sufferer may become possible – it eliminates, in other words, the theatrical stage within which human suffering may emerge as a sovereign reality that demands our emotion, reflection and action. In a manner similar to contemporary appeals and celebrities, Live 8 may be taking place on a 'stage', yet ultimately provides us with a 'mirror' through which our uneasy confrontation with human vulnerability is replaced by a more pleasurable engagement with people like 'us'. Our encounter with the charismatic figures of Bono and Geldof becomes, in this sense, a pedagogic encounter with aspirational versions of ourselves, insofar as, in the age of confessional celebrity, these mega-brands are both heroic figures to be admired from afar and domesticated in our lives as people like 'us', producing meaning about who we are and how we relate to the world beyond us (Thompson 1995; Marshall 1997).

At the same time, in the absence of visuals of suffering, our only encounter with human vulnerability in Live 8 is with the Korem survivor, Birhan Woldu. Even though Woldu's presence hints at this theatrical space, we need to remember that her presence signifies suffering as a triumphant memory, as evil that has already been overcome, rather than raising the question of justice as a contemporary requirement; in so doing, the Live 8 survivor contributes to cultivating the euphoria of achievement rather than raising unsettling questions about contemporary development and justice (see Orgad 2009 for the representation of survivors).

The post-humanitarian public of ceremonial humanitarianism runs, therefore, the risk of becoming a narcissistic public, insofar as it fails to recognize the humanity of vulnerable others and relies instead on a combination of self-recognition, through our engagement with charismatic rock stars, and technological 'cool', through the immediate gratification of online petitions, wristbands and concert tickets. Even though the vocabulary of justice proliferates in the post-humanitarian disposition, it is ultimately the quest for authenticity, or enchantment, and celebrity's strategic morality that defines the content of solidarity. As a consequence, ceremonial humanitarianism today moralizes the West through the massive reach of its thin content, which may empower publics as communities of 'cool' yet fail to engage them with the otherness of human vulnerability and to connect them with visions of social change.

Conclusion: towards a strategic morality of solidarity

Ceremonial humanitarianism is the most powerful genre of the humanitarian imaginary in that it has the unique capacity to integrate billions of people into its affective economy of solidarity. Using the two landmark rock concerts of Live Aid and Live 8 as case studies, I have examined how their ceremonial aesthetics, in line with the media script of the 'conquest', produced effects of charisma and enchantment, so as to engage the West with performances of solidarity.

Two historical transformations of the humanitarian imaginary characterize the trajectory of these rock concerts: the shift from moral universalism to strategic morality and the shift from compassionate to post-humanitarian publics. The shift towards strategic morality suggests that common humanity is now giving way to a morality of political efficiency, which situates the authenticity of humanitarianism within a framework of a post-populist 'realpolitik', whilst the shift towards post-humanitarian publics suggests that solidarity becomes increasingly technologized, that is, it relies on tokens of 'cool', such as wristbands, digital screens or concert tickets, and simultaneously renders the witnessing of human vulnerability irrelevant to solidarity.

These two transformations point, in turn, to a humanitarian imaginary that replaces theatricality, the social space of spectatorship where questions of politics and otherness appear as possibilities for collective reflection and action, with narcissistic pleasure, a return to the western self as both the subject and object of collective enchantment. This is an imaginary where publicness and fandom merge into a radically ambivalent agency, one that is both empowering, in that its sheer numbers make a loud statement of solidarity, and subduing, insofar as this activism, embedded as it is in the disenchanted enchantment of contemporary spectatorship, reflects less a body politic and more a pleasure-seeking yet knowing fandom – a public that, to paraphrase Silverstone, shares its private passion without public commitment.

In uncritically accepting the structures of capitalism as a precondition for its activism, post-humanitarianism thus runs the political risk of celebrating and relegitimizing these structures. And in failing to implicate vulnerable others in the cosmopolitan vision of the West, it also runs the moral risk of forgetting that solidarity is about acting on distant others, not because they are like 'us' but precisely because they defy our own conception of humanity.

6 News

Introduction: the moral appeal of news

The last genre of the humanitarian imaginary that I explore, the news, differs from the previous ones in that it does not usually involve direct calls to solidarity and, in this sense, it occupies a rather peripheral position to the communicative practices of the aid and development field. Insofar as the news provides one of the most important stages for human vulnerability to appear in the West, however, often also resorting to emergency appeals for action, the genre fully participates in the humanitarian imaginary – the dispersed communicative structure that mundanely habituates the West into dispositions of solidarity with distant others.

As a stage for the presentation of distant suffering, then, the news inevitably struggles with the immanent aesthetic and moral paradoxes of the imaginary, even though these paradoxes tend to be formulated through distinct questions and to find resolution in a distinct set of discursive choices that are particular to journalism. The key question here revolves around the tension between an ethics of the profession and an ethics of human life: should the journalist stop and help the wounded or continue reporting on their misfortune?[1]

Often described as irreconcilable, these competing moral positions ultimately find resolution in the act of journalistic witnessing: 'I was appalled at what I was doing . . .', confesses Pulitzer prizewinning photographer Kevin Carter on shooting the first public execution in South Africa captured on camera. 'But then people started talking about those pictures . . . maybe my actions hadn't been at all bad. Being a witness to something this horrible wasn't necessarily such a bad thing to do' (quoted in Evans 2004: 41). It is precisely this capacity of the news to bring distant suffering close to home and invite us to respond to it, I argue in this chapter, which renders journalism one of the most crucial moralizing forces in the West (Muhlmann 2008).

Even though witnessing indeed constitutes a strong moral justification for journalism, the nature of witnessing itself is today dramatically transformed through the use of new technologies and the changing professional cultures of reporting (Allan and Zelizer 2002; Deuze 2004, 2006). For some, new media have facilitated connectivity with and action on distant suffering, yet for others they fragment global connectivity, creating multiple but insulated communities of 'our own'. As a consequence, witnessing loses its moral force – the force of presenting human misfortune as a cause for solidarity. As Beckett and Mansell put it, 'Emerging forms of journalism may . . . enable(s) stories about distant others to be told and better understood.' However, they note, 'although convergent media platforms create opportunities for new exchanges, there are reasons to question whether the potential will be met' (2008: 92).

In the spirit of this sceptical optimism, it is the changing nature of journalistic witnessing as a space of humanitarian performance and its implications for the moralization of western publics that I explore in this chapter. Taking my starting point in a conception of journalism as a 'ritual' of communication (Carey 1989), I explore how witnessing changes as it moves from television to post-television genres, bringing about novel journalistic narratives and new performances of solidarity with vulnerable others.

To this end, I draw on major pieces of disaster (earthquake) reporting in the BBC from the past 35 years, focusing on *television news* (the earthquakes of Tangshan, 1976, Mexico, 1985 and Turkey, 1999) and on *post-television news*, which have recently bifurcated into *convergent news* (the earthquakes of Kashmir, 2005 and Haiti, 2010) and in *live blogging* (Haiti, 2010). My comparative analysis of the narrative performativity of these pieces of news shows that there are significant discontinuities in the modes of witnessing that the genre makes available to its publics across time. Whereas all classes of news remain recognizable as 'accounts and explanations of events presented by news organizations' (Tuchman 1973: 112), the generic shift from television to post-television journalism, enabled by the intense technologization of our culture, also marks a narrative shift *from professional to ordinary testimony* and, therefore, from *hybrid narratives*, mixing professional and non-professional testimony, to *hypertextual ones*, driven by input from 'ordinary' witnesses.

Post-television genres pose, therefore, a challenge as to how we are to understand their narrative properties and their impact on the performances of solidarity in the West. As they are becoming increasingly central to our news consumption patterns, particularly but not exclusively amongst the young (Deuze 2001), it is important to turn analytical attention to their emerging properties, treating their transformations as reflections of broader aesthetic and moral transformations in the humanitarian imaginary.

The theatricality of journalism

> 'Good journalism in the field is about bearing witness to events that others may wish to hide or ignore; or which are simply too far out of sight for most people to care about.'
>
> BBC College of Journalism website[2]

Witnessing and journalism

In describing good journalism as a form of 'bearing witness', the BBC draws attention to a crucial function of the news not only as reporting on events but as engaging people's potential to care. In further specifying witnessing as an act of disclosure, something others may 'hide' or something that is 'too far out of sight', the BBC simultaneously situates journalism within a theatrical conception of publicity as a 'space of appearance' (more in chapter 7).

Distinct, though not completely separate, from deliberative conceptions of publicity that emphasize the role of journalism in informing audiences or shaping public opinion, this theatrical conception of publicity draws attention to the arrangement of separation between those who act on the scene of suffering and those who watch at a distance; in so doing, it throws into relief the reliance of journalism on performance, on the images and stories of suffering that situate events within symbolic regimes of emotion and action so as to make a specific demand on their publics: to take a stance or do something. It is by raising this imperative to act on the theatrical space of journalism that the news participates in the humanitarian imaginary of the West as a particular 'ritual of communication' – one that consists of 'narratives of dramatic action in which the reader joins a world of contending forces as an observer of the play' (Carey 1989: 21) – notice Carey's use of a 'theatrical' metaphor for the news as an arrangement of separation between 'dramatic action' and its 'observers'.

Rather than free-floating story-telling, however, these narratives are strictly controlled by institutional economies of regulation that subject the genre to the test of truth. This means that 'dramatic action' on suffering should incorporate the moral claim to a response but it should also be presented as objective information that allows spectators to judge the suffering as worthy of our response. Reflected in the concept of witnessing itself, this dual requirement refers both to the act of seeing as a proof of the facts on suffering (the objective dimension of witnessing) and to seeing as an emotive testimony to the 'unspeakable' horror of suffering (the reflexive dimension of witnessing; Oliver 2001).

Journalism as empire

It is the coexistence of these requirements, the objective and the reflexive, variously articulated as they are in the communicative practice of the news, that construes distant suffering in diverse performances of dramatic action. Whereas objectivity brings into focus the management of authenticity in the act of witnessing, reflexivity draws attention to the regimes of emotion and action that witnessing seeks to evoke, either in the form of denunciation against the injustice of suffering, in the presence of a persecutor, or in the form of care and philanthropic sentiment, in the presence of a benefactor (Boltanski 1999).

In the case of natural disasters, like earthquakes, news stories focus on the presence of benefactors, that is, INGOs and aid volunteers, that appear to act on the spot in order to comfort acute needs in the aftermath of a disaster. As a consequence, INGOs, such as the Red Cross, act both as authenticating and as reflexive voices in such news stories, showing the extent to which the relationship between journalism and humanitarian agencies has always been one of interdependent symbiosis (Benthall 1993; G. Cooper 2007). This is because, in inhabiting the zone of suffering in moments of crisis, humanitarian actors share with journalists the unique responsibility to witness the facts and publicize them in the West. This symbiosis, however, can be conflictual as the power to report ultimately rests with the journalist, often obliging NGOs to compromise or 'package' their message in particular ways so as to have a chance of publicity; rather than straightforward, the relationship between the two is troubled with tensions (Cottle 2009: 146–53).

Such tensions in the power relationship between these key agents of witnessing reflect a more fundamental issue with the mediation of human suffering. This is the power of western journalism to classify suffering into hierarchies of place and human life, privileging some disasters as worthy of western emotion and action but leaving others outside the space of appearance (Galtung and Ruge 1965) – a power that I have earlier theorized in terms of the critique of empire. Whereas some instances of suffering might never be witnessed as events worth reporting, what Joye (2010) calls 'neglected news', those that do get reported are subject to distinct 'pathologies' of witnessing: stories of suffering that focus on witnessing exclusively as a fact, for example, diminish the emotive capacity of the news, 'annihilating' the human quality of the sufferer, whilst stories that focus on witnessing as horror, 'appropriating' the sufferer as someone who shares our own humanity, may lean towards a commodified sentimentalism that reduces witnessing to voyeurism (Silverstone 2007).

What makes journalistic witnessing both an important dimension of the humanitarian imaginary and an object of harsh criticism, then, is not simply its capacity to bring distant suffering into the space of appearance per se, but the performative power of its rituals to constitute the West as a public, as a collectivity with a will to act, at the very moment that they claim to address it. 'Pathologies' of witnessing, in this sense, far from instances of individual malpractice, are systemic forms of bias, which tend to reinforce a sense of belonging to 'our' own local world – constituting 'communitarian' rather than 'cosmopolitan' publics (Chouliaraki 2006, 2008a,b).

New media, new journalism?

It is, at least partly, against this critique of television as empire that the entry of new media into journalism has been hailed as a radical move. Relevant literature has focused, in particular, on the 'decentring' potential of citizen journalism, that is, its potential to bypass news gatekeepers and challenge the dominant flows of western broadcasting (Reese 2009).

Today, however, this radical potential is also claimed by traditional broadcasters, such as the BBC, which have been quick to appropriate the new media under their own moral vision. Talking of a 'day of broadcasting from Afghanistan', Richard Sambrook, Director of the BBC's Global News division, illustrates the use of new media as instruments of cosmopolitanization by recounting how 'one of our reporters took a laptop and satellite phone into the village of Asad Khyl', making it possible for BBC website users to interact with Afghan villagers: 'these conversational links', he concludes, 'created a unique cultural connection' (Sambrook 2005).[3] Yet, even if the use of convergent technologies stretches the reach of global broadcasting in new ways, it is still the 'I' of the journalist that mediates their 'unique cultural connection'.

What constitutes a break from this monopoly of story-telling is the incorporation of citizen input into mainstream news, which increasingly comes to define the genre of news as a collaborative product. For networks such as the BBC, the lesson drawn from major news on human suffering, such as the 2004 tsunami or the 2005 London attacks, is that 'when major events occur, the public can offer us as much new information as we are able to broadcast to them. From now on, news coverage is a partnership' (2009).[4]

Distinguishing the online journalism of blogging and tweeting from the institutional journalism that appropriates voices of bloggers and tweeters into its news structure, Deuze refers to the latter as 'multi-media' or 'convergent' journalism: the online presentation of a 'news story package' that incorporates more than one media formats, including 'the spoken and written word, music, moving and still image, graphic animations, including interactive and hypertextual elements' (2004: 140). Driven by techno-commercial as well as professional interests, the rise of this journalism is nonetheless primarily invested by an ethico-political discourse, that of 'giving voice' to the public (Beckett 2008). Whereas the opening up of the new 'stage' of journalism has been welcome by humanitarian actors, as they can now perform their emergency pleas to the West without depending on journalists on the ground, there are concerns that this stage is becoming not only richer but also riskier, not only more 'democratic' but also more 'demotic', to use Turner's terms (2010).

This risk is closely connected to the theatrical paradox of authenticity, in that the inclusion of new voices raises anew the question of truth – if it is humanitarian workers or ordinary people who now tell the story of vulnerable others, how can we know that their story is real? This paradox stems from transformations in the control mechanism of news production from a journalism of 'indexing', which anchors the news to its official sources, to an event-driven journalism, which anchors the news in any source that happens to offer testimony and is, therefore, hard to contain through editorial control (Bennett, Lawrence and Livingston 2007). It is this relaxation of control over content that presents a major challenge for news networks, in that it raises the key question of how emerging news genres may be subject to the 'test of truth', that is to say, how they should appear both as objective information that respects the values of news organizations and as reflexive accounts that may move publics into action (Sambrook 2005).

To come full circle from this chapter's introduction, it is the question of how emerging practices of witnessing performed in the news can guarantee the authenticity of suffering and, thereby, act as a moralizing force in the humanitarian imaginary that concerns me in this chapter. After providing an overview of the historical controversy around the truth-claims of journalism ('The Controversy around Journalistic Witnessing'), I propose an analytical focus on the narrative aesthetics of the news genre and offer a comparative reading of news on major earthquakes, in the past 35 years (in The Analysis of Narrative Aesthetics' and in 'News Narratives: a Typology of Witnessing', respectively). If the analysis of news aesthetics is important in a study of witnessing, I argue, this is because the shift towards convergent narratives of 'dramatic action' do not only alter the claims to authenticity that the news makes but also have profound implications for the performances of solidarity available today in these news, that is 'for the ways we understand and visualize each other and the world around us' (Manovich 2001: 13–14; see 'The Authenticity Effects of News').

The controversy around television witnessing

The historical controversy of the authenticity of news revolves around three key performative practices of witnessing, what I below examine as 'detached', 'omnipresent' and 'committed' witnessing. In discussing distinct truth-claims, I also present the varying proposals of moral agency towards distant suffering each makes available in the humanitarian imaginary.

Witnessing in television news

My starting point in this overview is the age-old scepticism towards technology as a guarantee of the authenticity of suffering, characteristic of the critique of the spectacle. According to this critique, let us recall, the truth-claim of the news depends on the camera as a transparent medium that conveys facts beyond manipulation, but this truth is simultaneously undermined by a suspicion that the camera manipulates the very spectacle it comes to depict (McQuire 1998; Zelizer 2005). Since the early days of the profession, therefore, the voice of the journalist functioned as a guarantee for the truth-claims of the camera, rendering the journalist a key theatrical figure of the humanitarian imaginary – a figure who, by using the authority of personal testimony, performs 'the truth' by transforming a precarious 'seen' into the believable 'said' (Peters 2009: 26).

Performances of witnessing

Far from unproblematic, however, this 'I' that speaks has itself raised scepticism, posing the question of whether journalistic voice can, at all, act as a guarantee of the authenticity of suffering (Frosh and Pinchevski 2009). It is in response to this scepticism that television journalism has developed three distinct performances of witnessing, each of which situates the 'I' of the journalist into a different news narrative and, in so doing, seeks to construe a different collective 'we' of solidarity with vulnerable others. These three performances are *detached*, *omnipresent* and *committed witnessing*.

Detached witnessing replaces the 'I' of the journalist with a disembodied gaze that presents facts. Responding to critics of war propaganda that, following World War I, undermined faith in the value of news, what Lippman called 'the problem of modern news', the detached position uses third-person testimony as a guarantee of truth beyond points of view and, hence, as a device capable of unifying the public without the evocation of emotion. This third person authority informs the instantly recognizable frame of broadcast 'reporting', which produces authenticity by appealing to a neutral conception of communication as 'information conveyance and the surveillance of current events' without evaluative content (Cottle and Rai 2006: 171); see below for the BBC report on the Tangshan earthquake: 'Hundreds of thousands of people are feared dead following an 8.3 magnitude earthquake in China.'

Omnipresent witnessing acknowledges the moral value of the 'I' that authors the news and, therefore, takes its starting point in the subjective experience of the journalist whilst, however, retaining a conception of truth grounded on the factual world. It, therefore, seeks to render suffering a cause for emotion and action through a faithful reconstruction of the realm of facts and views that make up a story (Mulhmann 2008). It is in the narratives of investigative journalism that the omnipresent witness figures prominently (Cottle and Rai 2006) – a notable example being Michael Buerk's historical piece on the Ethiopian famine on the BBC in 1984. A key feature of such narratives is their mix of factual with fictional genres, which addresses news publics not as already unified behind a shared truth but as impartial spectators who reflexively engage with the moral plea of suffering; consider, for example, Buerk's opening line in the Ethiopian famine report: 'Dawn. And as the sun breaks through the piercing chill of night on the plain outside Korem, it lights up a biblical famine; now in the twentieth century.'

Committed witnessing is similarly grounded in the realm of facts yet primarily emphasizes the ethical duty of the journalist as an 'I' that not only describes but also judges – not simply reports but also takes sides. 'Committed journalism', says European Press Editor of Human Rights Watch Jean-Paul Marthoz, 'does not mean biased reporting or tampering with the facts. It does mean a realization that truth can only be found by shining a much brighter light on issues than the one commonly used by overly cautious diplomats or governments.'[5] Arising in the context of war and conflict reporting, this form of witnessing has led to the project of a 'journalism of attachment' (Bell 1998: 7) and is associated with the relatively rare news frame of campaigning – a frame that 'seeks to galvanize sympathies and support for its intervention' (Cottle and Rai 2006: 175). Approaching suffering as a cause for passionate engagement rather than neutral reporting, committed witnessing seeks to unify news publics not by the force of objective fact but by the truth of conviction (Tester 2001).

The scepticism towards objectivity

At the heart of all three performances of witnessing lies a conception of news authenticity as objectivity, a powerful yet fragile truth-claim that situates the moral force of witnessing on 'the intrinsic value of facts . . . that must be made available to members of the public so as to facilitate their efforts to engage with the pressing questions of the day' (Allan 2009: 61). Instead of equating objectivity with the rational empiricism of the detached witness only, the term refers to a more flexible realm of truth-claims that grounds news stories on the world of fact, but also relies on the voice of the journalist to mobilize the formation of an active 'we' (Muhlmann 2008).

The moral power of witnessing, in its three performances, however, is simultaneously challenged by the critique of journalism as empire. The first critique, *pace* Sambrook's celebration of 'global connectivity', castigates the role of corporate media for placing disaster news within a hierarchical matrix that ranks the newsworthiness of suffering along the lines of western priorities – a development intensified by the corporate 'rationalization' (cf. reduction) of the services of foreign reporting in news networks (Utley 1997; Hafez 2007; Harding 2009). Hierarchies of reporting, critics argue, point to the inadequacy of detached witnessing as a legitimate truth-claim of television news, insofar as 'detachment' is already embedded in a journalistic culture that selectively enables proposals for engagement with certain distant sufferers whilst withholding it for others: 'the blindness', as Campbell calls it, 'produced by a combination of the social economy of taste and the media system of self-censorship constitutes a considerable injustice with regard to our collective understanding of the fate of the other' (2004: 71).

In the second critique, the intense marketization of news reporting has had a detrimental impact on the visibility of INGOs as messengers of global altruism (Cottle 2009). Whereas, as the Michael Buerk example demonstrates, the visibility of such messages in the news is 'the only decisive factor' in endorsing a disaster as worthy of a response and, therefore, in the fate of its victims (Benthall 1993: 12), the increasingly aggressive market competition for live television means that such visibility is often absent. Rather than reporting on humanitarian crises in the spirit of omnipresent witnessing, the marketization of the media favours instead a commercial, sound-bite approach to suffering that turns the field of NGOs into 'a Darwinian marketplace where legions of desperate groups vie for scarce attention, sympathy and money' (Bob 2002: 37; also Cottle and Nolan 2007).

Finally, critics say, there is a fine line between committed witnessing and propaganda, as the former can easily mutate into the latter. A case in point is the 'embedded journalism' of the 2003 Iraq war, where the moral duty of conviction gave way to the infotainment format of 'journalists-following-the-troops' – format that privileges accounts of military achievement at the expense of explanatory context and critical analysis (Lewis 2004).

In summary, despite the commitment of television journalism to objectivity, all performances of witnessing, from detached to committed, are ultimately vulnerable to the effects of the market, turning distant suffering into sensational spectacle, 'an exercise in Pavlovian compassion' as we are all 'freshly torn by the day's allotment of collapsing buildings, fires, flood and terror' (Peters 2005: 227).

Witnessing in post-television news

Post-television journalism promises to overcome the critiques of empire and the spectacle so as to reclaim the news as a force of moralization in the humanitarian imaginary. It does so by replacing the journalist with the citizen as a guarantee of the authenticity of witnessing. Amateur videos on the tsunami (Gillmor 2004), the London bombings (Allan 2007) or the Burma protests (G. Cooper 2007) celebrate precisely this new promise to deliver news that is made by 'a citizen with a sense of loyalty to other citizens' (Harcup 2002: 103). Even though the nature of witnessing in post-television journalism has not yet been thoroughly studied, there is an ongoing debate over the centrality of the ordinary voice in post-television narrative (Pavlik 2001; Matheson 2004; Deuze 2004, 2006).

'Ordinary' witnessing

As opposed to the witnessing of the journalist, which prioritizes the 'intrinsic value of facts', the witnessing of the citizen is grounded on first-hand testimony and personal opinion. It is what we may call 'ordinary' witnessing – a performance that signifies a break with the monopoly of professional witnessing and the dangers of propaganda or marketization that come with it, in favour of a valorization of the 'person on the street' as the most appropriate voice to tell the story of suffering; recall, for instance, Sambrook's quote that 'when major events occur, the public can offer us as much new information as we are able to broadcast to them.'

The valorization of ordinary witnessing introduces into the news a different claim to authenticity that relativizes the empiricism of facts by placing it side by side with the empiricism of emotion. Rather than implying that a journalism of facts has now receded, the primacy of emotion suggests that the hierarchical boundary between professional and citizen notions of fact is blurred: it is not the verification and analysis of sources but the immediacy of experience that counts as news (Matheson 2004; Turner 2010).

A clear manifestation of the moralizing impact of ordinary witnessing on post-television journalism is found in clandestine user-generated content, as in the Burma protests (2007) and the Iran riots (2009) that managed to instantly disseminate images and stories of local violence across the globe, not only setting the western news agenda but also mobilizing a global activism of solidarity. Ordinary witnessing, in this sense, democratizes the space of appearance by breaking the monopoly of television news and enhancing the communicative repertoire of the humanitarian imaginary: 'as new actors enter the formerly privileged information-sharing sphere dominated by the mainstream media and aid agencies,' G. Cooper says, 'there are increased possibilities of more diverse stories being told, and more diverse voices being heard' (2007: 16; see also Chouliaraki 2008b).

Echoing the performance of committed witnessing, or journalism with a stance, the ordinary witness of convergence journalism nevertheless departs from it, insofar as its authority of moral commitment is not 'galvanized' by the scrutiny of facts but is authenticated solely by the force of conviction (Atton 2002: 122). By this token, even though the witnessing of television seeks to constitute its publics by using (various versions of) the 'I' 'to speak in the name' of a unified 'we', the witnessing of post-television journalism constitutes its publics by claiming to be precisely that 'we': ordinary witnessing is about people who 'are being represented by themselves' (Atton 2002: 122).

The scepticism towards testimony

Despite this move towards subjective testimony, post-television journalism still remains caught up in the controversy around authenticity. Far from celebrating the democratization of voice, the sceptical argument on convergent journalism associates subjectivism with the popularity of new media as vehicles of self-expression and their use as tools for the relegitimization of mainstream journalism in the face of a declining consumption in broadcast news (Deuze 2001; Beckett 2008).

Instead of reflecting a plurality of information and opinion, as it promises to do, critics argue, convergent journalism demonstrates a remarkable homogenization of content as similar news texts become recontextualized in different multi-media formats (Scott 2005; Manovich 2001). Even the authenticity of user-generated content that has been hailed as enabling global solidarity has ultimately shown, critics continue, both its inability to substitute professional news (Turner 2010) and the quality deficit that a retreating foreign correspondence service leaves behind (Halavais 2002). At the same time, as user-generated content is co-opted in major corporations for market purposes, convergent journalism becomes embedded in an all-pervasive entertainment logic that prioritizes sensationalism over in-depth analysis and turns the news into commodities: 'convergence in journalism', as Scott puts it, is not about progress in the technological dissemination of information but about 'a new strategy in the economic management of information production and distribution', for which the '*raison d'être* is profit' (2005: 101).

Post-television journalism, in summary, replaces the public value of objectivity, which reflects the possibility of a unified 'we' beyond points of view, with the market value of emotive self-expression, which prioritizes the dominance of 'the private, the ordinary, the everyday' (Turner 2010: 22). Even though, as I argued in chapter 1, new forms of technologized solidarities may emerge out of this trend, the 'we' of such solidarities, critics have it, tend to constitute insulated 'discourse publics' that orient themselves towards their own communitarian concerns rather than developing cosmopolitan sensibilities towards distant others.

The analysis of narrative aesthetics

The discussion on journalistic witnessing throws into relief the instability of the notion of truth in the news – an instability originating in the theatrical paradox of authenticity, between facts as they are and the constant suspicion of the spectacle or the empire. Suspended between objectivism and subjectivism, this theoretical discussion may question the performance of witnessing but stops short of problematizing authenticity itself as a 'given' property of witnessing – be this the authenticity of a professional or an ordinary 'I'. In presupposing that authenticity 'belongs' either to the realm of objectivity or of subjective testimony, what this discussion fails to account for is the narrative process by which authenticity is performed as a particular truth-claim in the course of the news story itself. In so doing, the theoretical discussion on news journalism further fails to critically analyse *how* the shift from television to post-television news comes to perform novel claims to authenticity and how these claims might impact on the formation of news publics. In order to engage with such critical analysis, let me now turn to a discussion of the performativity of the news as narrative.

Witnessing as narrative

The starting point for a narrative approach to witnessing lies in the performative conception of journalism as a ritual of 'dramatic action' that involves those who act at the scene of suffering and those who watch from a distance. Despite being part of the broader theatrical structure of the imaginary, journalism seeks to authenticate its truths not through personification or charisma, as previous genres did, but through its own distinct communicative practice of suffering as a cause. This is the practice of witnessing that, as I mentioned, combines disinterested viewing with an emotive response: 'a local suffering', Boltanski says, 'must be conveyed without deformation in such a way that it is there for anyone to examine it . . . and find themselves sufficiently affected by it to become committed and take it up as their cause' (1999: 31).

What this recognition of the theatrical presentation of the news suggests is that solidarity is not so much a spontaneous response to the 'facts' of suffering but arises instead in the course of the news as a narrative, that is, as a performance that both appeals to objectivity, conveying facts 'without deformation', and makes proposals of emotion, rendering publics 'sufficiently affected', that may lead to action. This dual requirement does not necessarily suggest that journalists always engage in news reporting by consciously working to bring together these two dimensions of the news. It suggests, rather, that the imperative to witness suffering as a 'cause for action' has historically informed the public presentation of suffering, so that changes in the articulation of these two narrative requirements can be seen as sensitive barometers for concomitant changes in the performances of witnessing in the news.

Authenticity, it follows, cannot be fixed once and for all as a single, ahistorical truth-claim of the news narrative, be this objectivity or testimony, but should be approached as a historically contingent truth-claim that, in turn, variously defines the conditions upon which witnessing is enacted and raises the question as to what kinds of publics these claims summon up in the humanitarian imaginary.

News as history

In this spirit, I take a historical perspective on the study of news (Rantanen 2009), focusing on BBC archive stories of major earthquakes in the time-span of the past 35 years.[6] To this end, I draw on the television/post-television distinction and, as established earlier, I discuss, in turn: (i) television narratives (Tangshan, China 1976; Mexico 1985; Turkey 1999); (ii) post-television/convergent narratives (Kashmir, Pakistan 2005, Haiti 2010); and (iii) post-television/live blogging (Haiti 2010).[7]

Whereas the distinction points to a technology-driven differentiation between television and post-television news, the focus clearly falls on the analysis of post-television, establishing a further differentiation between convergent and live blogging ones. The reason for this analytical bias is that whereas television, for instance in pre-satellite and satellite news, has been exhaustively studied, post-television news, for instance in terms of the impact of new media on self-expression, has only recently began to pose analytical challenges in the study of journalism. The point of the juxtaposition, then, is to identify the narrative properties of both journalistic regimes in order to examine how the move from one to another reflects broader shifts in the performances of witnessing available to news publics.

Given that the empirical material draws on the BBC web archive, the analysis of witnessing does not identify the implications of news narratives as they occur, inevitably impossible in a historical study of news, but focuses instead on how these implications are encoded in these narratives as a historical record of their time. Insofar as the BBC archives, from the 1976 Tangshan piece on the BBC's 'This Day' site to the 2010 Haiti 'As It Happened' site, present these news narratives 'as news', that is, in the temporality of the present, it is possible to treat them as records of the journalistic performances of witnessing they made available, at the moment of recording.[8] At the same time, insofar as television news now appears in online form, the analysis of television news as history is less about the reproduction of past news broadcasts online and more about the recontextualization of those broadcasts in online formats – particularly in the case of the 1999 satellite news on Turkey, where the element of 'liveness' is represented through a brief embedded 'live' video of its television footage.

The online recontextualization of television narratives further raises an important analytical argument in the historical analysis of news. By addressing how 'older' media, such as television, are appropriated and repurposed within post-television journalism, the analysis avoids a technological determinism that treats the narrative discontinuities of the news as radical ruptures between contrasting platforms. It adopts instead a discursive approach that focuses on the ways in which the convergence of these diverse media platforms comes to rearticulate the narrative modes of news in different ways (for the argument, see Peters 2009: 22). By this token, the study of journalistic witnessing as performance is here about both the relative stability of its narratives across time and the gradual changes in these narratives, under the pressure of shifting historical, including technological, circumstances.

Narrative aesthetics

This conception of news as narrative, as an 'authoring' of reality that inevitably involves the positionality of a voice, is not new. As Tuchman puts it, 'to say that news is a story no more, but no less, is not to demean the news, not to accuse it of being fictitious. Rather, it alerts us that news, like all public documents, is a constructed reality possessing its own internal validity' (Tuchman 1976: 96). The idea of 'constructedness' does not simply assert that the news is a story, albeit subject to specific truth-claims, but also that, as such, it entails an irreducible aesthetic dimension. This is so insofar as the news is made up by aesthetic choices that operate performatively, that is to say, by specific combinations of language, image and sound that do not simply reflect an external world but render this world a sensible and meaningful reality for those who engage with it. Rather than referring to high art, then, this view of aesthetics as narrative performance with moral effects foregrounds instead the act of witnessing as an act of theatrical representation in front of an audience, where every choice matters: the use of the third person or the passionate 'I' may report on similar 'facts' yet produce these facts as very different emotional and moral realities.

In this spirit, I propose a framework for the study of journalistic witnessing, what I have elsewhere called the 'analytics of mediation', that conceptualizes the news as an aesthetic practice with ethico-political implications (Chouliaraki 2006, 2008a). The inseparability of aesthetic quality from moral agency granted, it is useful to address these categories of the news story as analytically distinct. The distinction enables us, on the one hand, to identify the process through which witnessing, rather than an inherent property of the news, is itself performed through choices of image and language and, on the other, to explore how such aesthetic choices simultaneously construe western spectators in particular relationships of solidarity with vulnerable others.

The category of 'aesthetic quality' draws attention to two features of the news narrative: (i) its *multi-mediality*, which looks at the combination or 'repurposing' of the different forms of media in it; and (ii) its *narrative structure*, which explores the impact of multi-mediality on *the cohesive structure*, or the informational architecture of the narrative (Cottle 2006b), the *clause structure*, or the representation of authority in the news; and the *process structure* that looks into the representation of action on suffering, that is, who acts on whom in which capacity. Various configurations of these narrative dimensions of the news bring about different effects of authenticity and produce different forms of narrative realism – factual, testimonial or participatory.

The category of 'moral agency' draws attention to the performances of witnessing that the narrative aesthetics of the news make available to their publics. In line with the critique of empire, those pieces of news that are devoid of multi-mediality make available the performance of detached witnessing by construing suffering as a factual piece of information with little moralizing force; others enhance multi-mediality with interactive options that facilitate the communication of emotion and action and, thus, enable the performance of witnessing as committed. By exploring the ways in which performances of witnessing regulate our responsiveness to distant suffering, the analysis of moral agency aims, therefore, at identifying the kinds of publics that news journalism contributes to shaping – either by orienting us towards existing collectivities of emotion and action, communitarian publics, or by orienting us towards vulnerable others beyond the West, cosmopolitan publics.

News narratives: a typology of witnessing

My discussion starts with television and moves on to post-television news, examining each in terms of: (i) aesthetic quality, focusing on key properties of their narrative structure (cohesive, clause and process structure) and the forms of realism they give rise to; and (ii) moral agency, focusing on the modes of witnessing that each form of realism proposes as morally acceptable.

Television news narratives

Box 6.1 BBC News. Chinese earthquake kills hundreds of thousands, 28 July 1976

1976: Chinese earthquake kills hundreds of thousands
Hundreds of thousands of people are feared dead following an 8.3 magnitude earthquake in China. The quake has virtually destroyed the city of Tangshan, north-east of Beijing, and western sources believe the death toll may be much higher than the official figure of 240,000. Some believe the figure is more like 750,000. The Hong Kong Royal Observatory reports the earthquake was intense, although speculation of the magnitude of the quake ranges from 6.3 to 8.3. Around 2,000 people are believed to have died when the quake devastated the city's biggest hospital, according to sources quoting Chinese officials.

It is feared that many miners are buried alive in coal works in the industrial city, which has a total population of 1.6m. Diplomatic observers say that up to 80,000 people died in the first shock of the natural disaster. Up to 164,000 people have been severely injured, according to initial reports from the city. Tangshan was at the epicentre of the earthquake, although it badly damaged Tientsin. Tremors were also felt in Beijing, where residents were urged to live in the streets and keep to open spaces as it is not thought to be safe to return to their homes in the city.

The force of the quake has been so strong that people are reported to have been thrown into the air after roads, bridges, railway stations, homes and factories were completely destroyed. The quake has also knocked out power throughout the city, making rescue efforts difficult. When the earthquake struck Tangshan at 03.42 local time, more than a million people lay sleeping. The entire earthquake reportedly lasted approximately 14 to 16 seconds. It was followed by a 7.1 magnitude aftershock. Survivors have been digging through debris to answer the calls for help as well as find missing relatives. There is a deep-seated peasant belief that the 'Year of the Dragon' – which happens every 12 years – augurs ill. The survivors of the Tangshan quake are living in tents and are expected to be moved to winter shelters, the New China news agency has reported. Aircraft and lorries have been taking large quantities of relief supplies to help the relief effort. The authorities later hope to move people to simple houses, which can withstand tremors and are warm and rainproof before winter sets in. Chinese officials have rejected any offers of help from the outside world, saying that survivors have enough to eat and wear and there are sufficient medical supplies and doctors in the city.

'Any grave natural disaster can be overcome with the guidance of Chairman Mao' – spokesman for the *Red Flag Journal*

Aesthetic quality

The three pieces of news, in this category, move towards increasingly *multi-medial* configurations of information, reflecting variations internal to the development of broadcasting (see note 7 for links to texts for the Mexico and Turkey earthquakes). The 1976 text on Tangshan is purely linguistic and, in the absence of on-location images, its only visual element is a picture of the Chinese flag as a symbol of the nation. The 1985 text on Mexico is minimally multi-modal, in that it includes an image of the earthquake's aftermath, whereas the 1999 Turkey one further includes a hyperlink to video footage. The move towards an increasingly complex use of image and sound captures here a developmental trajectory of multi-mediality from pre-satellite news, which traditionally relied on the local agency of the diplomatic office (1976), to satellite news, which relies on technologies of instantaneous transmission (1999) and therefore moves towards 'liveness'.

Even though, as in the case of Turkey, live broadcasting proposes the possibility of 'reflexive identification', whereby the immediacy of the spectacle combined with the act of simultaneous watching produces an awareness of 'global connectivity' with distant others (Chouliaraki 2006: 178), the power of authoring all television narratives ultimately remains in the hands of the journalist. This authoring power of the journalist is clearly reflected in the *narrative structure* of the pieces. In terms of *cohesion structure*, the narratives follow the pattern of the 'inverted pyramid', whereby the first three sentences of each piece of news convey essential information, the 'what, where, when and how' of the earthquake, with the rest of the story elaborating on the state of destruction and relief efforts. An historical trope of the news genre, the inverted pyramid is instrumental in constituting the truth-claim to objectivity in that it reflects a conception of events as reducible to basic knowable facts (Schudson 1995).

In terms of *clause structure*, these pieces are characterized by the use of *categorical* or *'unmodalized' language*, *passive voice* and *reported speech*. Categorical language presents facts beyond doubt, as in 'Tangshan *was* at the epicenter of the earthquake', 'when the earthquake *struck* . . . more than a million people *lay sleeping*' (China); 'The quake *hit* the west coast near . . . Acapulco', 'It *lasted* for 50 seconds . . .' (Mexico); or 'The earthquake *struck* the industrialized city of Izmit . . .', 'whole districts *collapsed* . . .' (Turkey). The use of the passive voice or impersonal constructions deletes subjective agency in the narrative: 'hundreds of thousands of people *are feared* dead . . .' (China); '*it is feared* the death toll may rise . . .' (Mexico) or 'the earthquake *has left at least* 1,000 people dead . . .' (Turkey). Finally, notice that none of the examples figures the journalistic 'I' as a marker of personal testimony; instead, reported speech places the informational value onto external sources: '*Western sources* believe that . . .', '*Chinese officials* have rejected any offers . . .' (China) or '*Officials say* at least 170 people . . .', '*Television reports said* hundreds of people . . .' (Turkey), '"a part of the mountain just slid away, falling on the peasants . . ." *said Lieutenant* . . .' (Mexico). The rare use of direct quotes is reserved for official statements, rather than ordinary experience, such as *The Red Flag Journal*'s 'Any grave natural disaster can be overcome with the guidance of President Mao' or Turkish President Ecevit's 'May God help our country and its people.'

The *process structure* of the narratives is represented by the past tense, which construes the events as faits accomplis: 'died; . . . have been severely injured; . . . damaged . . . were felt' (China); 'has hit . . . was caused . . . were cut . . . littered . . . collapsed . . .' (Mexico) or 'were asleep . . . had no chance . . . collapsed' (Turkey). There are instances of present or perfect temporality, which point to the ongoing agency of local benefactors, government and its humanitarian services: 'The authorities *later hope to* move people . . .'; 'Aircraft and lorries *have been taking* large quantities of relief supplies' (China); 'rescue workers *digging through* rubble in a frantic search for survivors . . .' (Mexico); 'Rescue teams *have found* some people alive underneath the rubble . . .' (Turkey). Whereas satellite news (Turkey) progressively incorporates a contemporaneous temporality in the video link, the news narrative remains resolutely in the hands of the journalist; moreover, as this live element is now embedded in a video hyperlink, its temporality remains subordinate to the linguistic temporality of the past.

In summary, television news narrates distant suffering through an aesthetics of 'factual realism' – an aesthetics that follows the non-experiential logic of 'essentials first' and appeals to the authenticity of facts. There is significant gradation in the representation of magnitude and depth of the catastrophe, from minimal references, such as 'The force of the quake has been so strong that people are reported to have been thrown into the air' (China),[9] or 'Many people gathered on street corners, several weeping or fainting' (Mexico), to the live link of the Turkey earthquake which introduces elements of omnipresent witnessing – we see references to ordinary experience as part of the reporting brief. These bear, however, a rather restricted emotive force, insofar as they are subordinate to the authoring power of the journalist and are followed by no or limited visualization of the scene of suffering.

Moral agency

The witnessing performance of factual aesthetics is that of *detached witnessing* that relies on (i) the truth-claim to aperspectival objectivity, through the inverted pyramid (cohesive structure) and third-person testimony (clause structure); (ii) the desingularization of voice, through the use of official sources that marginalize ordinary accounts and the minimal use of imagery (clause structure); and (iii) the minimal temporalization of the dynamics of the event, through the use of the finite temporality of the past and the embedded use of a 'live' link (process structure).

Two implications follow from the performance of these news narratives as detached witnessing. The first is the 'othering' of the zone of suffering as a location beyond our reach and, relatedly, the 'de-emotionalization' of the relationship between this zone and the zone of western safety. Despite the elements of ordinary experience and the increasing presence of satellite visuality, both of which introduce a certain degree of ordinariness to the story, these pieces of news maintain *a strong boundary* between the zone of suffering and that of safety.

Post-television narratives: convergent news

Box 6.2 BBC News. Hundreds Die in South Asia Quake. 5 October 2005

Pakistan says more than 1,000 people may have died in a powerful quake that also hit north India and Afghanistan.
The 7.6-magnitude quake with the epicentre 80km (50 miles) north-east of Islamabad wiped out several villages.

At least 500 died in North-West Frontier province in Pakistan. More than 450 lost their lives in the disputed territory of Kashmir.

In Islamabad, people rushed to dig with bare hands to rescue those trapped when an apartment building collapsed.

Pakistani President Pervez Musharraf, who was visiting the site, said the quake was a 'test of the nation'.

Several countries have offered to send emergency aid.

In a message to Mr Musharraf, Indian Prime Minister Manmohan Singh said: 'While parts of India have also suffered from this unexpected natural disaster, we are prepared to extend any assistance with rescue and relief which you may deem appropriate.'

Severed legs

The earthquake, which was registered at 03.50 GMT, was felt as far away as the Afghan capital, Kabul, and India's capital, Delhi. Several aftershocks followed.

Maj. Gen. Shaukat Sultan, President Musharraf's spokesman, told the BBC: 'I would say it is massive damage that has been caused. I would say that the casualties may not be hundreds – but much more.'

Interior Minister Aftab Sherpao told local television: 'We have reports that several entire villages have been wiped out.'

The head of police in the North-West Frontier Province told AFP news agency 'between 550 and 600' people had died and the figure was likely to rise.

In Pakistani-controlled Kashmir, 250 bodies have been recovered of the more than 2,000 feared dead, an official told the BBC from the provincial capital, Muzaffarabad.

'All official buildings have collapsed,' he said.

Landslides have blocked all access roads to Muzaffarabad, where there is no electricity and telephones.

Islamabad collapse

Part of the upmarket Margala Towers residential complex collapsed in Islamabad.

One rescuer, Rehmatullah, said: 'I rushed down and for some time you could not see anything because of the dust . . . We pulled out one man by cutting off his legs.'

Karam Usmani, a 28-year-old sub-inspector with Islamabad police, told the BBC: 'I heard the cries of the people in the debris and with my bare hands I started to dig and I pulled out one dead body.

'But I managed to rescue another man of 35 and carried him on my shoulders to the ambulance.'

In Indian-administered Kashmir, 200 are confirmed dead – including 15 soldiers – and 600 injured.

The town of Uri close to the Line of Control that separates divided Kashmir was worst hit, with 104 dead.

The administration is working overtime to restore essential supplies like electricity and water disrupted by the earthquake, says the BBC's Altaf Hussain in Srinagar.

Aid talks

Ben Phillips of Oxfam told the BBC a meeting of relief organizations was under way and is liaising with the UN and the Pakistani government on supplying aid.

Mr Phillips said the initial requirement would be for tents, blankets, food aid and medical supplies.

In other reports around the region:

- A meeting attended by India's prime minister in the northern city of Chandigarh was stopped after his bodyguards ordered an immediate evacuation following the tremors.
- The 200-year-old Moti Mahal fort in Poonch district, Indian-administered Kashmir, has collapsed.
- One child was killed and six injured in a school collapse in Rawalpindi, Pakistan's information minister said.

Aesthetic quality

In contrast to the previous class of news, the Kashmir 2005 and Haiti 2010 pieces are characterized by a rich *multi-mediality* which reflects the increasing complexity of the news genre, as it moves beyond broadcasting towards convergence. Multi-mediality, the coexistence of media platforms on the online news page, facilitates the insertion of complex visual and aural material in the story, including interactive maps of the affected area, 'eyewitness links' with footage from ordinary people, 'audio accounts' of survivors (some transcribed as highlighted blurbs on the webpage), historical information and the live blog (given copyright restrictions by the BBC, these hyperlinks are only available online; see note 7).

As a consequence, the *cohesive structure* of the news becomes 'hypertextual', enhancing the flow of the linguistic story with options of interactive engagement with multiple, though not immediately available, information sources-as-links (Deuze 2006: 70). Hypertextuality is, at the same time, combined with the traditional cohesive marker of the news, the inverted pyramid, which still dominates the linguistic aspect of the narrative. The result is a hybrid structure that may resemble traditional news yet de-homogenizes its narrative, in that sources are now presented in terms of unrelated quotes without a tight sequential logic, and further allows for multiple modes of engagement with the text: reading, clicking and navigating, skimming through images.

The *clause structure* remains, as a result, dominated by categorical language that conveys facts, but the indirect quotes and passive voice of the previous class of news have now been replaced by the extensive use of direct quotes. This encompasses official voices, such as local government ('Pakistani President . . . said the quake was "a test of the nation"', Kashmir) but also international ones ('US President Barack Obama said his "thoughts and prayers . . ."', Haiti), which not only inject a sense of immediacy in the narrative but further 'globalize' the field of action. Importantly, the narrative now includes aid agencies and ordinary people's stories: 'One rescuer, Rehmatullah, said "I rushed down . . ."' (Pakistan) or 'Rachmani Domersant, an operations manager with the Food for the Poor charity, told Reuters that "You have thousands of people sitting in the streets with nowhere to go . . . running, crying, screaming"' (Haiti).

The *process structure* brings to the fore different proposals to action in the scene of suffering. In contrast to the finiteness of the previous category, these pieces retain a sense of urgent 'liveness', conveyed through the eternal present of eyewitness accounts, such as 'The cries of the people trapped in the debris haunt me. There are still many trapped there' (Pakistan) or 'Now it's dark outside, there is no electricity, all the phone networks are down . . .' (Haiti), in amateur recordings and audio links. Interactive options, asking for information ('Have you been affected by the earthquake?'), are available immediately after the event on the BBC website, as are links related to the geological and political history of the affected countries. The multiple temporalization of action is thus not only encoded in the grammar of the linguistic narrative, but further appears as a structural possibility in the hypertextual links it provides.

This configuration of narrative properties constitutes both stories in an aesthetics of 'testimonial realism' – a narrative aesthetics organized around the authority of the journalist but, this time, combining the realism of facts with the emotion of personal testimony. As a consequence, this class of news construes a *weak boundary* between the zone of suffering and that of safety. Two elements contribute to this weakening: (i) the emergence of eyewitness accounts, survivors' and NGOs', and documentary footage, which increase the visibility of suffering; and (ii) the hypertextuality of the narrative, which places events within a historical perspective and, importantly, offers interactive options that invite the West to act as a potential benefactor – communicating their views or donating to relief agencies.

Moral agency

The moral agency of testimonial realism emerges from a performance of *omnipresent witnessing* that relies on: (i) a *hybrid truth-claim* to aperspectival objectivity (through the authoritative structure of the inverted pyramid) and to subjective story-telling (through direct quotes and hyperlinks); (ii) the *hybridization of voice*, which invites engagement both with the specificity of the sufferer as a singular person and with the generality of the context of suffering as an object of international aid; and (iii) the *multiple temporalization* of action, which allows for engagement with the circumstances of the past, the urgency of the present and the future of beneficiary action.

Two implications follow from the performance of moral agency in terms of omnipresent witnessing: the construal of the zone of suffering as both distant from us and yet within our reach and, relatedly, the 'emotionalization' of the relationship between this zone and the western spectator, which offers outlets for beneficiary action. There is, however, a difference between the two examples: Haiti managed to capture the moral imagination of the West as the object of extensive altruistic action, whilst Kashmir did not (Franks 2006). Even though there are historical and political reasons for this asymmetry in coverage, the lack of the use of new media has also been singled out as an important reason for the poor news coverage in Kashmir: 'poorer news coverage', as Thelwall and Stuart put it, '[was] due to the much smaller number of western journalists available to cover Pakistan . . . and the lower quantity of first-hand eyewitness digital images, resulting in a lower "glitz" factor' (2007). In contrast, the Haiti earthquake took place in a media-saturated environment that provided an open and instantaneous online structure of information and action, unprecedented in disaster reporting. As Fox News commented: 'The power of Twitter to turn eyewitnesses into on-the-scene journalists stood out in the wake of the massive earthquake that struck off the coast of Haiti on Tuesday. Graphic photographs of Haitians covered in rubble promptly shot onto Twitter, far ahead of anything from the traditional news wire services' (14 January 2010).

It is to live blogging, as the news platform, par excellence, that aggregated citizen contributions and so greatly enhanced the visibility of suffering that I now turn. Instead of claiming that news publics engaged primarily with live blogging rather than with broadcast media as sources of information on Haiti, my argument is rather that news publics spread across these media, using each in different ways and for different purposes. Whilst broadcasting remained, therefore, a key source of information, live blogging acted as a source of updates and interaction (personal communication with BBC interactive hub).

Live blogging

Box 6.3 BBC, 'As It Happened', 13 January 2010

11.32 Caroline Hurford of the World Food Programme (WFP) said the agency's building in Port-Au-Prince was still standing and all staff are accounted for. WFP is airlifting 90 metric tonnes of high energy biscuits to neighbouring Dominican Republic – enough to feed 30,000 people for a week.

11.24 Reports say the capital, Port-au-Prince, was covered in a blanket of dust for about 20 minutes after the quake.

[Mobile phone footage of quake's immediate aftermath]

11.22 Louis Belanger, a spokesman for UK-based aid agency Oxfam, tells the BBC aid agencies will probably use the Dominican Republic's capital Santo Domingo as their hub to bring in aid as Haiti's main airport is out of action.

11.17 *Troy Livesay tweets*: 'Church groups are singing throughout the city all through the night in prayer. It is a beautiful sound in the middle of a horrible tragedy.'

11.13 Pope Benedict XVI calls on people to 'unite in prayer' for the victims of the quake.

11.08 'This is a huge humanitarian operation, no question about that,' Patrick McCormick of the UN's children's agency UNICEF tells the BBC.

Aesthetic quality

What differentiates live blogging from the previous classes of news is that its narrative structure is now fully driven by *multi-mediality* – the configuration of media that carry the new information. What gets reported is whatever reaches the BBC interactive newsroom as presentable information in whichever techno-platform it is, email, Twitter, video or blog entry (see note 7 for the news link).

As a consequence, there is a sharp increase of ordinary voice: 50 out of 115 stream entries are anchored on testimonies of suffering. Either through amateur recordings or through verbal accounts, this prominence of ordinary voice renders the suffering in Haiti a therapeutic practice – a highly emotive performance that vocalizes the trauma of the affected: '18.49 *Troy Livesay, Port-au-Prince, blogs*: Thousands of people are currently trapped. To guess at a number would be like guessing at raindrops in the ocean. Precious lives hang in the balance . . .'; '18.17 *Thomas Chadwick, Florida, US, emails*: I have an orphanage in Jacmel with 13 children. My wife is out there but I haven't been able to speak to any of them since an hour before the earthquake. I feel so useless.'

As a result of its intense multi-mediality, the *narrative structure* of the live blog differs substantially from that of convergent journalism. Its *cohesive structure*, in particular, is now organized along the lines of a timeline, that is, a temporally aggregated collection of self-contained entries in the form of informational 'updates': '10.53 *The International Federation of the Red Cross says* . . .', '11.01 *Former Haitian President is quoted by the AFP news agency as saying* . . .' Rather than a seamless story, unified around the objectivist logic of the inverted pyramid, the experiential narrative of the live blog is a fully decentred narrative, a 'bricolage' or a 'continuous and more or less autonomous assembly, disassembly and reassembly of mediated reality' (Deuze 2006: 66).

Narrative fragmentation is further characterized by a heterogeneous *clause structure* consisting of unconnected messages that share one common feature: they all contain references to their source identity: '11.17 *Troy Livesay tweets*,' '19.10 *The British Red Cross* in Haiti has set up a Flickr picture gallery.' This sequential annotation of sources points to the orientation of the stream towards 'who says what' rather than to the validity of the source, 'what is being said'. As opposed to the authority of the journalistic voice, in the third or first person, this clause structure reflects, therefore, the preference for a 'situated' and contingent truth-claim.

The *process structure* places the user squarely in the sphere of simultaneity by inserting into the narrative the dimension of 'crisis communication', that is, communication with a view to immediately acting on the urgency of suffering (Fearn-Banks 2007). It does so through the extensive presence of hyperlinks, which make possible new options for action at a distance. Beyond the 'Have you been affected by the earthquake?' invitation to email, there is now a new range of engagement options via photo and video uploads, Twitter sites and, importantly, donations. Whereas donation links obviously address the West as potential benefactors to the Haitian suffering, informational interactivity, as in 'Photos: Email yourpics @bbc.co.uk'; 'Video: Upload your video'; 'Twitter: HYS on Twitter', invites primarily the contributions of the affected as the principal source of news in the blog. Yet only seven out of 115 entries in the stream include this voice, all of them Twitter messages (fewer than 140 character-long phrases) plus a mobile phone video, whilst the majority of eyewitness accounts come from INGOs – approximately twenty messages. The remaining testimonial messages come from westerners indirectly affected by the earthquake or by Haitians who live in the West and, in some cases, in neighbouring countries (such as the Dominican Republican).

As a result, a key feature of live blogging is the hyper-temporalization of the news: even though it provides the option of historicizing distant suffering, in links such as 'Troubled history: Haiti and the US' or envisaging a hopeful future in 'Rebuild challenge', it remains primarily organized around real-time interactivity, which proposes instant action 'at the click of the mouse'.

The aesthetic quality of live blogging is, therefore, a 'participatory realism' which engages with distant suffering from the perspective of a dispersed but involved collectivity that actively taps into the BBC's interactive options (Nichols 2001 for the term 'participatory'). In so doing, 'participatory' realism challenges the 'I' of the journalist by placing it side by side with the separate 'I's of amateur users – the entry of the BBC journalist arriving in Port-au-Prince, for instance, is just one feed amongst others: '23.09 The *BBC's Andy Gallacher says*: "I've just arrived at Port-au-Prince and aid in now coming in, but very slowly indeed. There are just a few US Coast Guard and a few military planes here . . ."'

Moral agency

The moral agency of participatory realism emerges from a performance of 'ordinary witnessing', which relies on: (i) the *de-homogenization* of narrative consisting of real-time testimonies but without a coherent storyline; (ii) the *decentralization* of voice, which equalizes all contributions but renders the truth-claim of the news more contingent and situated; and (iii) the *hyper-temporalization* of suffering, which introduces the interactive simultaneity of 'crisis communication' but remains western in the voices of disaster.

The participatory realism of post-television news, in conclusion, is caught up in a paradoxical development. It appears to facilitate the ritual function of journalism, that is, the formation of a community of potential benefactors, but it does so on the condition that it transforms the news narrative of suffering beyond recognition. It is the consequences of this transformation for the performances of witnessing in the humanitarian imaginary today that I address next.

The authenticity effects of news: from narrative to database

The analysis of participatory news points to the fact that, whereas authenticity has always been part of the news, it is only post-television news that turns authenticity into an aesthetic problem. In a manner different to appeals, where authenticity also figures as an object of our contemplation, post-television news replaces television's logic of story-telling with a techno-textual logic, thereby also replacing dramatic action with the timeline, the source and the hyperlink are the new resources for communicating vulnerability.

Even though testimonial narratives also go some way in this process, they nonetheless retain elements of homogeneous story-telling in their use of the 'inverted pyramid' and the authorial voice of the journalist. It is the live blog that breaks with these elements and marks the culmination of the news as a participatory process with important implications on the performances of witnessing now available to us. I discuss two such implications: (i) the *technologization of witnessing*; and (ii) *the construal of a post-humanitarian public*.

The technologization of witnessing

The paradox of authenticity, inherent in all performances of witnessing, has been variously resolved in the different narratives that I have explored so far. The detached witnessing of television, as we saw, addresses technological suspicion by claiming authenticity beyond points of view, whereas the omnipresent witnessing of convergent journalism fences off suspicion by containing the totality of the points of view within a story. Both performances, however, continue to use the voice of the journalist as the ultimate guarantee of authenticity; as capable, that is, of closing the gap between the 'seen' and the 'said' for the publics they address.

Participatory narratives, in contrast, abandon authorial voice and turn to the truth of ordinary witnessing – a form of reporting that does not simply speak in the name of a public but claims to be that public itself. Even if this performance of witnessing evades the risk between the voice that speaks and the public it represents, it cannot escape, however, its own risky dislocations. Given its institutional appropriation by major news networks, ordinary witnessing has to manage another risk between the 'seen', which is contextual and experiential, and the 'said' which, once it reaches the BBC newsroom, becomes the object of editorial regulation.

From this perspective, post-television journalism should not simply be seen as facilitating the representation of ordinary voice, but also as regulating this voice in the process of representing it. The technologization of witnessing refers here precisely to this rearticulation of ordinary voice which, in the process of institutionalizing the 'seen' into the 'said', also changes the epistemic status of news from 'knowledge', voice attached to its experiential context, to 'information', decontextualized voice available for retrieval and use. Two processes contribute to this technologization of witnessing in participatory news: the *visibility of journalistic labour online*; and the *availability of interactive technology*. I have so far addressed these as properties of the narrative aesthetics of the news, but I now turn to them as traces of change in the institutional regulation of the news.

The *visibility of journalistic labour* reflects market changes in news gathering from a source-driven journalism oriented to the verification of information towards an event-driven journalism that is based on material from the zone of suffering. This is evident in the timeline, which replaces a hierarchy of importance (what the facts are) with a hierarchy of time (what comes in first). It is also evident in the annotation of sources, which replaces a hierarchy of status (what officials report) with a hierarchy of activism (whoever reports first). At the same time, the *availability of interactive technology* reflects changes in the authorship of news from a single-authoring newsroom, where editing involves the writing up of individual reports, towards a multi-skilled newsroom, where editing involves cross-media monitoring and repurposing of content in often 'collaborative' news reports (Deuze 2004).

These developments come to address market concerns not only with the declining public trust towards news but also with a declining profitability in the online news provision of major networks, where the co-option of the unpaid labour of citizen journalists becomes part of a corporate strategy to reinvent more attractive news models at low cost (Scott 2005). Rather than enhancing public participation, however, critics argue that the multi-skilling of newsrooms ultimately leads to a re-centralization of the news market as, in their attempt to attract audiences at minimal cost, networks now repurpose and recirculate similar content across different platforms. As a consequence, the consolidation of their position in the global market comes at the cost of producing news that is less than trustworthy but more of the same (Turner 2010).

Whilst there is no doubt that the move from 'business-to-consumer' towards 'peer-to-peer' news does obey the market priorities of the news industry, it nonetheless makes a difference in the power relations of the newsroom. For, independently of corporate agendas, the opening up to the voices of the people does endow online journalism with an irreducibly democratizing dimension (Gillmor 2004). This is perhaps most obvious in the role of INGOs in disaster reporting, where their 'unpaid labour' to online journalism is accompanied by new, unprecedented opportunities to have their voice heard: during the first 24 hours following the Haiti earthquake, it was INGOs that filled an important informational gap in the BBC live blog, only later covered by the voice of professional journalists. By using the multi-medial affordances of global networks, INGOs managed, thus, to break through the selective indifference of much television reporting and gain some control over the management of information in communicating disaster news (Cottle 2009). Suspicious, then, as the political economy of convergence journalism may be, participatory news seems to resonate positively with what Jenkins calls the 'cultural economy' of convergence – the promise of this type of news to offer non-professionals the chance to take some control of the agenda of the news (2004).

A crucial consequence of this new cultural economy that urgently requires our critical attention is, however, that its self-expressive structure replaces the logic of news as 'dramatic action' with a logic of the news as a 'database': a cumulative depository of entries without internal coherence but available for archival purposes (Manovich 2001). This remodelling of the news into an archival format is evident in the disintegration of the participatory narrative: the cohesive structure of bricolage, the clause structure of the fragment and the process structure of the embedded link – a logic of hypermediacy that treats the technological infrastructure of convergence as an explicit and integral part of the narrative aesthetics of news.

Participatory narratives are, in this sense, a collection of self-contained 'speech acts' that celebrate the voice of the eyewitness whilst making this voice available for immediate consumption or for subsequent use, in any order and any time. The use of the live blog as an online record for public access, appropriately entitled 'BBC: As it Happened', points precisely to the archival function of participatory narratives as a technological diary, which provides a chronology of events 'without analysis or interpretation' (Rantanen 2009: 6).

The technologization of witnessing points, here, to a shift not only in the technical media of news reporting but also, importantly, to a shift in the moral education of news publics – what Foucault refers to as technologies of the self. As I argued in chapter 1, technologies of the self do not operate via explicit moralizing talk about solidarity but by mundanely performing normative dispositions as to how we should feel, think and act towards distant others. Participatory news narratives work as technologies of the self, in this sense, to the extent that their morality of solidarity is today cumulatively articulated through the multiple 'we' voices of the people, thereby replacing an objectivist conception of the world as it is, characteristic of traditional news stories, with the subjectivist reality of the world as we saw it. It is this subordination of the story of distant suffering to many, small self-expressive stories that tends to undermine the theatricality of the genre and to produce live-blogging publics as post-humanitarian publics.

A post-humanitarian public

Post-humanitarianism is a public disposition of solidarity with vulnerable others that rests on the proliferation of personal testimony in the narration of distant suffering and invites an instantaneous, albeit discontinuous, 'point-and-click' activism. Central to this structure of solidarity is the increasing dispersion of the narrative structure of the news towards testimonial and participatory performances of witnessing. I discuss two implications of this narrative dispersion for the constitution of participatory news publics as post-humanitarian: (i) *the 'impossibility' of the public* and (ii) *the rise of therapeutic discourse.*

Far from implying that post-television narratives do not summon up their own publics, the idea of 'impossibility' refers rather to the ways in which the witnessing public can(not) be performed as a collective agency in these narratives. In this respect, the shift towards convergent journalism does not necessarily mean that post-television publics pay less attention to dramatic stories of television journalism and their objectivist claims to knowledge (Deuze 2005), but it does tell us something important about the changing status of witnessing as a radically situated and open-ended claim to knowledge :'less of a claim to what the readers want or to know what an event means' and, instead, 'a site of multiple knowledge and of breadth of knowledge of the world' (Matheson 2004: 461). It is this 'aporetic' nature of witnessing, that is, the (narrative) awareness that distant suffering can never be adequately narrated as a twin claim to objectivity and emotionality – 'without deformation' and in such a way that people 'find themselves sufficiently affected by it', in Boltanski's terms – but will always remain a partial and contingent story, that throws into relief the 'impossibility' of performing the public in post-television news.

This is so in that the post-television shift from 'dramatic' to 'aporetic' witnessing replaces the arrangement of separation between watching and acting with an arrangement of potential co-performance, as users are now able to co-author the story of suffering, and, in so doing, it breaks down the theatrical model of representing suffering in the news. This public is post-humanitarian, then, in the sense that it imagines itself as an actor not on the grounds of narratives of 'dramatic action' that potentially engage them with other actors in the space of appearance, what Mulhmann (2008) calls 'a journalism of unification', but on the grounds of disconnected, '*petit* narratives' that engage each one as an individual with the interactive technologies of the news, in a 'journalism of decentring'.

This individuation of authorship undoubtedly resonates well with monitorial and voluntarist forms of citizenship that, like post-television news, move away from claims of 'representing the public' and see public participation as authentic self-expression in the context of what Hartley calls 'conversational democracy' (2010, drawing on Coleman 2005; see also Schudson 1998). The question that concerns me here, however, is what kind of conversation this form of public participation constitutes in the face of distant suffering – a question that leads me to the second feature of the post-humanitarian public: the rise of therapeutic discourse.

Ordinary witnessing rests upon an intense vocalization of the trauma of disaster. This vocalization of trauma, as I argued earlier, introduces into the news a therapeutic discourse that makes claims to what Taylor (1995) calls recognition: the right of the affected to render their suffering visible and, thereby, legitimate to all in the theatrical space of the imaginary – as in '*Jovenel Presume, Massachusetts, US, emails:* Since the quake, I have lost all communication with my family. My mum is there. She was due to fly back today . . .' '20.57 In a moving report on its website, Haitian Radio Metropole describes the devastation: "The streets of Port-au-Prince are nothing more than a gaping wound, where corpses are tangled with the remains of houses, shops . . ."'

These references to powerlessness, despair, physical and emotional pain but also death constitute claims that call up the post-television news public as a sphere of compassionate addressees – and where humanitarian agencies make a distinct contribution in both providing aid and asking for public response. Whereas journalistic accounts may appear as forms of response to this 'conversational democracy' of the humanitarian imaginary, such claims to recognition simultaneously throw into relief the capacity of ordinary witnessing to go beyond 'conversational' speech acts and to function as performances of solidarity within a therapeutic discourse of common humanity – a discourse that thematizes our 'shared mental and physical vulnerability' across hierarchies of place and human life and thereby 'projects forms of solidarity across the boundaries of established communities' (Linklater 2007b:

138). In so doing, post-television news comes to problematize the strong boundary that television news sets between the zones of safety and suffering and to facilitate a cosmopolitan imagination that extends the solidary sensibilities of western publics beyond its existing communities of belonging.

Yet, despite the proliferation of ordinary witnessing in the news, the vast majority of testimonies from the affected comes from the West – only eight web-stream entries by 'average people' come from Haiti (and it remains unclear as to how many of these come from Haitians) while the remaining forty-two are attributed either to western NGOs or to westerners who are indirectly touched by the earthquake.

Such inequality in the voices of witnessing undoubtedly follows patterns of uneven distribution and use in mobile technologies (Beckett and Mansell 2008), yet my argument on the dominance of western voices draws attention to a different, though related, point: a shift in journalism as a ritual of communication from constituting 'watching' television publics, united around 'dramatic action' on distant suffering, towards 'multi-tasking' post-television publics, united around online conversations on distant suffering. Far from claiming that television has disappeared as a source of engagement with the news, my point is rather that television is now one amongst a range of media that western publics engage with in the course of disaster reporting 'surfing the web, searching databases, responding to email, visiting chat rooms' (Lievrouw and Livingstone 2002: 10).

In the process of this dialogical yet discontinuous engagement, a new boundary between the zones of safety and suffering may be re-emerging as news publics 'talk' about distant suffering to one another, publicizing their trauma and seeking recognition, but in fact reconstitute and reproduce a western sphere of altruistic publicness. Rather than originating from or being oriented towards vulnerable others, then, this circuit of publicness takes those others as its subject of communication whilst it places a circle of western addresses like 'us' at the centre of its rituals of communication. The post-humanitarian publics of participatory news, in this sense, can be characterized as narcissistic publics, that is, publics that turn their awareness of the 'impossibility' of journalistic witnessing as a moral act into what Deuze calls an 'over-zealous faith in ourselves' and privilege 'our' own individuated performances of 'traumatized citizenship' over alternative, historical and contemporary correlations of suffering, identity and citizenship in disaster locations.

What is missing is a move beyond the urgent temporality of simultaneity towards a historicization of the suffering in Haiti in terms of the political power relations that inevitably bear on the outcomes of a natural catastrophe, including references to the colonial and post-colonial history of the nation. Such history, as James clearly shows, is responsible not only for its profound poverty but also for the dominance of therapeutic discourse, both outside and within the nation, as an instrumental form of public communication that consistently construes Haiti as the permanent object of humanitarian aid and dependence upon the West (James 2004).[10]

In seeking to redress, then, the political and ethical deficits of television news, evident in the pathologies of 'annihilation' and 'appropriation' discussed in the Introduction, post-television news may be producing its own distinct 'pathology' of witnessing, 'ventrilocation': the trauma of the sufferer may now become a powerfully legitimate moral claim in the space of appearance, but only on the condition that the voice of the sufferer is situated in the West and is performed through a resolutely communitarian moral imagination.

Conclusion: objectivity or therapy?

My analysis of the changing performances of witnessing from television to post-television news is informed by the assumption that such changes do not simply signal shifts in journalistic culture or news reporting but are, precisely, performative acts that also transform the dispositions of solidarity available in the humanitarian imaginary today. Crucial to this transformation is the shift from factual to participatory news narratives, which further reflects transformations in the theatrical presentation of suffering from 'detached' to 'ordinary' witnessing – from objectivity to testimony.

Whereas, in its reliance on the testimony of people like 'us', this shift promises more inclusive communicative structures that potentially cosmopolitanize the West, my analysis simultaneously warns against an important risk of post-television news. Its reconfiguration of the production–consumption relationships in journalism, I argue, may not necessarily challenge existing hierarchies of place and human life but may actually reproduce these hierarchies in the course of addressing them. Central to this critique of participatory journalism is the receding role of theatricality in the communication of solidarity.

The theatrical conception of journalism, grounded as it is on an arrangement of separation between those who act on the scene of suffering and those who watch at a distance, relies on an authorial voice that orchestrates the performativity of the news around narratives of dramatic action. Whereas television news upholds this theatrical model, post-television news, I have shown, introduces a therapeutic model of journalism which, in giving voice and recognition to ordinary contributions on distant suffering, replaces objectivity with a proliferation of truth-claims none of which take epistemological priority over others – the impossibility of witnessing, in this class of news, resting precisely on the presentation of suffering as a 'stream of other voices . . . dizzy multiplicity of interpretations of experience in the hope of achieving intimacy with violence' (Mulhmann 2008: 233, 235).

It is this collapse of objectivity into a 'stream of voices' that lies behind the moral imagination of post-humanitarism: in the name of an authenticity of the ordinary, narratives of suffering as dramatic action give way to self-reflexive, discontinuous and technologically mediated moves of online activism that construe western publics as performers of personal trauma (Eagleton 2009 on the link between narcissism and objectivity).

Post-television narratives, however, should not be seen as an autonomous class of news that exists on its own but as one class of news that exists in relationships of complementarity and tension with television news, each engaging their publics with distinct claims to truth and proposals for action – theatrical and anti-theatrical. Insofar as both classes form part of the humanitarian imaginary and its inherent paradoxes, both classes will continue to reproduce their own distinct pathologies of witnessing, annihilation, assimilation, ventrilocation, rendering journalism yet another ongoing site of struggle over the communication of vulnerability that our public culture makes available to us.

Indeed, what the preceding empirical chapters have demonstrated is how four different genres of the humanitarian imaginary, appeals, celebrity, concerts and news, negotiate the paradoxes of the imaginary by subtly but surely moving from a theatrical towards an anti-theatrical performance of human vulnerability and how, in so doing, they come to produce post-humanitarian dispositions of solidarity. In which ways can we explain this transformation in the aesthetics and ethics of solidarity in the context of modern humanitarianism? And can we theorize anew the possibility of cosmopolitan solidarity in the post-humanitarian era? It is these questions that the next and last chapter of this book turns to.

7 Theatricality, Irony, Solidarity

Introduction: the historical shifts of humanitarianism

The humanitarian imaginary is a communicative structure that disseminates the imperative to act on vulnerable others through a wide repertoire of popular genres – from appeals to news and from celebrity to concerts. Whilst humanitarianism is organized around the direct action of institutions of global governance, IOs and INGOs, this communicative structure is crucial insofar as it systematically represents the global South to the West, inviting us to act ourselves on vulnerable others through practices of speaking and paying.

It is this communicative structure of humanitarianism, mundanely cultivating dispositions of solidarity in the West, which has been the object of my study. Diversified as it is through the multiple practices of popular culture, such structure remains essentially theatrical in that it relies on spectacles of suffering in order to perform aspirational dispositions of solidarity. Amnesty appeals, celebrity activism, journalistic reporting and rock concerts are all, I have argued, part of a theatre of pity that seeks to confront us with vulnerable others with a view to inspiring our action on their condition. Yet, as I have also demonstrated, there are problems with the theatrical communication of solidarity.

Whereas the theatre of suffering introduces into this communicative structure the suspicion of technology, raising the question of whether mediated suffering is true fact or manipulated fiction (in line with the critique of spectacle), pity inspired by the spectacle introduces into the structure the problem of agency, raising the question of whether public action should aim at saving lives or changing society (in line with the critique of empire). It is these questions around the authenticity of the spectacle and around the morality of solidarity, constantly resurfacing in any attempt to represent a cause, that compelled me to approach humanitarianism not just as a series of messages but as a dynamic field of communicative paradoxes, as a humanitarian 'imaginary'.

By analysing four dominant genres of humanitarianism, I sought to demonstrate how these paradoxes of the imaginary are negotiated and provisionally settled at two key historical 'moments': its emergence and its contemporary state. What my analysis showed is that there is substantial change in the ways that both the authenticity of suffering and notions of solidarity with vulnerable others are performed across time – a change that I am now about to theorize as a paradigmatic shift from *solidarity as pity* to *solidarity as irony*. Rather than a rupture, however, this shift is the progressive outcome of longer-term institutional, technological and political changes in the humanitarian field which, as discussed in chapter 1, consist of the instrumentalization of the aid and development market and the rise of mediated self-expression in the post-Cold War context of the 'end of ideologies'.

Today, this shift is evident in the truth-claims of suffering, which move from an emphasis on suffering as external reality, validated by objective criteria of authenticity, to suffering as subjective knowledge, validated by psychologically grounded criteria of authenticity. It is also evident in a shift in the moral agency of suffering from a disposition that is oriented towards the distant other, acknowledging human vulnerability as a cause for our action, to a disposition that is oriented towards the self, acknowledging consumerism as a key motivation of our humanitarian engagements – discussed earlier as the post-humanitarian disposition.

What I attempt to do next, then, is understand and evaluate this paradigmatic shift towards post-humanitarianism by addressing the following questions: what do these changes in the authentication of suffering tell us about the kind of public life we inhabit today? Is cosmopolitan solidarity still possible in this age of 'feel good' activism? And how can we imagine alternative ways of performing solidarity with vulnerable others?

I first discuss post-humanitarianism as a paradigm shift from a solidarity of pity to that of irony, claiming that, whilst post-humanitarianism resonates with basic features of the ironic condition, as developed in Rorty's account of solidarity (1989), it also points to crucial limitations of irony as a desirable culture of solidarity (in the section 'Post-humanitarianism: Solidarity as Irony'). This is, I contend, because irony is not simply a cultural sensibility characteristic of our times. It is also an ambivalent political project firmly grounded on the neoliberal 'spirit' of capitalism – a politics that, in seeking to maximize the commercial and technological efficiency of the imaginary, risks transforming our moral bonds with vulnerable others into narcissistic self-expressions that have little to do with cosmopolitan solidarity (in 'Post-humanitarianism as Neoliberalism'). In response, I propose an account that goes beyond pity and irony in order to argue for a solidarity of agonism – a solidarity that no longer focuses exclusively on our own feelings about the sufferer's pain but on creating what Arendt calls 'a common, shared world' wherein collective action to change the conditions of suffering may become both thinkable and possible in the West (in 'Beyond Irony: Solidarity as Agonism).

Post-humanitarianism: solidarity as irony

Given the complex overdetermination of its economic, technological and political dimensions, the post-humanitarian imaginary cannot possibly be defined through one single attribute of its genres. If the post-humanitarianism of appeals resides in the performativity of its texts, inviting reflection on our own lifestyle vis-à-vis the vulnerable other, that of celebrity is manifested in his or her embodied performance of a confessional intimacy that displaces the voice of the sufferer onto the emotional world of the star. And whereas the post-humanitarianism of the news abandons journalistic objectivity for snippets of personal testimony, on Twitter or in mobile phone snapshots, that of concerts replaces the oppositional romanticism of rock with the pragmatism of elite politics.

What renders the moral disposition performed by these genres post-humanitarian, then, are neither its links with the entertainment industry nor its reliance on new technologies alone – though see pp. 182–6 for a return to both. Rather, what marks the post-humanitarian disposition is a profound shift in the epistemic basis of humanitarianism away from the moral gravity of distant suffering-qua-suffering and towards a reliance to 'our own' truths as a guarantee of the authenticity of suffering. Emerging in different guises across the genres of the imaginary, this moral disposition appears to be both a consequence of and a response to the universalisms of pity, which, in the form of either charitable giving or denunciatory critique, were premised upon unquestionable moral truths – salvation or revolution. It is, as I argued throughout this book, the problematization of these universal truths that have, at least partly, led to scepticism towards solidarity and have contributed to compassion fatigue. The lesson drawn from such fatigue by IOs and INGOs seems to be that, since external truths are now met with doubt, the spectacle of suffering should better turn such doubt into its very motivation for action.

This fatigue of universalisms, at the heart of contemporary ethics, indeed marks, according to Rorty, an important shift from traditional conceptions of solidarity grounded on the belief in 'humanity as such' towards a solidarity manifested precisely as self-doubt: 'doubt about their [the people's] own sensitivity to the pain and humiliation of others, doubt that present institutional arrangements are adequate to deal with this pain and humiliation, curiosity about possible alternatives' (1989: xvi). It is this affirmation of self-doubt as the driving force of, rather than as an obstacle to, solidarity that post-humanitarianism comes to reflect. Turning the paradox of authenticity inherent in the theatre of pity from problem into resource, epistemic doubt further situates this post-humanitarian ethic within a broader historical condition, what Rorty calls the 'culture of irony' (1989).

Grounded as it may be on self-doubt, the culture of irony differs nonetheless from the radical relativism of postmodern culture in that it recognizes in human suffering that minimal, yet crucial, moral claim to solidarity that remains irreducible to any language game and defines the nature of sociality in our culture. Solidarity as irony, in this sense, flourishes within a world of situated meanings and values not in the form of a universal truth, as rationalist philosophies would have it, but in the form of stories of suffering that, by way of 'sentimental education', mundanely cultivate the virtue of 'being kind to others as *the only social bond that is needed*' (Rorty 1989: 93, emphasis added).

What is ironic, then, about this mode of solidarity is a certain knowingness about the inescapable constraints under which solidarity is today practised. Even though it claims the status of a 'first principle', in that it is the question 'Are you in pain?' that constitutes our moral life, solidarity cannot possibly be performed as a transcendental obligation towards the 'mass of mankind [sic]' (Rorty 1989: 164). It can only be performed as a contingent belief that, much as it may guide the course of our everyday lives, always remains limited by the constraints of history – societal and personal. This move beyond the solidarities of conviction, premised on the claim that 'a belief can be . . . thought worth dying for', and towards a solidarity of self-doubt, whereby 'this belief is caused by nothing deeper than contingent historical circumstance' (1989: 189), lies at the heart of the ironic disposition of solidarity.

Vulnerability and show business: the rhetorical irony of the humanitarian imaginary

This 'dispositional' irony of post-humanitarianism is reflected in the aesthetic properties of its communicative genres – what we may call, accordingly, the 'rhetorical' irony of the humanitarian imaginary (for a discussion, see Szerszynski 2007: 340–3). Whereas the only instance of rhetorical irony I have so far identified is the irony of appeals, irony is, in fact, a constitutive property of all contemporary practices of the imaginary.

The rhetorical irony of appeals, let us recall, relies on various forms of semiotic juxtaposition which create a distance from our own privileged existence and urge us to reflect on the poverty of the South not through moral argumentation but through the affective estrangement that these forms of distance enable. Rhetorical irony is, in this context, an elliptical form of communication that remains silent on the vulnerable other so as to gesture towards the knowingness of the West – a savvy consumer of the mega-brands of the United Nations and Amnesty International, fully familiar with the advertising tropes through which these brands promote themselves in the media market.

Beyond the strategic intertextuality of INGO branding, however, rhetorical irony further resides in the intertextual references of celebrity advocacy and solidarity concerts. Both these genres of the imaginary, in different ways, work by capitalizing on the performativity of celebrity so as to invest the cause with the star aura of Angelina Jolie or Bono. In celebrity advocacy, this process relies on Jolie's 'impersonation' of suffering, which brings together her public persona with her voicing (or personification) of the sufferer's condition. What is distinctive about Jolie's impersonating style, as opposed to Hepburn's, is the deliberate fusion of her humanitarian profile as a spokesperson for the voiceless with her professional status as a Hollywood star and her private status as an individual of legendary wealth. Rhetorical irony here relies on a different kind of juxtaposition which, rather than performed in text, as in appeals, is now performed by the celebrity herself – the juxtaposition between her solidarity with the poorest of the world and her own extraordinary existence as one of the richest.

In a similar manner, the solidarity concert relies on the performance of 'charisma', which enables rock stars such as Bono and Geldof to seduce their publics both as fans loyal to rock music and as citizens who express solidarity with vulnerable others. Irony, here, resides in the juxtaposition between the enchantment of rock music and the acute corporatization of the concert, further confirming the philanthro-capitalist claim that humanitarianism is at its most effective when practised by the rich and famous. Both cases bring forth the systemic paradox of humanitarianism, namely, that the power of celebrity activism is premised upon the very divide between utter destitution and extreme wealth that such activism brings into focus. It is again, here, people's bitter knowingness of the close alliance between solidarity and show business that becomes the condition for, rather than an obstacle to, the communication of a cause.

Such knowingness further informs the practice of journalism as a co-creation between professionals and media users, including humanitarian INGOs. What convergent journalism introduces into the dominant news-making culture is, as I argued, a break with the truth-claims of television news; rather than accepting the authority of journalistic objectivity, news publics are all too aware of the agenda-setting power of the industry and use their platforms strategically to provide alternative accounts of events. The rhetorical irony of the Haiti earthquake live blogging rests, in this sense, in the rise of ordinary testimony in BBC news, which may claim to represent a democratic 'bricolage' of the voices of disaster, yet capitalizes upon the technological wealth of the West and speaks its voice.

What this discussion demonstrates is that rhetorical irony, the aesthetic dimension of post-humanitarianism, does not simply appeal to a pre-existing public already aware of the precarious truths of solidarity but, as the performativity of the imaginary suggests, rhetorical irony creates this sceptical disposition through its very representations of suffering. Semiotic juxtapositions, non-linear narratives and intertextual performances are, in this sense, some of the aesthetic choices through which the systemic paradox of humanitarianism becomes part of the dispositional irony of the imaginary today.

Lifestyle solidarity: the dispositional irony of the humanitarian imaginary

Yet, even if dispositional irony cannot exist without its rhetorical manifestations, neither do such manifestations emerge in a vacuum. It is the historical conditions of humanitarianism, the historicity of the imaginary, that enable the emergence of irony as a key aesthetic trope – in a move between performativity and history that, in chapter 3, I have theorized as a 'dialectics of change'.

Instrumentalization, the managerial practices and knowledges of humanitarianism, technologization, the use of new media as vehicles of self-expression, and the retreat of 'grand narratives' are, let us recall, the three key changes in the humanitarian imaginary that have led to the rise of irony as a key paradigm of humanitarian communication today. Whilst the rhetorical aspects of these transformations are evident in the aesthetic properties of humanitarian practices, as discussed above, their moral and political aspects are evident in the individuated ways by which western publics are asked to perform solidarity: the online activism of campaigns, the post-populist advocacy of celebrity and the proliferation of e-testimonies in disaster journalism.

This individuated activism, often justified as an effective response to compassion fatigue, has been contrasted to the robust culture of mass protest in the 1960s and 1970s and criticized as an atrophy of civil society that needs to return to politics proper (e.g., Marks & Fischer 2002). The ironic disposition that informs contemporary activism, however, invites a more complex approach to the changes of the humanitarian imaginary that neither the compassion fatigue thesis nor the return-to-politics call are able to grant. In order to better understand these changes, I now revisit two aspects of the moral agency of humanitarianism, as they developed in the course of time: the shift *from collective to lifestyle agency* and the shift *from the vulnerable other to the self* as a cause for action.

A conception of moral agency as collective is evident in the early humanitarian appeals of pity, where communication centred around the evocation of 'grand emotions', indignation against the perpetrators of injustice and empathy towards their victims – Amnesty International spearheading the former strategy through protest demonstrations and massive letter-writing to undemocratic regimes, in the 1960s and 1970s. Even though not all genres enable similar forms of hands-on activism, all nonetheless evoke their publics as a collective actor. Live Aid addresses a politically oppositional audience that romantically aspires to join forces so as to 'feed the world', whilst the UN celebrity, by addressing her audience in the name of the organization she represents (remember Hepburn's ambassadorial style), calls up not only a transnational order of governance but also the figure of the 'global public' as an actor with significant legitimizing power; disaster reporting, finally, belongs to a 'journalism of unification' that uses objectivity as the device to gather its audiences around 'the' truth of suffering and, thus, tends to construe a unified West beyond points of view.

Lifestyle agency, in contrast, emerges in today's appeals that encourage a light-touch activism, where online petitions or donations are part of the multitasking of everyday desk life and where care for vulnerable others may take place through tweeting one's feelings, following celebrity online or buying the 'Make Poverty History' wristband. Solidarity is here embedded in a public culture of consumption and an ethos of mutual benefit with minimal effort.[1]

This public ethos points to the second major shift in moral agency across time – one that not only posits the individual self as the source of solidarity, but further legitimizes this self, rather than the vulnerable other, as the justification for action. This other has been, let us recall, a central figure in the appeals of pity, where both 'negative' and 'positive' performativities were criticized for failing to humanize the sufferer, whilst solidarity concerts were equally met with suspicion for sublimating distant suffering and depoliticizing the causes of famine. Celebrity advocacy and journalism, in their different ways, also thematized the vulnerable other as a cause for action: Hepburn, through a dispassionate form of witnessing that backgrounded her own status so as to allow the voice of the sufferer to be heard, and the journalist, through detached and testimonial forms of witnessing that focused on the realities of earthquake victims.

The presence of the vulnerable other tends, in contrast, to recede in contemporary humanitarian genres. Appeals shift towards a focus on 'us' rather than the other, or represent this other in aesthetic genres associated with new media fiction – computer games or advertising; similarly, concerts abandon the representation of vulnerability as part of a post-colonial politics of the West and focus instead on celebrity and the triumphant imagery of beautiful survivors. In a parallel process, celebrity advocacy adopts a confessional style of communication that indistinguishably fuses the voice of the sufferer with that of the star, whilst convergent journalism replaces the voice of the news with dispersed citizen voices, locating therapeutic discourse at the centre of its narratives of suffering.

By moving away from a collective, other-oriented conception of agency, dispositional irony further marginalizes the key 'why' question. Instead of employing moral argument to justify action of suffering, dispositional irony favours a variety of eloquent short cuts: the organizational brand, the celebrity catchphrase, the concert star or the bricolage of e-postings. Motivated by the ambition to minimize self-doubt, lifestyle solidarity becomes instead an effortless extension of everyday life that responds to our individual consumer needs whilst minimizing our engagement with human vulnerability.

Post-humanitarianism as neoliberalism

The irony of post-humanitarian practices is an empirical manifestation of Rorty's normative theory of solidarity. Rather than a utopian ideal, flourishing only in philosophical imagination, irony emerges today through these popular practices as a palpable proposal for moral agency that routinely defines the ways we perform solidarity in the West. If their strategies of authenticity turn the doubt of the self into a source of the truth of suffering, their strategies of moralization turn the desires of the self into a cause for action on suffering.

What these post-humanitarian strategies introduce into western public culture, I argue, is a utilitarian rationality at the heart of its ethics of solidarity – a shift from the idea that doing good to others without expecting a response is both desirable and possible to the idea that doing good to others is desirable when there is something to gain from the act. Whilst no form of solidarity is devoid of a self-oriented component, as a number of theorists beyond Rorty have argued, there is a distinct quality to the utilitarian solidarity of post-humanitarianism.

Unlike the collectivist solidarity of pity, where personal benefit is situated within an other-oriented moral vision or deferred in a future temporality (in the solidarities of salvation and revolution), the solidarity of irony is conceived as personal benefit within one's own life project and is consumed in the here and now. It favours an instantaneous engagement with celebrity appeals, concerts, online news or graphic animation appeals and invites immediate gratification through forms of e-activism. Far from claiming that these genres determine the responses of their publics in fully predictable ways, a question open to empirical research, their rhetorical patterns indicate that lifestyle solidarity responds to the challenges of compassion fatigue by replacing an ethos of longer-term commitment with a closer-to-life altruism of the everyday – what Eagleton playfully refers to as 'the banality of goodness' (2009: 273).

Even though spectacle and commodity have always been integral components of the humanitarian imaginary, the utilitarian solidarity of post-humanitarianism, I contend next, reflects and reproduces a specifically *neoliberal* conception of humanitarianism that replaces conviction with consumption (Rose 1999; Lemke 2001). Neoliberalism is broadly defined as the generalization of the market logic beyond the sphere of commercial exchange, recasting 'non-economic areas and forms of action in terms of economic categories' with a view to legitimizing the logic of economic profit over other forms of political or moral legitimacy (Lemke 2001: 198), but two specific features of neoliberalism are particularly relevant to post-humanitarianism: its *pragmatism*, which turns the communication of solidarity into artful story-telling, rather than also using it as a resource for judgement on the politics of vulnerability; and its *privatism*, which situates acts of solidarity within the private realm and aims at empowering consumers, rather than cultivating dispositions of other-oriented care.

Pragmatism: the marginalization of judgement

Humanitarian stories where famine is framed by our own experience of what 'not eating' is about, where distant disaster is mediated through an 'I'm-praying-for-them' tweet from London and where the necessity for health policies in Africa is narrated through a celebrity's fears about her own adopted child tell us much more than the cause that they attempt to communicate. They tell us something about the ways in which we come to imagine the world outside ourselves. Emanating from and, in turn, confirming a culture of self-doubt, this is a pragmatic imagination that, rather than relying on principles upon which we must act, relies instead on the stories we tell one another as the best possible justification for action. If, indeed, as Rorty puts it, 'there is no synoptic view of culture which is more than a narrative account of how our culture managed to get where it now is' (2008: 67), then the pragmatism of post-humanitarianism consists in a rejection of universal discourse about the world and a celebration of ourselves as the only possible source of morality.

Solidarity as story-telling

Building upon the belief that the sources of knowledge cannot be located outside personal experience, a key premise of nineteenth-century pragmatist philosophy, neo-pragmatism radicalizes this subjectivist conception of knowledge by further claiming that there can be no grand narrative that justifies moral action beyond the cultural repertoire of stories that help us imagine ourselves as actors of solidarity within our own communities of belonging.

In its celebration of the contingency of all knowledge, neo-pragmatism converges with the radical politics of deconstruction – the latter also placing the challenge of universal truths at the centre of its project of social critique. Yet, unlike the politics of deconstruction which challenges philosophical universals so as to ultimately attack neoliberal politics for using those universals to mask unequal relations of power, neo-pragmatism defends the political project of neoliberalism as the best option we have (Geras 1995; Eagleton 1990).

It is Rorty's figure of the 'liberal ironist' that best exemplifies the neo-pragmatist ethos (1989: 15). Much like the post-humanitarian activist who expresses her/his solidarity with distant others from the comfort of their living room, the liberal ironist situates what Rorty calls the 'vocabulary of justice' within a context of 'standard bourgeois freedoms', which enable the liberal ironist to both remain sceptical of any truth-claims as to the reality of those others and, simultaneously, to act upon their suffering as part of her/his own personal project of self-fulfilment. If, therefore, the imperative to reduce suffering marks the liberal's commitment to the public realm of solidarity, the question of justification that informs this moral imperative is treated as inherently unresolvable in the public realm and, hence, as belonging to the private realm of the ironist. Rorty's 'private irony, liberal hope' formulation captures this seemingly paradoxical moral subjectivity that nonetheless dominates the humanitarian imaginary today: whilst public hope can be sustained by our altruistic response to the question 'Are you in pain?', it is private irony that informs such response insofar as our solidarity relies not on our conviction of a common humanity but on sentimental stories of suffering that touch our feelings (1989: 73–95).

An important consequence follows from this. In situating public action within a rationality of private scepticism, the neo-pragmatist imagination separates the cultural dimension of solidarity, where emphasis falls on self-expressive stories that speak of our commitment to vulnerable others, from the political dimension of solidarity, where emphasis falls on understanding human vulnerability as a question of injustice. Whilst, as I argued in chapter 2, these two dimensions of the humanitarian imaginary are always implicated with one another, their post-humanitarian separation privileges the cultural over the political. If it is through stories of suffering that we become accustomed to a 'vocabulary of justice' rather than through the argumentative justification of justice, then solidarity becomes exclusively a matter of training the soul rather than a matter of understanding the causes of suffering and debating our responses to it.

It is precisely this view of solidarity as sentimental education that dominates the post-humanitarian imaginary. Catalysed by processes of technologization, humanitarian communication has today ceased to appeal to the imagery of vulnerable others and to justification for action about these others, and relies instead on mediated self-expression – 'artful' stories that speak to the private ironist. The introspection of campaigns, the intimate life of celebrity, the disenchanted enchantment of the concert and the therapeutic discourse of disaster reporting are all, in this sense, claims to authenticity that abandon earlier references to the truth of emaciated bodies or factual discourse so as to ground public action on the truth of the self.

Yet, we might ask, how does such truth provide a place through which we can recognize the vulnerable other as an other with her or his own humanity? Or wherefrom we could reflect critically upon our own culture and upon the power relations that this culture perpetuates on a global scale? Instead of addressing such questions, neo-pragmatism favours what Singer calls a 'complacent' view of culture as devoid of power relations and social conflict (1972/2008: 1822–42).

Solidarity as artistic critique

In order to fully grasp the implications of this complacent ethos for the humanitarian imaginary, it is crucial to locate the triumph of Rorty's neo-pragmatism within the trajectory of instrumentalization – the historical process by which the humanitarian field gradually came to adopt the managerial practices of the corporate sphere. Even though instrumentalization is often criticized for allowing the market to colonize the aid and development field, in fact its impact amounts to more than a one-sided domination of the field by corporate forces.

Instrumentalization, as I mention in chapter 1, should best be approached as a complex process that is driven by the radical critique of past practices and aims at transcending such critique through the dynamic management of its communicative apparatus (Boltanski & Chiapello 2005). In order to pursue its strategic interest, that is to formulate an ever-stronger justification of humanitarianism in the global market, instrumentalization works, thus, by reflexively appropriating and re-employing the critical discourses already formulated against earlier humanitarian performances – what, in chapter 2, I discussed as the critique of the spectacle and the critique of empire. If the critique of the spectacle, Boltanski and Chiapello's 'artistic critique' of capitalism, challenges the claims to authenticity that mediated communication makes to distant suffering, the critique of empire, their 'social critique' of capitalism, challenges the historical relations of capitalism that are responsible for existing divisions in wealth and well-being across the globe (Boltanksi & Chiapello 2005: 165–7).

The instrumentalization of the humanitarian field, I suggest, has today incorporated these two challenges in ways that thematize artistic critique as an explicit dimension of its communicative practices, whilst rendering social critique peripheral to them. This is evident in the authentication strategies of post-humanitarianism which openly problematize the authenticity claims of earlier styles of humanitarian communication. The hyper-real aesthetic of campaigns, for instance, problematizes the photorealism of earlier textualities of suffering, whereas the hyper-celebritization of UN advocacy breaks with Hepburn's somewhat formal 'ambassadorial' style in favour of Jolie's emotional, 'saturated' self that leaves no doubt as to the authenticity of her performance. Similarly, concerts abandon their reliance on the facts of vulnerability to rely instead on charismatic celebrity as a readily authenticated figure of solidarity, whilst the ordinary voices of online news are a response to the 'manufactured' truths of traditional reporting. At the same time, in avoiding the question of 'why', these new practices marginalize the presence of social critique – appeals flag the brand rather than the cause, journalism privileges testimony over analysis and celebrity frames 'big picture' argument through confessional discourse or enchanted consumerism.

This does not mean that the vocabulary of justice is absent from these genres. Far from it. It could be argued, in fact, that it is the very proliferation of this vocabulary that enables post-humanitarian performances to emerge in the first place: the elliptical character of humanitarian branding, for instance, presupposes our familiarity with a vocabulary of justice and taps upon our already existing awareness of human rights as a cause for action; the entrepreneurial activism of Jolie rests on criticisms of Hepburn's morality of salvation, which prioritized the alleviation of suffering at the expense of questions of development; Live 8 similarly relies on a bold move to link mass entertainment with the political agenda of fair trade and, finally, convergent journalism links the co-creation of news with the rationale of the de-westernization of journalism.

Even though these insinuations of a vocabulary of justice could be seen as performing what Benhabib (2007) calls a series of 'democratic iterations', that is, a chain of ethico-political claims that catalyse debate and action in the mediated public realm, they do not, in fact, constitute a resource for the exercise of judgement. What renders judgement marginal to these messages is the fact that these iterations do not raise the question of justice as a systemic paradox of the West. Informed as they are by the neutral discourse of human rights as individual entitlements, be these the entitlement of a prisoner to be executed or of the survivor in the rock concert, these references to justice not only disconnect suffering from questions of systemic inequality but further subordinate it to an instrumentalized discourse of western self-empowerment. The democratic iterations of these performances are, in this sense, fully embedded in the story-telling conventions of the post-humanitarian genres and always formulated as subordinate to a 'vocabulary of authenticity' as the only legitimate source of knowledge of the world.

As a consequence, rather than providing us with the resources to judge the predicament of vulnerable others, these performances present us with short cuts to judgement, hinting at justice but always tending towards corporate persuasion: Amnesty International promotes its global brand to maximize consumer loyalty; Jolie, a mega-brand of the film industry, increases the authority of the star system; Live 8 renews the legitimacy of the digital media industry; and the BBC markets citizen journalism as the 'new democracy' of global broadcasters. This marginalization of judgement, in turn, allows little space for accounts of humanitarianism that may touch on solidarity as a project for social change. By being prevented, as McCarthy puts it, 'from even thinking . . . the thought that the basic structures of society might be inherently unjust in some way, that they might work to the systematic disadvantage of certain social groups' (1990: 367), the neo-pragmatist moral imagination favours both historical amnesia and apolitical activism.

Privatism: the marginalization of empathy

Online petitions, ethical consumption and citizen reporting are some of the key performances of ironic solidarity available in post-humanitarianism. In their refusal to engage our capacity for judgement, these proposals speak directly to the liberal ironist – a western figure reluctant to act out a solidarity of conviction, yet harbouring a visceral moral sense that guides our own altruistic response to human suffering.

Narcissistic publics

Even though this commitment to vulnerable others situates the lifestyle solidarity of the ironist within the public realm, the disposition of the liberal ironist remains resolutely private, insofar as justification of action on vulnerable others is ultimately a matter of personal empowerment.

Closely linked to the new affordances of self-expression inherent in interactive media, this is evident in appeals, which promise to enhance our social conscience ('This is not the Atkins diet' or 'Be Humankind'), or ensure the impact of our actions ('Your petitions are more powerful than you think', AI), and in convergent journalism, where the therapeutic sharing of personal experience is celebrated as the power of ordinary people to author the news. Similarly, both celebrity performances, in their different ways, capitalize on the empowering potential that identification with global stars bears upon audiences – Live 8 is about enhancing our social conscience through the cool consumerism of rock, whilst Jolie functions as the ultimate role model of lifestyle solidarity.

If, then, pragmatism is responsible for cutting judgement off the public expression of solidarity, privatism is further responsible for construing this judgement as the exercise of our free choice within our own 'self-created, autonomous, human life' (Rorty 1989: xiv). It is this conception of solidarity as free choice that informs the utilitarianism of post-humanitarian communication. Utilitarianism, I have already argued, turns the moral imperative to act on vulnerable others without asking back into an imperative that ultimately anticipates rewards for the self – consumer empowerment and celebrity pleasure. Yet, post-humanitarianism is utilitarian in one more sense. Insofar as solidarity is presented as a matter of choice about how to live our lives, rather than (also) as a practice of how we may imagine vulnerable others as others with humanity, then the communication of solidarity ceases to be about habituating publics into ways of engaging with the world beyond our own and becomes an effort to better connect with ourselves so as to be able to act on others. The new emphasis on celebrity confessions, ordinary testimony, enchanted spectacle or self-reflexivity shows, indeed, that emotional introspection lies at the heart of contemporary solidarity.

The neoliberal privileging of artistic over social critique here goes beyond just marginalizing rational argument in favour of corporate catchphrases. It also marginalizes the reality of suffering in favour of stories about 'us' as the only authentic voice that can speak about the world at large. This move is narcissistic, then, insofar as the turn to the self blurs the boundary between 'us' and the world, rendering our emotions the measure upon which to evaluate the experience of others: 'social relationships of all kinds', as a consequence, become or 'are real, believable and authentic the closer they approach the inner psychological concerns of each person' (Sennett 1977: 259). Mirroring these psychological concerns, the narcissistic agency of post-humanitarianism is exhausted in online clicks on the 'donate', 'sign a petition', 'like' and 'buy' links that, in the name of self-empowerment, subtly inserts the desires of the self into ever-expanding circuits of consumption. Neoliberal capitalism manages, in this way, to shape the post-humanitarian self precisely by 'making the economic self emotional and emotions more closely harnessed to instrumental action' (Illouz 2007: 23).

Rather than exercising free will, post-humanitarianism is, I argue, a technology of the self that has come to regulate our will within the field of instrumental relations that today defines the humanitarian imaginary in the first place. Branding, celebrity and Twitter journalism may, indeed, be occasions for self-expression but, at the same time, they are also commercial discourses that craft their publics primarily as consumers – of advertising, entertainment and the news. In blurring this crucial boundary between the means and ends of solidarity, what post-humanitarianism proposes is a civic disposition that may be hinting at a vocabulary of justice, yet ultimately remains incapable of going beyond the promise of pleasurable consumption.

Ethnocentric cosmopolitanism

Solidarity as personal preference does not only construe the West as a narcissistic public. It also construes the vulnerable other as a quasi-fictional figure – an individual inhabiting what Rorty calls 'the world of literary culture' (1989: 80). Just as the solidarity of the ironist belongs to the realm of the private, whereby choices appear to be made independently of the field of social forces that define it, so the vulnerability of the other is also regarded as a private matter: the prisoner about to be executed in the AI appeal, the destitute refugee in the celebrity story, the earthquake orphan in the NGO email or the survivor in the concert all enter the realm of public performance as 'strange' figures of undeserved suffering that invite our response.

What these figures lack is historicity. Even though they may be linked to past facts and a rhetoric of dignity, they are not presented as historical beings who inhabit an unequal world and experience the dire consequences of its inhuman distribution of resources, material and symbolic. The post-humanitarian sufferer is, consequently, a private sufferer not in the sense that her/his stories lack a 'vocabulary of justice' but, rather, in the sense that this vocabulary becomes, again, subordinate to stories about 'us'. Appeals aestheticize (or avoid) the presence of the poor, convergent news fragments the sufferer's voice through the voices of people like 'us', celebrity appropriates this voice through her or his own affective personification of their suffering and the concert is more about the cool of rock rather than the cause of solidarity. Just as there is a separation between the cultural and political dimensions of solidarity, which ultimately marginalizes judgement in favour of self-empowerment, there is here an equivalent insulation between the public and private dimensions of the vulnerable other which renders her/his suffering public but keeps his/her history and aspirations out of view.

As a consequence, post-humanitarianism may aim at combating fatigue towards traditional iconographies of suffering but simultaneously deprives this sufferer of her/his own humanity. As the empire theorists remind us, the quality of humanity cannot be taken for granted as a universal property of our species but is constructed through particular performative practices, which selectively humanize certain figures rather than others, in the humanitarian imaginary. By construing the sufferer through the fictional aesthetics of branding or by ventriloquizing her/his voice through that of celebrity, what post-humanitarianism manages to do is to unequally distribute the quality of humanity among its communicative figures. It over-humanizes the benefactor, who always lies at the centre of the economic and cultural power of the West, but systematically dehumanizes the sufferer, who already lies outside such centres of power and visibility.

Post-humanitarianism enacts, in this sense, an ethnocentric cosmopolitanism that reserves the vocabulary of justice for those who belong to the national spheres of western politics but uses an apolitical and dehumanizing discourse in the transnational sphere of development politics. Instead of enabling us to hear their voice and get an insight into their lives, it treats distant others as voiceless props who cannot, in themselves, become anything more than shadow figures in someone else's story.

The privatism of post-humanitarianism, in summary, manifests itself both in its conception of western publics, where solidarity is construed as a matter of self-empowerment, and in its conception of the vulnerable other, which deprives her/his suffering of a vocabulary of justice and so of the possibility for it to be part of a politics of social change.

The tearful celebrity, the rock concert, the Twitter hype and the graphic animation are, I suggest, prototypical performances of post-humanitarianism which limit our resources for reflecting upon human vulnerability as a political problem of injustice and minimizes our capacity of empathy with vulnerable others as others with their own humanity. In proposing a solidarity of self-empowerment, where our preference for a cause depends on our affiliation to a brand or the star appeal of a celebrity, post-humanitarianism simultaneously treats western publics more as a means to the accomplishment of certain ends – sign, donate or buy online – and less as ends in themselves – as citizens who may engage with distant suffering because we believe in a better world. In the solidarity of irony, as McIntyre would put it, 'others are always means, never ends' (1981/2006: 24).

Beyond irony: solidarity as agonism

Pity and irony, the two historical paradigms of the humanitarian imaginary, fail to legitimize the moral imperative to act on vulnerable others. Pity is associated with a solidarity of moral universalism, which is today challenged by a widespread scepticism towards all given 'truths', and irony is associated with a solidarity of moral particularism, which relies upon private choice and utilitarian calculation. Whilst the latter emerges as a critique of the former, neither paradigm offers a politically and morally productive proposal for solidarity.

After reviewing 'The Ironic Critique of Pity', just below, I put forward an alternative proposal of solidarity as 'agonism', which is inspired by Hannah Arendt's account of public action as a matter of imaginative judgement. To this end, I return to the concept of the theatre as the most appropriate structure for imagining distant others as subjects of solidarity. This is, I argue, because the theatre can stage the spectacle of suffering not only as a practice of artistic critique, characteristic of irony, but also, importantly, as a practice of moral and political critique ('The Theatricality of Solidarity'). Finally, having coming full circle to the empirical focus of my work, the communicative genres of the imaginary, where I discuss how each one might be changed to inform this practice of critique, I end this book by reflecting on the quality of 'being good' that agonistic solidarity proposes to us ('Conclusion: On Being Good')

The ironic critique of pity

The solidarity of irony arises out of a historically specific 'spirit' of capitalism, neoliberalism, which generalizes the entrepreneurial logic of economic activity onto other spheres of social action and thereby renders solidarity a matter of consumerist choice. Whilst the technological activism of such solidarity may have increased donation rates, it has also privileged the pursuit of pleasures of the self over the morality of otherness and justice; in this imaginary, as Boltanski and Chiapello put it, 'nothing is worth protecting from commodification by mere virtue of its existence . . . and everything, accordingly, will be an object of commerce' (2005: 466). This pervasive instrumentalization of humanitarianism, however, does not occur in a vacuum. It comes to respond, as we know, to the post-Cold War retreat of 'grand narratives' which, amongst other things, challenged the 'objectivity' of suffering in the early genres of pity.

Pity, this ironic critique has it, misrecognizes the inevitable partiality of its own story-telling as a universal truth and thereby perpetuates global relationships of power under the noble guise of 'grand emotion'. 'Negative' and 'positive' appeals, let us recall, reflect a long history of neocolonial and interventionist humanitarian policies of the West, which sought to communicate the otherness of suffering under the unifying tropes of bare life (in negative) or assimilated humanity (in positive imagery), at the expense of misrepresenting distant others. Similarly, the objectivity of broadcasting may claim to present suffering as it is, yet its narrative choices selectively humanize certain sufferers rather than others, thereby contributing to the reproduction of global hierarchies of place and human life. If western citizens are worthy lives whilst non-western ones are unworthy, then pity can be just as ethnocentric and narcissistic as irony is (Chouliaraki 2006, 2008a,b).

Going beyond the figure of the sufferer, the ironic critique of pity further problematizes the subjectivity of the spectator. Similarly entangled into the often unexamined certainties of 'objective' representation, the spectator of distant suffering often becomes arbitrarily collectivized in the totalizing figure of the 'western actor' – be this figure the guilty westerner confronted with the imagery of emaciated children, the kind-hearted benefactor in Hepburn's testimonies or the impartial news viewer of early disaster reporting. Such construals of the western actor as a unified collectivity of conviction, irony claims, remain blind to the plurality of enactments of solidarity by particular actors in specific spaces and times – an argument that echoes the post-colonial critiques of the solidarity of revolution in chapter 1.

Rather than privileging a solidarity that allows both figures of suffering to emerge as historical beings, struggling with the moral and political dilemmas of their time, the paradigm of pity covers up such dilemmas in universalist discourses that take for granted the apolitical *agape* of salvation or the selective internationalism of revolution. At the heart of these positions, as I argued in chapter 1, lies the Enlightenment belief in common humanity, which irons out the plurality of discourses and practices of solidarity in the name of a self-assured yet orientalist moralism. The cosmopolitan ethics of pity, as Tomlinson puts it, belongs to 'a vision of technocratic,

Enlightenment universalism, largely untroubled by concerns of cultural difference . . . and populated by orderly, rational, co-operative moral agents who had transcended all cultural particularity' (2011: 355).

Irony, from this perspective, offers a useful critique of pity in that it shows how its self-righteous universalisms not only fail to sustain a legitimate claim to solidarity but lead, directly, to a generalized suspicion of certainties – Rorty's self-doubt. From the ironic standpoint, then, compassion fatigue is not so much a fatigue of the excess of human suffering that transcends our individual capacity to feel for or act on it, but rather, as I put it in chapter 3, a fatigue of the excess of moralizing discourses around which we are called to organize our feelings and actions towards suffering. This is an important inversion of responsibility because, in shifting the blame from the apathy of the West towards the failing performative practices through which the West is invited to engage with vulnerable others, irony draws attention to the genres of suffering as a crucial site upon which the politics of solidarity is played out.

Compatible with my conception of humanitarianism as a social imaginary, a relatively malleable communicative structure that produces various moral imaginations of solidarity, the ironic critique of pity offers a similar, performative view of solidarity that emphasizes the role of communication in the formation of moral dispositions. Unlike irony, however, which draws upon the depoliticized morality of human rights so as to legitimize a market-driven disposition of solidarity, I focus instead on the need to repoliticize the meaning of solidarity itself. The question I explore next, therefore, is *how* the humanitarian imaginary may be able to navigate beyond pity and irony so as to escape both the totalizing vision of the past and the neoliberal grip of the present. My starting point is, predictably perhaps, the communicative structure of the theatre.

The theatricality of solidarity

Irony and pity are not only different paradigms of solidarity but also distinct communicative structures of the humanitarian imaginary. Pity, I have argued, relies on the theatrical distance between stage or screen and spectator so as to enable us to imagine how someone else's suffering might feel like for her/him but also to imagine ourselves as actors upon this suffering. Whilst still operating with the metaphor of the stage or screen, irony has effectively eliminated the distance between spectator and stage that is instrumental in the politics of pity, its theatricality, and introduced, instead, a new distance – the distant within oneself: between one's conscience and one's lifestyle habits, in appeals, between one's voice and the voice of others like 'us', in post-television news, between one's desire for celebrity and the celebrity's impersonations of suffering others in celebrity advocacy. It is precisely by substituting the stage of the other with a mirror of the self that the post-humanitarian imaginary ends up as a theatre without theatricality.

The main consequence of the shift from a theatrical politics of pity to an anti-theatrical politics of irony is that the latter's spectacles of suffering give up their force as moral education. They cease, that is, to propose ways of feeling and thinking that may move us beyond the boundaries of our communities of belonging. Irony diminishes the educative force of the theatre because, in celebrating self-expression and in marginalizing the question of why, it severs the duality between feeling and thinking necessary for relationships of solidarity to be established with suffering others. The theatre, in contrast, functions as moral education precisely because it relies on this continuous enactment of both emotion and judgement in order to invite such relationships.

It is Arendt's theatrical conception of the public realm as a 'space of appearance', where 'everything . . . appears in public and can be seen and heard by everybody', that best captures the moralizing force that the theatricality of suffering may have upon the West (Villa 1999). Even though Arendt is suspicious of empathy as a private emotion that corrupts politics proper, her own vision of solidarity, Silverstone argues, does acknowledge that the spectacular element of 'appearing' for everybody to see, inherent in all public performance, is a necessary condition for the civic education of the cosmopolis (2007).

At the same time, aware of the radical asymmetries of the modern world, Arendt's claim is not that we all equally participate in the 'space of appearance' but, rather, that the task of actively construing this space as open for all to appear in is a moral stake in its own right and itself an act of solidarity. This is because it is only through such an inclusive space that the world can emerge as distinct from each one of us and acquire an 'objective' quality – it can become 'common to all of us and distinguished from our own privately owned place in it' (Arendt 1958/1998: 52). It is not surprising, then, that Arendt's critique of contemporary societies focuses on denouncing the reduction of plurality in the space of appearance and, importantly, its concomitant loss of the 'objectivity' of the world: 'What makes [contemporary] mass society so difficult to bear is not the number of people involved . . . but the fact that the world between them has lost its power to gather them together, to relate and to separate them' (1958/1998: 52–3).

This is an apt critique of the humanitarian imaginary, as both pity's appeal to common humanity and, particularly, irony's appeal to self-empowerment turn the space of appearance into a site of our own 'grand emotions' or our own private pleasures and, in so doing, exclude vulnerable others from our field of visibility. Both paradigms have, in other words, lost the power 'to relate and separate' people. The metaphor of the 'space of appearance', in contrast, performs the double act of relating and separating: it both brings 'us' and 'them' close together and, at the same time, keeps us apart from one another. It is, therefore, this space that should serve as our starting point for a new imagination of solidarity, 'agonistic' solidarity.

Even though agonism has been associated with a particular form of liberal democratic politics, radical democracy, that does not explicitly incorporate the theatrical dimension in its account of democracy (Laclau & Mouffe 1985; Mouffe 1992), my conception of agonistic solidarity relies heavily on the pedagogical process by which the theatre regulates both our affective proximity to and contemplative distance from vulnerable others, constantly seeking to engage us with the two key requirements of solidarity – emotion and argument.

Central to this educative potential of the theatre is the power of imagination, a symbolic process that, as I explained in chapter 2, complicates the dominant but impoverished conception of humanitarianism as spectacle and, in so doing, avoids the unproductive categorization of all imagery of suffering as commodity or simulacrum. By relying on a more complex view of humanitarian communication as performance that, depending on variations in its 'mise en scène', invites different responses towards vulnerable others, the theatre habituates us into dispositions of solidarity through the two key functions of theatrical imagination: the mobilization of empathy and the challenge of judgement (Marshall 1984 for these two dimensions of spectatorship).

Empathy, let us recall, draws attention to the force of the spectacle of suffering to set up an emotional relationship of identification between those who watch and those who suffer. This may take the form of tender-heartedness towards the benefactor and anger towards the persecutor (in pity) or gratification of the self (in irony), yet always relies on those performative strategies of the theatre that render the spectacle of suffering authentic in the eyes of its spectators. Judgement refers to the force of the spectacle to establish a contemplative distance between those who watch and those who suffer, raising the question of why, in a dual sense: why *this* suffering is important and what there is to do about it but also why suffering, *as a symptom of injustice*, is perpetuated and what can be done to change its conditions of existence. This aspect of spectatorship, let us recall, relies on performative strategies of moralization that may present the scene of suffering as either an irrelevant event or as a legitimate cause on which we may act. It is the dual function of spectatorship, in Moyn's words, to allow 'both for the recognition of the other's point of view and preserve a space for criticizing that point of view' (2006: 404) that renders the theatre an appropriate communicative structure for agonistic solidarity. Let me now briefly discuss each dimension in turn.

Empathy

This function of the theatre is about the welling up of emotion and emerges through our encounter with suffering others, staged as this is through the various performances of humanitarianism – the imagery of emergency appeals, the narratives of disaster news, the performance of rock stars or the witnessing of celebrity. Even though agonism inevitably relies on such dramatizations to evoke empathy, it differs from pity in that it refrains from regarding common humanity as the only source of empathetic emotion, and from irony, in that it does not give up the possibility of empathetic emotion altogether. Agonism, instead, grounds empathetic imagination upon what Arendt calls 'imaginative mobility', that is, the performance of the vulnerable other as a sovereign actor endowed with her/his own humanity.

The *inclusion of the sufferer's voice* is instrumental to the process of humanization because, as we already know, the quality of humanity cannot be taken for granted but is actively constructed through the presentation of the sufferer as an actor in the scene of suffering. It is, therefore, the way in which the sufferer's voice participates in the dramatization of suffering that can make a difference to our affective engagement with it; for, as Villa puts it, solidarity does not solely depend upon 'the rigorous logical unfolding of an argument . . . but rather [on] imaginative mobility and the capacity to represent the perspective of others' (1999: 96).

Despite Arendt's suspicion of sympathetic emotion, therefore, her 'imaginative mobility' can and should be theorized as an important dimension of empathy insofar as it draws attention to the importance of 'the perspective of others' in 'seeing and understanding everything that is too far as though it were our own affair' (Arendt 1994: 323). *Contra* irony, this position enables the vulnerable other to take centre-stage as an historical agent, that is, as someone who is seen to speak and act in her/his own context, striving to make a difference under systemic constraints of injustice. It is also because, *contra* pity, the inclusion of the other escapes the comfortable sensationalisms of bodily destitution or assimilated self-determination, characteristic of moral universalisms, and opens a space where this other may appear in often uneasy and discomforting performances, which nonetheless invite our empathy.

This is not easy. So far, the humanitarian imaginary has engaged with the other in a narcissistic manner – either through the sentimentalisms of pity, where the other is a site for the manifestation of our moral certainties, or through the self-absorption of irony, where the other is eclipsed in favour of our own voices. A crucial stake of agonistic solidarity is, in this context, to break with these different forms of subjectivism and to turn, instead, on the objectivity of the theatrical stage, where the other speaks to us through his/her own voice, 'so that', as Sen argues, 'each person's beliefs and utterances are not inescapably confined to some personal subjectivity that others may not be able to penetrate' (2009: 118). Estrangement is one representational trope that can produce more complex and, perhaps, more discomforting performances not only of others but also of ourselves – performances that, as I argue below, can today become available in the new mediated spectacles of the humanitarian imaginary.

Judgement

The second dimension of the theatre mobilizes the faculty of judgement and emerges through our encounter with moral argument as to why it is important to act on suffering. By raising the question of why, judgement challenges the separation between private justification and public self-expression inherent in the paradigm of irony. Far from private, as I have shown, the promise to self-empowerment that justifies post-humanitarian action is itself constitutive of this action and cannot be arbitrarily separated from it. The moral imperative to 'Be Humankind', for instance, construes action as the private choice of a western consumer, yet remains itself fully public insofar as it bears effects not only upon the performance of solidarity as a consumerist practice of brand recognition or celebrity fandom, but also upon vulnerable others by silencing their voices and annihilating their humanity.

The neoliberal attempt to separate private from public dimensions of solidarity should, in this sense, be seen as itself serving a specific project of power that ultimately legitimizes the instrumental rationality of the market that informs such action: 'by restricting irony and ironists to the private sphere,' Critchley (drawing on Connolly) says, 'Rorty might be said to refuse the possibility of a critique of liberal society that would use the strategy of public irony to uncover the power relations of liberalism, in the first place' (1994: 6). Instead, then, of approaching solidarity from a pragmatic perspective, as a claim to action that denies its own interest, agonism proposes that solidarity is a claim always driven by interests and, consequently, always open to struggle over which of these claims are to be heard and seen, praised or criticized, accepted or rejected: 'being seen and heard by others', as Arendt puts it, 'derive their significance from the fact that everyone sees and hears *from a different position*' (emphasis added). The voicing of standpoints (claims to public interest), rather than self-expressions (claims to private morality) is, therefore, crucial to a solidarity of agonism.

Far from arguing that humanitarian communication should become a heavy-handed lesson in the complexities of development, the requirement of judgement suggests that, *contra* irony, agonistic solidarity becomes explicit about the social values that inform its calls to action and problematizes human vulnerability as a question of global injustice, collective responsibility and social change. This means that instead of the commercialized genres of post-humanitarianism that keep the justification of action on suffering implicit, justice becomes a recurrent and systematic reference in humanitarian communication.

Interfering in the current struggle over the boundaries between humanitarianism and politics, today 'more visible' than ever, I argue that the explicit iteration to justice is the only morally legitimate alternative to the neoliberal 'spirit' of the imaginary and its depoliticizing effects – as, for instance, in the failure of 'Make Poverty History' campaign, which exhausted its potential for judgement to armband activism: 'in place of the values of economic injustice on which the campaign strategy was plotted,' as Darnton puts it, 'the consumerist values embodied in advertising, celebrities and fashion took centre stage' (2011: 40). Far from the consumerist buzz around brands, then, judgement here is about a particular form of public story-telling – 'telling stories that accord permanence to fleeting actions, crafting them into events whose meaning *can be open to public deliberation*' (Arendt 1961/1993: 73; emphasis added).

Judgement further suggests that, *contra* pity, agonism does not treat the meaning of solidarity as a universal truth, for, as Sen puts it, there may be many standpoints to injustice, various manifestations of collective responsibility and multiple visions of social change: 'there is no automatic settlement of differences between distinct theories here,' he says, 'but it is comforting to think that not only do proponents of different theories of justice share a common pursuit, they also make use of common human features that figure in the reasoning underlying their respective approaches' (2009: 415). It is precisely these features, namely 'to understand, to sympathise, to argue', Sen concludes, that makes it possible for us to escape privatism and become public, that is, to pursue consensus, practise deliberation or agree that we disagree. The debate around the meaning of human rights, for instance, as elaborated in mainstream views on development as 'good governance' and competing ones on development as 'freedom' (Sen 1999, 2009), 'capabilities' (Nussbaum and Sen 1993; Nussbaum 2011) or 'responsibility' (Giri 2003), is one of the domains in which a plurality of standpoints as to how the West can most effectively act on distant others can be debated in public. Even though each of these standpoints articulates its own universal truth, their public juxtaposition carves out a communicative space, wherein each simultaneously appears as a particular claim and becomes the object of judgement. It is, as Albrow and Seckinelgin put it, 'the fundamentally polysemic, polycentric diversity in the ideas of justice that animate civil society actors. . . . It is,' they continue, 'this diversity that can be the fertile bed for the full and free communication on which future cooperation depends' (2011: 4).

Similarly to empathy, such processes of judgement also require the objective space of the theatre in order to take place – a space of 'impartial spectatorship', to use Sen's preference for Adam Smith's vocabulary, wherein 'people can engage in debates about the correctness of the claims made by different persons' (Sen 2009: 118). Instead of appealing to the consumerist pleasures of online activism which, out of fear to switch off public support, avoids engagement with standpoints, agonistic solidarity insists that it is only by seeking to confront publics with meaningful dilemmas of action in concrete cases of suffering that the humanitarian imaginary may be able to catalyse civic disposition of solidarity beyond the West.

In conclusion, agonistic solidarity suggests that empathy alone, necessary as it may be for sympathetic identification, is an insufficient condition for solidarity insofar as, without judgement, emotion tends to collapse either into sentimentalism, as in pity, or into self-absorption, as in irony – both narcissistic engagements with distant others. Judgement, in contrast, introduces into the theatrical staging of solidarity the demand for impartial reflection: 'solidarity,' Arendt says, 'though it may be aroused by suffering, is not guided by it . . . ; compared with the sentiment of pity, it may appear cold and abstract, for it remains committed to "ideas" rather than to any "love" of men' (1963/1990: 84). Arendt's definition usefully foregrounds the value of a moral imagination of solidarity, which relies on the objectivity of the theatre to invite us to think harder about the values we stand for and enact. Important as this move from an 'artistic' towards a 'social' critique of capitalism may be, however, a key question remains: how might we today move beyond the existing performances of post-humanitarianism and imagine solidarity not only as a disposition but also as embodied action?

Action

Throughout this book, I have argued that the communicative practices of humanitarianism have a performative force: they are not 'mere words' to be consumed but act upon the world by constituting this world in meaning at the moment that they claim to represent it. This view also lies at the heart of

Arendt's view of public action as theatrical action. Indeed, her definition of the space of appearance considers the theatre to be not only a space where everything is there for all to see but also a space where 'seeing' and 'being seen' are not stable positions, fixed once and for all, but relatively flexible positions that may alternate with one another: 'the public realm', as she puts it, 'is constituted by the critics and the spectators, not the actors and the makers. And this critic and spectator sits in every actor' (Arendt 1982: 63).

This interchangeability of positions does not of course imply that spectators and sufferers empirically occupy alternate positions in an unproblematic manner. What it means, rather, is that construing the position of the spectator as if she/he were an actor is itself an important dimension of the pedagogical force of the theatre and should, therefore, become a key part of the performative repertoire of humanitarian genres. This is because, as Marshall puts it, the theatre does not simply enable us, spectators, to imagine vulnerable others as sovereign others with a voice but also helps us imagine ourselves as actors who respond to the spectacle of suffering (1984: 598). It is this internalized regard of others upon ourselves as-if we were actors on the scene of suffering, Smith's 'impartial spectator', that in fact constitutes the moralizing force of the theatre as judgement (1759/2000: 110).

Instead, then, of considering the moral imagination of the theatre to be solely a matter of engaging with distant others, we should see such imagination as also engaging us with our fellow spectators who, like us, raise their voice, debate their case and potentially act together with us in the name of a cause. The performances of agonism are, in this sense, not only about empathetic judgement but, in so being, also about public debate. Even though the retreat of solidarities of conviction, where activism was part of a robust civil culture, may be making the vision of mass politics rather hard to imagine today, agonistic solidarity must and can insist on the pedagogic potential of staging the spectator as actor – as someone capable of seeing him/herself thinking with and acting in a collective 'we' of other actors for a common cause (see Dayan 2001 for a similar point).

This is because public action, prototypically reflected in protest and donation practices, becomes most effective when it combines the symbolic power of words with the physical power of bodies – a process that Boltanski further describes in terms of the incorporation of speech in bodily gestures and movements; the presence of others, and the sacrifice of other possible actions (1999: 185). By thus incorporating physical action, in the form of a demonstration or a commemoration, effective speech goes beyond words to display values and commitments that may be hinted at but cannot be fully articulated in the online activism of post-humanitarianism.

Often described as a move from online to offline activism, this link between performance and collective action lies at the heart of the political efficacy of solidarity. Dahlgren talks about this move as the outcome of 'civic agency', a process of 'stepping into the public sphere, making sense of media representations of relevant developments and discussing current events with others; from there other actions may be taken' (2009: 76). Acknowledging that much of this mediated publicness takes place in the fleeting world of online interactions, Dahlgren does not nostalgically long for heroic forms of activism exercised by a fully informed citizenry. What he emphasizes, rather, is the importance of maintaining the symbolic space within which such activism can today remain a possibility.

For this to happen, agonistic solidarity needs to challenge the complacent performances of online activism that dominate the ironic genres of INGO branding and celebrity advocacy. Whilst the former reduces the radical potential of judgement inherent in 'estrangement' to self-empowering consumerism, the latter glorifies a post-populist model of activism and risks reducing civic agency to entertainment. Online activism needs, instead, to incorporate the dimension of 'political socialization' into its messages of solidarity: 'if internet-related practices are to improve the general preconditions of democratic engagement,' as Couldry, Livingstone and Markham put it, 'then internet-related habits must be articulated in a stable way with habits of political socialization (whether the latter remain stable or are themselves changing)' (2008: 113).

Two of the clearest examples of such online political socialization are the global protests in support of the Burma monks' protests in Rangoon, 2007, and against the Iranian election violence, 2009. Both are instances of transnational solidarity that broadly relied on user-generated content circulated in social networking and convergent journalism platforms. The technologization of solidarity demonstrates here its politicizing (rather than merely narcissistic) potential, in that it provides spaces of witnessing, catalyses deliberation and coordinates action across borders (Cammaerts & Carpentier 2007; Cammaerts 2008).

On a grander scale, the Middle East uprisings from Tunisia and Egypt to Bahrain, Oman and Syria (2011) similarly capitalized on the extensive use of new media to connect various peoples with their distinct visions of solidarity and justice in an unprecedented mass mobilization with real political effects. Such activism, which will no doubt soon get intense scholarly scrutiny, is characterized by three features of agonistic solidarity: they portray the sufferer as having a voice of her/his own without subjecting such voice to a single universalist narrative of change; they shift the positions of spectator and actor, rendering those who witnessed the uprising of others into actors of their own cause; and combine the online theatricality of suffering, in mediated imageries of violence, with the offline action of the physical spaces, prototypically Cairo's Tahrir Square, where tens of thousands joined their voices in a historic act of effective speech.

Compelling as the Middle East examples of agonistic solidarity are, however, they reflect a sensibility that lies far from the non-heroic disposition of managing the present, dominant in the neoliberal West. In our self-doubting cultures, I argue, what is needed is subtle but crucial rearticulations in the performative practices of humanitarianism, integrating empathy and judgement as the two crucial resources for our engagement with human vulnerability. By way of conclusion, I now return to estrangement as a promising performative trope that may act as a starting point for the mobilization of agonism in various genres of the imaginary.

Estrangement

Estrangement is a key performative strategy in the context of agonistic solidarity, both in that it is compatible with the dominant self-reflexive sensibility of the West and in that it is capable of capitalizing on this reflexivity to challenge more radically routine practices of denial and complicity in the West: 'The opportunity for self-knowledge is certainly worthwhile, but . . .', Gilroy suggests, 'it must take second place behind the principled and methodical cultivation of a degree of estrangement from one's own culture and history' (2004: 75). However, even though, as Sen reminds us, estrangement is embedded in Adam Smith's 'impartial' spectator as a position that enables us 'to view our sentiments from a certain distance from us' (2009: 45), the post-humanitarian use of the term has lost this productive potential.[2] This is because post-humanitarianism uses estrangement as a benign strategy of 'distance from the self', where reflecting on own habits and values is about 'feeling good' or 'being empowered' rather than (also) about challenging these values and the ways in which they may bear upon the world beyond us. What is needed for this to happen is, first, *exposure to otherness*, to a quality of humanity that invites empathy not through the various appropriations of otherness, characteristic of pity or irony, but precisely by challenging our notions of what or who the human is; and, second, *engagement with argument*, not in terms of the moral certainties of pity or the brand logos of irony, but as a systematic deliberation around social values and their justifications for solidary action.

With regard to *appeals*, one example that comes closer to an estranged representation of humanity, albeit not to the exposition of an argument, is Amnesty International's 'We Unsubscribe' appeal on torture. Entitled 'Waiting for the Guards', the appeal depicts a handcuffed and hooded prisoner who, squatting as he is between two cardboard boxes in the stress position, struggles to keep his balance. The appeal, as Amnesty says, 'is not acted and shows a performance artist being forced to enact the "Stress Position" used on actual prisoners'. Two features are characteristic of this appeal: the use of theatrical photorealism and the reversal of humanization. *Theatrical photorealism* refers to the use of realistic imagery that, unlike the imagery of pity, makes explicit its own constructed character yet, at the same time, in avoiding graphic animation, does not deprive suffering of its corporeal dimension. In explicitly referring to the acting-out of torture, the appeal self-consciously makes use of the theatricality of suffering in order to activate the full repertoire of sympathetic identification: empathy for the sufferer and indignation for the persecutor. Whilst the first sequence of the appeal concentrates on the immense physical strain that the stress position places on the human body, through close-ups of the prisoner's struggling muscles and the sound of his heavy breathing, the second turns to the torturer who, in the same physical space, uses his mobile phone to speak with his own child, with affection and care.

The reversal of humanization refers, therefore, to this symbolic process by which the sufferer is endowed with a sense of his own humanity whilst the westerner appears as an ambivalent figure, both like 'us' and thoroughly dehumanized. The sufferer's humanity is signified almost exclusively through the body language of extreme strain which, at the very moment of torture (and because of it), manages to register an extreme form of conditional agency. As the sufferer painfully struggles to balance his body on the cardboard box so as to avoid falling, his subjectivity similarly hovers between the tropes of bare life and dignified struggle without privileging any of the two. This liminal subjectivity, reflecting as it does the very instability inherent in all representations of humanity, relies on theatrical acting so as to momentarily invite us to feel his strain. The torturer, at the same time, is visualized as a person like 'us', dressed casually and appearing bored in the hours of inaction as he waits for his victim to succumb. The contrast between his banal goodness as a father, who asks his daughter to 'blow him a kiss', and the banal evil of his professionalism as, upon ending the phone call, he delivers a powerful blow to the victim's body, relies again on the theatricality of this appeal to problematize the moral boundaries between the familiar and the alien – the self as an other. It, importantly, also articulates the possibility for staging the West in ways that profoundly unsettle comfortable distinctions between good and evil.

Even though the appeal throws into relief the educative potential of theatrical estrangement as a practice that confronts us both with the humanity of otherness and with the otherness of the self, it remains resolutely post-humanitarian, in that its elliptical communication fails to contextualize the event beyond a minimal invitation to e-activism. Whereas empathy emerges here through a struggle between identification and disidentification, what is missing is the framing of torture in terms of a vocabulary of justice that links up with the question of how current global forms of governance perpetuate not only economic inequalities but also various forms of political violence around the world.

It is admittedly difficult to speak of estrangement in *celebrity advocacy* because its practices rely precisely on an unquestionable hegemony of the market-driven popular culture in the West. A process of challenging the certainties of this culture can take place, however, on the condition that IOs' dominant practices and knowledges become themselves the object of critical re-evaluation. This is important to the extent that crucial aspects of what chapter 1 discussed as the neoliberal practices and knowledges of the aid and development field are intimately connected to questions of IOs' legitimacy. Focusing, for instance, on the ways in which UN policies impact upon the institution's legitimacy and image, Alleyne argues that the UN's 'image problem stems not from a complacent world public that needs to be nudged to action by famous sports and entertainment figures but from skepticism about how it does its work' (2005: 183). Whilst the role of civil society in UN development policies privileges, as we saw, equal 'brand partnerships' between the UN and its western celebrity-ambassadors, civil actors on the ground enter, in contrast, into deeply 'asymmetrical' relationships with the UN, based not on respect for cultural difference and historical specificity but on the one-sided promotion of the UN's own conceptions of economic development and civil life as 'universal'.

A critical re-evaluation of the role of the UN in the sphere of global politics would, in this sense, inevitably also require a new approach to celebrity – one that may rely on a shift of emphasis away from the dominant figures of show business and towards new types of celebrity amongst those local activists whose heroic work makes a difference in their own communities of belonging: 'When contemplating the political clout of celebrity,' as Alleyne puts it, 'it is actually more worthwhile to liberate oneself from Annan's limited US understanding of celebrity as money and fame and consider the ways in which international progressive forces can create their own celebrities' (2005: 108). The strategic use of the Nobel Prize as an authoritative means through which solidarity activism in the South may generate celebrity status in the West, as the examples of Desmond Tutu and Rigoberta Menchu Tum convincingly demonstrate, is one example of what we may call *celebrity estrangement* – a reflexive distance from philanthro-capitalism and a gradual familiarization with internationally unknown figures who have managed to earn global reputations through their involvement in the shaming of inhumane regimes and the struggle for justice. Instead of privileging the impersonation of suffering by a western celebrity, which reproduces the systemic paradox of humanitarianism in that it, ultimately, glorifies extreme privilege and dehumanizes extreme deprivation, estrangement, here, celebritizes the voices of vulnerability themselves, and, in so doing, both offers the possibility of profoundly humanizing those vulnerable others and of politicizing their causes.

It is important, at the same time, to consider how, rather than wholly rejecting the role of celebrity in neoliberal philanthro-capitalism, we should rethink the specific ways in which its massive capital, financial and symbolic, can best be put to use in the humanitarian field. One of the few pieces of academic research on the value of celebrity as a UN brand, for instance, challenges commonsense assumptions about the efficacy of celebrity in raising the newsworthiness of often neglected emergencies but, at the same time, comments on the impressive success of celebrity advocacy in selected or 'targeted groups': 'though unable to make the front pages, celebrity advocacy can raise millions of dollars and encourage targeted groups to mobilize around opportunities for action, often without the vast majority of the United States noticing anything' (Thrall et al. 2008: 382). In line with my own argument, what Thrall et al. draw attention to, here, is the post-populist character of celebrity politics, which is less about spearheading massive strategies of sentimentalist broadcasting and more about lobbying and fund-raising through narrow-casting in the 'corridors of power' – a practice that, needless to say, needs to be carried out in the spirit of a fully transparent accountability.

A final example of estrangement, in the context of *convergent journalism*, is the *Guardian*'s 'Katine' project, which involved the long-term reporting of a development initiative in north-east Uganda, led by AMREF and Farm-Africa (2007–10).[3] A complex online performance, the 'Katine' project offers links to multiple stakeholders, including local residents' stories, NGOs and local governments' contributions, as well as the history of the village, the day-to-day progress of the project and its sustainability prospects for future development. Combining the temporality of the longue durée with these multiple micro-temporalities embedded within it, the project managed to enhance the journalism of development, both by inviting western self-expression, in that it crowd-sourced expert voices for specialist advice to the project and, crucially, by offering visibility to the problems of the residents of the village.

What renders 'Katine' a performance of estrangement is that, unlike post-humanitarian stories, it shares none of the narcissistic comfort that lies at the heart of the seductive persuasion of branding, the voyeuristic sentimentalism of celebrity or the therapeutic reverberation of online emotion. By contrast, 'Katine' is about discomforting stories: they show us how new media may disempower as well as empower local people, how people's expectations and NGOs' strategies may clash and bring projects to a grinding halt, how local government as much as international bureaucracy may stifle hope but also how things can, against all odds, be hopeful: 'Katine', as Jones says, 'shows that actually doing development is difficult . . . You are shown that development is less than perfect. But you are also shown that there is positive change' (Jones 2010: 18).

At the same time, 'Katine' also includes a broad array of voices of vulnerable others in its online reporting. By following testimonies of people's lives in their own words, this multi-media performance places the vulnerability of these people in the historical world of social conflicts and everyday struggles and, further, nuances our understanding of Uganda itself as a complex and challenging context of development. Rather than situating their vulnerability in the fictional universe of post-humanitarianism, this routine inclusion of local voices in the newspaper's story enables precisely that imaginative move towards the standpoint of the other, which makes it possible for us to consider their vulnerability as an object deserving our imaginative judgement.

Far from a comprehensive list of 'best practice', what these examples highlight is how estrangement, a trope already inherent in the performances of the imaginary as distance from the self, might help to educate us into habitual ways of feeling and thinking that are characteristic of agonistic solidarity. Like all examples, these are also partial, fragmented and incomplete; and there are other genres of the imaginary, such as cinema, documentary and the performative arts, that may also greatly contribute to nurturing the humanitarian imaginary. Their shortcomings granted, however, my hope is that the imperfection of these examples, together with others, might become a starting point for a new moral imagination of solidarity.

Conclusion: on being good

The humanitarian imaginary, I have proposed in this book, needs to reinvent itself as a communicative structure that is neither about our common humanity nor about our own feelings for distant others. Whilst these moral discourses reflect distinct 'moments' in the historical trajectory of humanitarianism from a classical liberal towards a neoliberal spirit of capitalism, their proposals to solidarity fail to move the West beyond narcissistic and increasingly corporate discourses of solidarity.

Despite my emphasis on the decisive role that the market has played in the rise of post-humanitarianism, however, my story of the four key genres of the imaginary has refrained from adopting the pessimistic argument of the critical school. The starting point of my analysis, as I said in chapter 2, is not an a priori denunciation of economic forces, either in the form of inhuman empire or commodified spectacle. In the spirit of Foucault's advice to study historical practices as discursive formations with performative effects of power, my starting point is, rather, the tensions and discontinuities that arise as the humanitarian imaginary constantly renegotiates the forces of the market, technology and politics, in the course of late modernity. Given that these complex forces are historically co-nascent with humanitarianism, I argued, global capitalism should not be seen as an adversary of cosmopolitan solidarity but as its necessary yet fragile condition of possibility. The systemic paradox of humanitarianism, explored in chapter 1, is, in this sense, nothing more than a claim to humanity that is produced by capitalism's own inhumanity (Cheah 2006).

However, instead of despairing for the inhumanity of modernity, as the critical school does, or accepting this paradox as an inevitable given, as the neoliberal ironists advise, my intention is, rather, to draw attention to *historical variation* in the production of humanity under inhuman conditions. This is because I believe that it is the study of such variation that makes it possible for us to better understand and critically evaluate how the market, politics and technology come together to transform the moral dispositions of our public life – how they turn solidarity from a collectivist politics of conviction into a lifestyle politics of reflexivity. Whereas the humanitarianism of early genres, as I have shown, belongs to a classical liberal imaginary that relies on an objective conception of suffering to enact a politics of pity, contemporary genres challenge this objectivity in favour of a subjectivist politics of irony.

If I strongly defend a return to the theatre as the privileged communicative structure of humanitarianism, then, this is because I also believe that neither the universal sentimentalism of pity nor the particularist pragmatism of irony can properly perform the crucial function of the imaginary, namely, the moral education of the West. This can only take place through a spectatorial imagination that both engages us with the humanity of the other and invites judgement on moral argument about this other. Rock concerts and corporate branding cannot replace this educative function nor can citizen journalism convey a deeper understanding of the realities of suffering beyond its experiential immediacy. Their solidarity, as a consequence, is an essentially ethnocentric solidarity that imagines the other in the self and treats argument as irrelevant to solidarity.

Breaking with these ironic textualities means breaking with the neoliberal assumption that we all know about justice and, therefore, we need not be explicit about it. On the contrary, I insist, we need to be invited, time and again, to engage both with the other and with the plurality of values that might inform our action on her/his suffering. Rather than denying it, we need to acknowledge the existing politicization of humanitarianism and to render its systemic paradox even more visible than it already is. This exercise in perpetual reflexivity, which keeps exposing the moral ambivalence of humanitarianism's liberal roots, is the best option we have for keeping the possibility of systemic change alive.

This is why we need the 'in-between' of the theatre, be it the discomforting image, the anonymous solidarity activist or the multi-media narrative. It is this in-between that connects us imaginatively with a distant world that is not and should not be reduced to the world we comfortably inhabit. It is this in-between that enables us to raise the crucial questions, now almost forgotten, of justification (why is this important?), antagonism (what is right and wrong?), complexity (is donating enough?), otherness and historicity (what makes these people who they are?) that may turn us from utilitarian altruists to cosmopolitan citizens. Without this agonistic engagement with otherness, I argue, there are no moral dilemmas to struggle with, no sides to take, no stakes to fight for, no hope to change the conditions of suffering.

This is not an easy task to manage. Not only because the humanitarian imaginary needs to balance a delicate act between judgement without over-rationalization, emotion without sentimentalism and an awareness of its paradoxes without surrendering the hope of representation. But because we, too, have to balance an equally delicate act between being good to others whilst being sceptical about any justification for such goodness that transcends ourselves. And this is perhaps the most important reason why we, ironic spectators, need the theatre now, more than ever – it may not make us become good but, as W. H. Auden put it, it can at least prevent us from imagining that we already are.

Notes

Chapter 1 Solidarity and Spectatorship

1 See www.allaboutyou.com/lifestyle/live-for-the-moment-actionaid-58250 for the 'Find your Feeling' appeal (accessed 29 December 2011). Permission was not granted for the use of a visual of the appeal in this book.

2 I here use 'epistemic shift' and 'paradigm shift' interchangeably to emphasize the emergence of a new rationality and practice of solidarity that drastically differs from previous ones. Such emergence, however, does not involve a revolutionary replacement of the old by the new but is instead an incremental and dispersed process, where irony coexists with pity (see Best and Kellner 1997: x–xii for a discussion of the terms epistemic and paradigmatic shift).

3 See www.professionalfundraising.co.uk, October 2009.

4 See www.professionalfundraising.co.uk, October 2009.

5 See McCleary and Barro (2007) and Barnett and Weiss (2008) for these numbers and for discussions on the significance of this increase in the humanitarian sector.

6 See Natsios (1995); Simmons (1998) and Cooley and Ron (2002) for the density argument in the sector.

7 See Poster (1975); Eagleton (1975, 1985) for discussions on Marxian humanism; see West (1969) for the affinity between Adam Smith and Karl Marx's views on the political economy of alienation.

8 See www.nobelprize.org/nobel_prizes/peace/laureates/1999/msf-lecture.html (accessed 8 October 2011)

9 www.professionalfundraising.co.uk, October 2009 (accessed 8 September 2011).

10 www.professionalfundraising.co.uk, October 2009 (accessed 8 September 2011).

11 Inherent in this conception of the theatre, from Aristotle to Smith and d'Alembert, or from Arendt to Nussbaum and Ranciere, is the idea of performance not simply as entertaining spectacle but also as a site of moral education. This idea originates in the close affinity between the communicative mechanisms of the theatre and politics, both of which rely on the separation between watching and acting as an aesthetic space where public dispositions are performed: 'politics as such', like the theatre, Bayly says, 'does indeed require a scene, a stage, some actors, some spectators, a text and, in effect, the entire aesthetic paraphernalia of the theatrical assemblage' (2009: 22). This is a theme I return to in chapter 7 in order to propose a theatrical view of solidarity as agonism.

12 See Zerilli (2005: 164) for a conception of reflexive judgement, in Arendt, that resonates with Smith's 'impartial spectator'. See Marshall (1984) for Smith's theory of spectatorship organized not only around empathy, or involved spectatorship, but also, importantly, around judgement, or impartial spectatorship. Chapter 7 further elaborates on this distinction.

Chapter 2 The Humanitarian Imaginary

1 See Mitchell (1986: 160–208) for 'the anti-ocular prejudice' of the critical school, including Habermas as well as Marxian and post-Marxian/post-structuralist thought.

2 My use of the term 'humanitarian imaginary' draws upon Castoriades but is further influenced by elaborations of the term in Charles Taylor's sociological description of modernity in terms of 'modern social imaginaries' (2002); Norman Fairclough's approach to the 'imaginary' (2003) as a regime of normative meanings, which defines the ways we should think, feel and act at specific points in time; and Craig Calhoun's critique of the dominant perception of humanitarian aid in terms of an apolitical 'emergency imaginary' (2010).

Chapter 3 Appeals

1 See 'Code of conduct on images and messages relating to the third world' (April 1989), where NGOs were advised to be 'attentive to messages that over-simplify or over-concentrate sensational aspects of life in the third world'.

2 This idea of 'estrangement', as a literary and cultural device of self-knowledge that operates by rendering the familiar strange, is central to Adam Smith's theory of spectatorship and, specifically, to his concept of the impartial spectator. In order to understand the other, Smith claims, we need to view her/his interests 'neither from our own place nor yet from his [sic], neither with our own eyes nor yet with his, but with the eyes and from the place of a third person, who has no particular connexion with either, and who judges with impartiality between us' (1759/2000: 135). For relevant elaborations on the term 'estrangement' see Gilroy (2004: 75); Sen (2009: 45). The use of 'estrangement' with specific reference to the mediated representation of the stranger in 'our' media is discussed in Silverstone (2007: 136) and its use with reference to the domestic as if it were distant and strange is discussed in Orgad (2011: 401–21). For a further discussion on theatrical estrangement as part of agonistic solidarity, see chapter 7, note 2.

3 AI 'Bullet. The Execution' appeal was created by advertising agency AOCPROD and was launched on French television as the AI 2006 global report on executions was published Paris; it won the Golden Lion at the Cannes Festival in ad productions (2007).The 'No Food Diet' appeal is part of a series of outsourced productions, which includes celebrity interviews and on-location visits to Africa, as well as the use of Hollywood film trailers such as the humanitarian *Blood Diamond* (Warner Bros 2006). 'Be Humankind' was originally created as a TV commercial ad by Rkcr/y&r for Oxfam, UK and released April 2008.

Chapter 4 Celebrity

1 See R. M. Press (1992), 'A visit of compassion to Somalia'. *The Christian Science Monitor*, 5 October. Available at: www.csmonitor.com/1992/1005/05141.html (accessed 8 October 2001)

2 See UNHCR Press Release (2001), Angelina Jolie named UNHCR Goodwill Ambassador for refugees. *The UN Refugee Agency*, 23 August. Available at: www.unhcr.org/3b85044b10.html (accessed 8 October 2011).

3 Oliver Buston, European Director of DATA, a Bono-founded organization (standing for Debt, AIDS, Trade and Africa) that lobbies at elite and grass-roots level with a view to influencing humanitarian politics. In P. Vallely (2009), 'From A-lister to Aid-worker: Does celebrity diplomacy really work?' *The Independent*, 17 January. Available at: www.independent.co.uk/news/people/profiles/from-alister-to-aid-worker-does-celebrity-diplomacy-really-work-1365946.html (accessed 8 October 2011).

4 My discussion on Hepburn draws on three main sources: UNICEF's website and mission footage; television and press interviews and the actress' official biography (Walker 1995). My discussion on Jolie focuses, similarly, on her UNICEF website, including mission footage and the actress diary notes; and selected interviews in global press and television networks.

5 *Moralization* refers to the educative process by which celebrity provides exemplary moral dispositions for publics to identify with, whereas *ethicalization* refers to the self-formative process by which celebrity composes himself or herself as a particular moral subject – thereby also becoming available as an exemplary public self in the process of moralization.

6 Press Conference on Somalia, 1992. See www.audrey1.org/biography/22/audrey-hepburns-unicef-field-missions (accessed 8 October 2011)

7 Press Conference on Somalia, 1992. See www.audrey1.org/biography/21/audrey-hepburn-unicef-overview (accessed 8 October 2011)

8 See J. Roberts (1992), 'Interview / Envoy for the starving: Audrey Hepburn: James Roberts meets the actress determined to help Somalia's children'. *The Independent*, 4 October. Available at: www.independent.co.uk/opinion/interview--envoy-for-the-starving-audrey-hepburn-james-roberts-meets-the-actress-determined-to-help-somalias-children-1555466.html (accessed 8 October 2011)

9 Statement issued upon Hepburn's UNICEF appointment, May 1988. See www.cf-hst.net/UNICEF-TEMP/Doc-Repository/doc/doc401478.PDF (accessed 08 October 2011)

10 See CBS interview at *This Morning*, 3 June, 1991. Interview transcript available at: www.ahepburn.com/interview4.html (accessed 8 October 2011)

11 See J. Roberts (1992), 'Interview / Envoy for the starving: Audrey Hepburn: James Roberts meets the actress determined to help Somalia's children'. *The Independent*, 4 October. Available at: www.independent.co.uk/opinion/interview--envoy-for-the-starving-audrey-hepburn-james-roberts-meets-the-

actress-determined-to-help-somalias-children-1555466.html (accessed 8 October 2011)

12 See Educational Broadcasting – The MacNeil/Lehrer NewsHour, 5 November 1992. Interview transcript available at: www.ahepburn.com/interview5.html (accessed 8 October 2011).

13 See Educational Broadcasting – The MacNeil/Lehrer NewsHour, 5 November 1992. Interview transcript available at: www.ahepburn.com/interview5.html (accessed 8 October 2011).

14 See L. Garner (1991), 'Lesley Garner meets the legendary actress as she prepares for this week's Unicef gala performance'. *The Sunday Telegraph,* 26 May. Available at: www.ahepburn.com/article6.html (accessed 8 October 2011)

15 Press conference after her first UNICEF mission on Ethiopia, 1988. See www.audrey1.org/biography/22/audrey-hepburns-unicef-field-missions (accessed 8 October 2011).

16 UNICEF co-ordinator of Goodwill Ambassadors, Christa Roth. See www.ahepburn.com/work10.html (accessed 8 October 2011).

17 See M. Miller, D. Pomerantz and L. Rose (eds) (2009), 'The world's 100 most powerful celebrities list'. *Forbes.com,* 06/03/09. Available at: www.forbes.com/2009/06/03/forbes-100-celebrity-09-jolie-oprah-madonna_land.html (accessed 8 October 2011).

18 See 'Actress Angelina Jolie: "I was wacko, emotionally, during this movie"', *Daily Mail,* 23 November 2008 Available at: www.dailymail.co.uk/home/you/article-1087028/Angelina-Jolie-I-think-looks-getting-better-age.html (accessed 8 October 2011).

19 MTV Series Documentary *The Diary,* featuring 'The Diary of Angelina Jolie and Dr Jeffery Sachs in Africa' (2005).

20 See 'Sarah Sands: we need Angelina Jolie – she's the antidote to despair', *The Independent on Sunday,* 18 November 2007. Available at: www.independent.co.uk/opinion/commentators/sarah-sands/sarah-sands-we-need-angelina-jolie-ndash-shes-the-antidote-to-despair-400797.html, and Mark Malloch Brown 'The 2006 Time 100: Angelina Jolie', *The Time,* 8 May 2006. Available at: www.time.com/time/specials/packages/article/0,28804,1975813_1975847_1976577,00.html (accessed 8 October 2011)

21 See ABC News 'Jolie on motherhood and mental health', 17 October 2002. Available at: http://abcnews.go.com/2020/story?id=124372&page=1 (accessed 8 October 2011).

22 Introduction to Jolie A. (2003), *Notes from my Travels.*

23 See R. Cohen (2008), 'A woman in full'. *Vanity Fair,* July 2008. Available at: www.vanityfair.com/culture/features/2008/07/jolie200807 (accessed 8 October 2011).

24 The Clinton Global Initiative Annual Meeting, New York, September 26–28, 2007.

25 See ABC News 'Jolie on motherhood and mental health', 17 October 2002.

Available at: http://abcnews.go.com/2020/story?id=124372&page=1 (accessed 8 October 2011).

26 See Mark Malloch Brown, 'The 2006 Time 100: Angelina Jolie', *The Time*, 8 May 2006. Available at: www.time.com/time/specials/packages/article/0,28804,1975813_1975847_1976577,00.html (accessed 08 October 2011)

27 See Illouz (2007) on the therapeutic sentimentalism of Oprah Winfrey; 't Hart and Tindall (2009) on Geldof's anger; Littler (2008) on Jolie's tearful appearances.

28 See Couldry and Markham (2007) for an empirical study showing no evidence of the claim that engagement with celebrity may act as a lead-in to engagement with social issues; Alleyne (2005) for the 'intellectual vacuum' of UN's celebrity-driven policy-making.

29 See McDougall (2006), 'Now charity staff hit at cult of celebrity', in *The Observer*, 26 November. Available at www.guardian.co.uk/society/2006/nov/26/internationalaidanddevelopment.internationalnews (accessed 8 October 2011)

Chapter 5 Concerts

1 See Monbiot (2005), 'And still he stays silent', in the *Guardian*, 6 September. Available at www.guardian.co.uk/world/2005/sep/06/g8.climatechange (accessed 5 September 2011).

2 See Dayan and Katz (1992), Silverstone (1994), Couldry (2003), Cottle (2006a) for the performativity of media rituals.

3 See Dayan (2009) for this dilemmatic formulation.

4 See Pruce (2010), *Culture industry and the marketing of human rights*. Available at: http://ssrn.com/abstract=1654575 (accessed 4 September 2011).

5 See Coleman (2010), 'From the Archive: Missionary zeal in a world of famine,' in the *Guardian*, 15 July 1985. Available at: www.guardian.co.uk/theguardian/2010/jul/16/archive-missionary-zeal-1985?INTCMP=SRCH (accessed 5 September 2011).

6 BBC News Online (2005), 'On this day – 1985: Live Aid makes millions for Africa'. Available at: http://news.bbc.co.uk/onthisday/hi/dates/stories/july/13/newsid_2502000/2502735.stm (accessed 5 September 2011).

7 See G. Jones (2005), *Live Aid 1985: A day of magic*. CNN, 6 July. Available at: http://webcache.googleusercontent.com/search?q=cache:isvkqR6oOwQJ:articles.cnn.com/2005-07-01/entertainment/liveaid.memories_1_tv-live-aid Geldof%3F_s%3DPM:SHOWBIZ +audience+of+live+aid&cd=5&hl=en&ct=clnk&gl=uk&source=www.google.co.uk (accessed 5 September 2011).

8 BBC News (1984), Michael Buerk on Ethiopian famine, 23 October (video). Available at: www.youtube.com/watch?v=XYOj_6OYuJc (accessed 5 September 2011).

9 See R. Bennett (2011), 'Bob Geldof: Live Aid, Live 8 & Me'. *Mojo Magazine*, 4

January. Available at: www.mojo4music.com/blog/2011/01/bob_geldof_live_aid_live_8_me.html (accessed 3 September 2011).

10 See R. Bennett (2011), 'Bob Geldof: Live Aid, Live 8 & Me'. *Mojo Magazine*, 4 January. Available at: www.mojo4music.com/blog/2011/01/bob_geldof_live_aid_live_8_me.html (accessed 3 September 2011).

11 See Geldof interview in *Melody Maker*, 15 July 1978, quoted in Hague, Street and Savigny (2008: 13); see also Tester (2010: 14–16) for a similar argument.

12 See Bennett, R. (2011) Bob Geldof: Live Aid, Live 8 & Me. *Mojo Magazine*, 4 January. Available at: www.mojo4music.com/blog/2011/01/bob_geldof_live_aid_live_8_me.html (accessed 3 September 2011).

13 See A. Darnton (2011), 'Aid: why are we still stuck in 1985?' *Guardian*, 28 March. Available at: www.guardian.co.uk/global-development/poverty-matters/2011/mar/28/aid-public-perceptions (accessed 5 September 2011)

14 See G. Jones (2005), *Live Aid 1985: A day of magic*. CNN, 6 July. Availabe at: http://webcache.googleusercontent.com/search?q=cache:isvkqR6oOwQJ:articles.cnn.com/2005-07-01/entertainment/liveaid.memories_1_tv-live-aid Geldof%3F_s%3DPM:SHOWBIZ +audience+of+live+aid&cd=5&hl=en&ct=clnk&gl=uk&source=www.google.co.uk (accessed 5 September 2011).

15 The BBC was responsible for the concert feed in UK and Europe, and ABC for the USA.

16 BBC News Online, 8 November 2004, 'Stars recall Live Aid spectacular'. Available at: http://news.bbc.co.uk/2/hi/entertainment/3979461.stm#midge (accessed 5 September 2011).

17 BBC, 'Have your say: Live Aid memories July 2005'. Available at: www.bbc.co.uk/music/thelive8event/haveyoursay/liveaidmemories.shtml (accessed 5 September 2011).

18 BBC News Online, 8 November 2004; Stars recall Live Aid spectacular. Available at: http://news.bbc.co.uk/2/hi/entertainment/3979461.stm#midge (accessed 5 September 2011).

19 BBC News (1985), 'On this day – 1985: Live Aid raises millions'. *BBC News* (video). Available at: http://news.bbc.co.uk/player/nol/newsid_6520000/newsid_6522700/6522735.stm?bw=bb&mp=wm&news=1&ms3=6&ms_javascript=true&bbcws=2 (accessed 5 September 2011).

20 See C. Bialik (2005), 'When it comes to TV stats, viewer discretion is advised'. *The Wall Street Journal*, 21 July. Available at: http://online.wsj.com/public/article/SB112180840215889963-XaNnhJ_OnHUIP4vyjpyugnjtIeA_20071216.html (accessed 5 September 2011).

21 See O. Gibson and S. Laville (2005), 'Live 8: old white guys singing the wrong tune?' *Guardian*, 4 June. Available at: http://webcache.googleusercontent.com/search?q=cache:SgJjmZtpcA4J:www.guardian.co.uk/uk/2005/jun/04/arts.hearafrica05+Geldof+fuck+off+Live+8&cd=8&hl=en&ct=clnk&gl=uk&sourc+e=www.google.co.uk (accessed 6 September 2011).

22 See B. Wheeler (2004), 'Bono pushes the right buttons'. *BBC News Online,* 30 September. Available at: http://news.bbc.co.uk/1/hi/uk_politics/3701414.stm (accessed 5 September 2011).
23 ABC News Online (2005), 'Live 8 concerts turn a profit', 29 October. Available at: www.abc.net.au/news/2005-10-29/live-8-concerts-turn-a-profit/2134506 (accessed 5 September 2011).
24 See O. Gibson and S. Laville (2005), 'Live 8: old white guys singing the wrong tune?' *Guardian,* 4 June. Available at: http://webcache.googleusercontent.com/search?q=cache:SgJjmZtpcA4J:www.guardian.co.uk/uk/2005/jun/04/arts.hearafrica05+Geldof+fuck+off+Live+8&cd=8&hl=en&ct=clnk&gl=uk&source=www.google.co.uk (accessed 6 September 2011).
25 See R. Bennett (2011), 'Bob Geldof: Live Aid, Live 8 & Me'. *Mojo Magazine*, 4 January. Available at: www.mojo4music.com/blog/2011/01/bob_geldof_live_aid_live_8_me.html (accessed 3 September 2011).
26 See B. Geldof (2005), 'Geldof's year'. *Guardian*, 28 December. Available at: www.guardian.co.uk/politics/2005/dec/28/development.live8 (accessed 5 September 2011).
27 See J. Traub (2005), 'The statesman'. *The New York Times*, 18 September. Available at: http://faculty.washington.edu/jwilker/353/bono.pdf (accessed 5 September 2011).
28 See G. Monbiot (2005), 'Bards of the powerful'. *Guardian*, 21 June. Available at: www.guardian.co.uk/politics/2005/jun/21/development.g8 (accessed 5 September 2011).
29 E. Stretch (2005), 'Live 8: Greatest show on earth: It's our time to stand up for what'. *Sunday Mirror*, 3 July. http://findarticles.com/p/articles/mi_qn4161/is_20050703/ai_n14683852/indArticles / News / Sunday Mirror / Jul 3, 2005 (accessed 5 September 2011).
30 Live Aid in Live 8: www.dailymotion.com/video/xhmcv_live8-bob-geldof-speech_news (for Geldof) and www.dailymotion.com/video/xhmir_live8-the-girl-birhan-woldu_news (for Birhan Woldu).
31 See E. Richardson (2002), 'Bono-Fire'. *O, The Oprah Magazine*, February. Available at: www.oprah.com/spirit/Bono-A-Global-Rock-Star-and-Activist (accessed 5 September 2011).
32 See G. Monbiot (2005), 'A truckload of nonsense'. *Guardian,* 14 June. Available at: www.guardian.co.uk/world/2005/jun/14/g8.politics (accessed 5 September 2011); and see O. Gibson and S. Laville (2005), 'Live 8: old white guys singing the wrong tune?' *Guardian*, 4 June. Available at: http://webcache.googleusercontent.com/search?q=cache:SgJjmZtpcA4J:www.guardian.co.uk/uk/2005/jun/04/arts.hearafrica05+Geldof+fuck+off+Live+8&cd=8&hl=en&ct=clnk&gl=uk&source=www.google.co.uk (accessed 6 September 2011).
33 See Monbiot, G. (2005) Live 8 – An opportunity lost? *Three Monkeys Online*, June. Available at: www.threemonkeysonline.com/als/_live_8_george_monbiot_critique.html (accessed 5 September 2011).

34 See J. Duffy (2005), 'So what happened?' *BBC News*, 2 November. Available at: http://news.bbc.co.uk/1/hi/magazine/4397936.stm (accessed 5 September 2011).

Chapter 6 News

1 See, for example, the CNN's Anderson Cooper controversy during his Haiti earthquake reporting: http://gawker.com/5451459/anderson-cooper-saves-boy-as-cnns-haiti-coverage-reaches-strange-apotheosis
2 See impartial witness section: www.bbc.co.uk/journalism/ethics-and-values/impartiality/witness.shtml.
3 See 'Citizen journalism and the BBC', Nieman report, downloadable at: www.nieman.harvard.edu/reportsitem.aspx?id=100542
4 See 'Citizen journalism and the BBC', Nieman report, downloadable at: www.nieman.harvard.edu/reportsitem.aspx?id=100542 .
5 www.bu.edu/globalbeat/syndicate/Marthoz050599.html
6 These cases belong to the list of the deadliest earthquakes of the past 100 years, with Tangshan as the second deadliest (255,000 deaths); Haiti as the fourth (230,000 deaths); Kashmir as the seventeenth (79,000 deaths); the Mexico and Turkey earthquakes have been the deadliest ones in the modern history of these countries.
7 By narrating some of the most tragic instances of natural disaster outside the West, these pieces of news function as 'paradigmatic'; that is, they can be used as exemplars that 'highlight more general characteristics' of their class (Flyvebjerg 2001: 80–1). The content of their news reports are available in the BBC online archive and can be accessed at the following addresses: Tangshan earthquake (1976): http://news.bbc.co.uk/onthisday/hi/dates/stories/july/28/newsid_4132000/4132109.stm
Turkey earthquake, BBC 1999: http://news.bbc.co.uk/onthisday/hi/dates/stories/august/17/newsid_253400/2534245.stm
Kashmir earthquake (2005): http://news.bbc.co.uk/1/hi/world/south_asia/4321490.stm
Mexico earthquake, BBC 1985: http://news.bbc.co.uk/onthisday/hi/dates/stories/september/19/newsid_4252000/4252078.stm
Haiti earthquake (2005): http://news.bbc.co.uk/1/hi/8455629.stm
Haiti webstream (or live blog; 2010): http://news.bbc.co.uk/1/hi/8456322.stm
8 The 'BBC On This Day' site, where the story comes from, is BBC's online archive consisting of major news texts that spanning the 55-year period 1950–2005 as the BBC presented them or, in the absence of original footage, would have presented them 'as if the event had only just occurred, drawing on archive media, old newspapers and historical reference books'. (http://news.bbc.co.uk/onthisday/hi/dates/stories/july/28/newsid_4132000/4132109.stm)
9 In the case of Tangshan, western aid was impossible, as the 'cultural revolution' kept communist China insulated from the capitalist West.

10 See Al Jazeera's live blog on Haiti, however, for a historicizing perspective along these lines: http://blogs.aljazeera.net/americas/2010/01/13/why-haiti-earthquake-was-so-devastating.

Chapter 7 Theatricality, Irony, Solidarity

1 See Barnett et al. (2010) for a positive account of the 'moralization of consumption' that has managed to subject hitherto non-problematized spheres of consumer activity to critical scrutiny and link mundane consumption practices with civil tactics, i.e. Fair Trade. My argument emphasizes, rather, the constraints upon solidarity that the corporatization of humanitarian communication brings about. Even though market and morality are constitutive of the public realm of Enlightenment modernity, I argue, historical variation in the articulation between the two suggests that the 'moralization of consumption' is increasingly linked, in a dialectical manner, to the 'corporatization of ethics' (Chouliaraki and Morsing 2010).

2 Let us recall that Adam Smith places 'estrangement', as a quality of his 'impartial spectator', at the heart of his morality of spectatorship (see also ch. 3, n. 2). In the context of theatrical performance and literary theory, estrangement is further explored as an aesthetic and ethical practice in the works of Brecht, Benjamin, Shklovsky, Meyerhold and Piscator but also, importantly, Jakobson and Bakhtin (Jestrovic 2006).

3 www.guardian.co.uk/katine/villagevoices. The website won the 'One World Media' award for its outstanding new media output (2008).

References

Abrahamsen, R. (2003) 'African studies and the postcolonial challenge'. *African Affairs* 102(407): 189–210.

Adorno, T. W. (1938/1991) 'On the fetish character in music and the regression of listening', in J. M. Bernstein (ed.), *The Culture Industry: Selected Essays on Mass Culture*. London: Routledge, pp. 26–52.

Adorno, T. W. and Horkheimer, M. (1942/1991) 'The schema of mass culture', trans. N. Walker, in J. M. Bernstein (ed.), *The Culture Industry: Selected Essays on Mass Culture*. London: Routledge, pp. 61–97.

Agamben, G. (1998) *Homo Sacer: Sovereign Power and Bare Life*. Stanford, CA: Stanford University Press.

Ahmed, S. (2004) *The Cultural Politics of Emotion*. Edinburgh: Edinburgh University Press.

Ainley, K. (2008) 'Individual agency and responsibility for atrocity', in R. Jeffery (ed.), *Confronting Evil in International Relations: Ethical Responses to Problems of Moral Agency*. Basingstoke: Palgrave, pp. 37–60.

Alberoni, F. (1962/2006) 'The powerless elite: theory and sociological research on the phenomenon of the stars', in D. P. Marshall (ed.), *The Celebrity Culture Reader*. London: Routledge, pp. 108–23.

Albrow, M. and Seckinelgin, H. (2011) 'Introduction: globality and the absence of justice', in M. Albrow, H. Seckinelgin and H. Anheier (eds), *Global Civil Society 2011: Globality and the Absence of Justice*. London: Palgrave Macmillan.

Allan, S. (2007) 'Citizen journalism and the rise of "mass self-communication": reporting the London bombings'. *Global Media Journal: Australian Edition* 1(1): 1–20.

Allan, S. (2009) 'The problem of the public: The Lippmann-Dewey debate', in S. Allan (ed.), *The Routledge Companion to News and Journalism*. London: Routledge, pp. 60–70.

Allan, S. and Zelizer, B. (eds) (2002) *Journalism After September 11*. London: Routledge.

Alleyne, M. (2005) 'The United Nations' celebrity diplomacy'. *SAIS Review* 25(1): 175–85.

Arendt, H. (1951/1979) *The Origins of Totalitarianism*. New York: Harcourt Brace Jovanovich.

Arendt, H. (1958/1998) *The Human Condition*. Chicago: University of Chicago Press.

Arendt, H. (1961/1993) *Between Past and Future*. Harmondsworth: Penguin Books.

Arendt, H. (1963/1990) *On Revolution*. London: Penguin Books.

Arendt, H. (1982) *Lectures on Kant's Political Philosophy*, ed. R. Beiner. Chicago: University of Chicago Press.

Arendt, H. (1994) *Essays in Understanding 1930–1954: Formation, Exile and Totalitarianism*, ed. J. Kohn. New York: Harcourt Brace & Company.

Aristotle (1987) *De Anima*, trans. L. Lawson-Tancred. London: Penguin.

Aristotle (1997) *Poetics*, trans. and with commentary by S. Halliwell London: Duckworth.

Aristotle (2002) *Nicomachean Ethics*, trans. and with commentary by S. Broadie and C. Rowe. Oxford: Oxford University Press.

Arvidsson, A. (2006) *Brands: Meaning and Value in Media Culture*. London: Routledge.

Atton, D. (2002) *Alternative Media*. London: Sage.

Auslander, P. (1998) 'Seeing is believing: live performance and the discourse of authenticity in rock culture'. *Literature and Psychology* 44(4): 1–26.

Bajde, D. (2009) 'Rethinking the social and cultural dimensions of charitable giving'. *Consumption Markets & Culture* 12(1): 65–84.

Barker, C. (2002) *Alain Badiou: A Critical Introduction*. London: Pluto Press.

Barnett, C., Cloke, P., Clarke, N. and Malpass, A. (2010) *Globalizing Responsibility: The Political Rationalities of Ethical Consumption*. Chichester: John Wiley & Sons.

Barnett, M. (2005) 'Humanitarianism transformed'. *Perspectives on Politics* 3(4): 723–40.

Barnett, M. and Weiss, T. G. (eds) (2008) *Humanitarianism in Question: Politics, Power, Ethics*. Ithaca, NY: Cornell University Press.

Baudrillard, J. (1983) *Simulations*. New York: Semiotext(e).

Baudrillard, J. (1988) *Jean Baudrillard: Selected Writings*, ed. M. Poster. Cambridge: Polity.

Baudrillard, J. (1993) *The Transparency of Evil: Essays on Extreme Phenomena*, trans. J. Benedict. London, New York: Verso.

Baudrillard, J. (1994) 'No reprieve for Sarajevo'. *Liberation*, 8 January. Available at: www.egs.edu/faculty/jean-baudrillard/articles/no-reprieve-for-sarajevo/ (accessed 26 September 2011).

Bayly, S. (2009) 'Theatre and the public: Badiou, Rancière, Virno'. *Radical Philosophy* 157: 20–9.

Beck, U. (2006) *Cosmopolitan Vision*. Cambridge: Polity.

Beckett, C. (2008) *Supermedia*. Chichester: Wiley-Blackwell.

Beckett, C. and Mansell, R. (2008) 'Crossing boundaries: new media and networked journalism'. *Communication, Culture & Critique* 1(1): 92–104.

Bell, M. (1998) 'The journalism of attachment', in M. Kieran (ed.), *Media Ethics*. London: Routledge, pp. 15–22.

Benhabib, S. (2007) 'Democratic exclusions and democratic iterations: dilemmas of "just membership" and prospects of cosmopolitan federalism'. *European Journal of Political Theory* 6(4): 445–62.

Bennett, A. (2001) *Cultures of Popular Music*. Buckingham, Philadelphia: Open University Press.

Bennett, J. (2001) *The Enchantment of Modern Life: Attachments, Crossings, and Ethics*. Princeton: Princeton University Press.

Bennett, W. L. (2003) 'New media power: the internet and global activism', in N. Couldry and J. Curran (eds), *Contesting Media Power*. Lanham: Rowman & Littlefield, pp. 17–37.

Bennett, W. L., Lawrence, R. G. and Livingston, S. (2007) *When the Press Fails: Political Power and the News Media from Iraq to Katrina*. Chicago: University of Chicago Press.

Benthall, J. (1993) *Disasters, Relief and the Media*. London: I. B. Tauris.

Best, S. and Kellner, D. (1997) *Debord and the Postmodern Turn: New Stages of the Spectacle*. Illuminations: The Critical Theory Website. Available at: www.cddc.vt.edu/illuminations/kell17.htm (accessed 8 August 2011).

Biccum, A. (2007) 'Marketing development: Live 8 and the production of the global citizen'. *Development and Change* 38(6): 1111–26.

Biel, R. (2000) *The New Imperialism: Crisis and Contradictions in North–South Relations*. London: Zed Books.

Bishop, M. and Green, M. (2008) *Philanthrocapitalism: How the Rich Can Save the World*. London: Bloomsbury.

Bob, C. (2002) 'Merchants of morality'. *Foreign Policy* 129 (March/April): 36–45.

Boltanski, L. (1999) *Distant Suffering: Politics, Morality and the Media*. Cambridge: Cambridge University Press.

Boltanski, L. (2000) 'The legitimacy of humanitarian actions and their media representation: the case of France'. *Ethical Perspectives* 7(1): 3–16.

Boltanski, L. and Chiapello, E. (2005) *The New Spirit of Capitalism*, trans. G. Elliott. London: Verso.

Boorstin, D. J. (1961) *The Image: A Guide to Pseudo-events in America*. New York: Harper & Row.

Bourdieu, P. (1977) *Outline of a Theory of Practice*. New York: Cambridge University Press.

Butler, J. (1993) *Bodies That Matter: On the Discursive Limits of 'Sex'*. London: Routledge.

Butler, J. (1997) *Excitable Speech: A Politics of the Performative*. London and New York: Routledge.

Butler, J. (2006) *Precarious Lives: The Powers of Mourning and Violence*. London: Verso.

Calhoun, C. (2002) 'Imagining solidarity: cosmopolitanism, constitutional patriotism, and the public sphere'. *Public Culture* 14(1): 147–71.

Calhoun, C. (2008) 'Cosmopolitanism in the modern social imaginary'. *Daedalus* 137(3): 105–14.

Calhoun, C. (2009) 'The imperative to reduce suffering: charity, progress and emergencies in the field of humanitarian action', in M. N. Barnett and T. G.

Weiss (eds), *Humanitarianism in Question: Politics, Power, Ethics*. Ithaca: Cornell University Press, pp. 73–97.

Calhoun, C. (2010) 'The idea of emergency: Humanitarian action and global (dis)order', in D. Fassin and M. Pandolfi (eds), *States of Emergency* Cambridge, MA: Zone Books.

Cammaerts, B. (2008) *Mind the Gap: Internet-Mediated Practices Beyond the Nation State*. Manchester: Manchester University Press.

Cammaerts, B. and Carpentier, N. (2007) (eds) *Reclaiming the Media: Communication Rights and Democratic Media Roles*. Bristol: Intellect.

Campbell, D. (2004) 'Horrific blindness: images of death in contemporary media'. *Journal for Cultural Research* 8(1): 55–74.

Carey, J. (1989) *Communication as Culture: Essays on Media and Society*. New York and London: Routledge.

Castoriadis, C. (1975/1987) *The Imaginary Institution of Society*. Cambridge: Polity.

Castells, M. (2009) *Communication Power*. Oxford: Oxford University Press.

Chandler, D. (2002) *Rethinking Human Rights: Critical Approaches to International Politics*. Basingstoke: Palgrave.

Chandler, D. (2009) 'Critiquing liberal cosmopolitanism? The limits of the biopolitical approach'. *International Political Sociology* 3: 53–70.

Cheah, P. (2006). *Inhuman Conditions: On Cosmopolitanism and Human Rights*. Cambridge, MA: Harvard University Press.

Chouliaraki, L. (2006) *The Spectatorship of Suffering*. London: Sage.

Chouliaraki, L. (2008a) 'Mediation as moral education'. *Media, Culture & Society* 30(6): 831–52.

Chouliaraki, L. (2008b) 'The symbolic power of transnational media: managing the visibility of suffering'. *Global Media and Communication* 4(3): 329–51.

Chouliaraki, L. and Fairclough, N. (1999) *Discourse in Late Modernity*. Edinburgh: Edinburgh University Press.

Chouliaraki, L. and Morsing, M. (2010) (eds) *Media, Organisations and Identity*. London: Palgrave.

Christian, L. G. (1987) *Theatrum Mundi: The History of an Idea*. New York: Garland Publishing.

Cmiel, K. (1999) 'The emergence of human rights politics in the United States'. *The Journal of American History* 86(3): 1231–50.

Cohen, S. (2001) *States of Denial: Knowing about Atrocities and Suffering*. Cambridge: Polity.

Cohen, S. and Seu, B. (2002) 'Knowing enough not to feel too much: emotional thinking about human rights appeals', in M. P. Bradley and P. Petro (eds), *Truth Claims: Representation and Human Rights*. New Brunswick, NJ: Rutgers University Press, pp. 187–201.

Coleman, S. (2005) *Direct Representation: Towards a Conversational Democracy*. London: IPPR.

Collier, P. (2007) *The Bottom Billion*. Oxford: Oxford University Press.

Compton, J. R. and Comor, E. (2007) 'The integrated news spectacle, Live 8, and the annihilation of time'. *Canadian Journal of Communication* 32(1): 29–53.

Cooley, A. and Ron, J. (2002) 'The NGO scramble: organizational insecurity and the political economy of transnational action'. *International Security* 27(1): 5–39.

Cooper, A. F. (2007) 'Celebrity Diplomacy and the G8: Bono and Geldof as Legitimate International Actors'. Working Paper No. 29, The Centre for International Governance Innovation, University of Waterloo. Available at: www.cigionline.org/sites/default/files/Paper_29-web.pdf (accessed 8 August 2011).

Cooper, G. (2007) 'Anyone Here Survived a Wave, Speak English and Got a Mobile? Aid Agencies, the Media and Reporting Disasters since the Tsunami'. The 14th *Guardian* lecture, Nuffield College, Oxford University, 5 November 2007.

Corbridge, S. (1993) 'Marxisms, modernities and moralities: development praxis and the claims of distant strangers'. *Environment and Planning D: Society and Space* 11(4): 449–72.

Cottle, S. (2006a) 'Mediatized rituals: beyond manufacturing consent'. *Media, Culture & Society* 28(3): 411–32.

Cottle, S. (2006b) 'Between display and deliberation: analyzing TV news as communicative architecture'. *Media, Culture & Society* 28(2): 163–89.

Cottle, S. (2009) *Global Crisis Reporting*. Milton Keynes: Open University Press.

Cottle, S. and Nolan, D. (2007) 'Global humanitarianism and the changing aid-media field'. *Journalism Studies* 8(6): 862–78.

Cottle, S. and Rai, M. (2006) 'Between display and deliberation: analysing TV news as communicative architecture'. *Media, Culture & Society* 28(2): 163–89.

Couldry, N. (2003) *Media Rituals*. London: Routledge

Couldry, N. and Markham, T. (2007) 'Celebrity culture and public connection: bridge or chasm'. *International Journal of Cultural Studies* 10(4): 403–21.

Couldry, N., Livingstone, S., and Markham, T. (2008) '"Public connection" and the uncertain norms of media consumption', in K. Soper and F. Trentman (eds), *Citizenship and Consumption*. London: Palgrave Macmillan, pp. 104–20.

Cowen, T. (2000) *What Price Fame?* Cambridge, MA: Harvard University Press.

Critchley, S. (1994) 'Deconstruction and pragmatism – is Derrida a private ironist or a public liberal?' *European Journal of Philosophy* 2(1): 1–21.

Crouch, C. (2004) *Post-Democracy*. Cambridge, Malden: Polity.

Dahlgren, P. (2009) *Media and Political Engagement: Citizens, Communication and Democracy*. Cambridge and New York: Cambridge University Press.

Darnton, A. with Martin, K. (2011) 'Finding frames: new ways to engage the UK public in global poverty'. London: Bond. Available at: www.findingframes.org/Finding%20Frames%20New%20ways%20to%20engage%20the%20UK%20public%20in%20global%20poverty%20Bond%202011.pdf (accessed 1 October 2011).

Dayan, D. (2001) 'The peculiar public of television'. *Media, Culture & Society* 23(6): 743–65.

Dayan, D. (2008) 'Beyond media events: disenchantment, derailment, disruption', in M. E. Price and D. Dayan (eds), *Owning the Olympics: Narratives of the New China*. Michigan: University of Michigan Press, pp. 391–402.

Dayan, D. (2009) 'Quand montrer c'est faire'. *Divinatio* 29: 155–78.

Dayan, D. and Katz, E. (1992) *Media Events: The Live Broadcasting of History*. Cambridge: Harvard University Press.

Dean, M. (1991) *A History of Poverty*. London: Routledge.

Debord, G. (1967/2002) *The Society of the Spectacle*, trans. K. Knabb. Canberra: Hobgoblin Press.

Debray, R. (1995) 'Remarks on the spectacle'. *New Left Review* 214: 134–41.

deChaine, D. R. (2005) *Global Humanitarianism: NGOs and the Crafting of Community*. Lanham, MD: Lexington Books.

Deuze, M. (2001) 'Online journalism: modeling the first generation of news media on the World Wide Web'. *First Monday* 6(10). Available at: http://firstmonday.org/htbin/cgiwrap/bin/ojs/index.php/fm/article/view/893/80 (accessed 8 August 2011).

Deuze, M. (2004) 'What is multimedia journalism?' *Journalism Studies* 5(2): 139–52.

Deuze, M. (2005) 'Towards professional participatory story-telling in journalism and advertising'. *First Monday* 10(7). Available at: http://firstmonday.org/htbin/cgiwrap/bin/ojs/index.php/fm/article/view/1257/1177 (accessed 8 August 2011).

Deuze, M. (2006) 'Participation, remediation, bricolage: considering principal components of a digital culture'. *The Information Society* 22: 63–75.

de Waal, A. (1997) *Famine Crimes: Politics and the Disaster Relief Industry in Africa*. Bloomington: Indiana University Press.

de Waal, A. (2008) 'The humanitarian carnival: a celebrity vogue'. *World Affairs Journal*, Fall 2008. Available at: www.worldaffairsjournal.org/articles/2008-Fall/full-DeWaal.html (accessed 8 August 2011).

Dieter, P. and Kumar, K. (2008) 'The downside of celebrity diplomacy: the neglected complexity of development'. *Global Governance* 14(1): 259–64.

Dogra, N. (2007) '"Reading NGOs visually" – implications of visual images for NGO management'. *Journal of International Development* 19: 161–71.

Douzinas, C. (2007) *Human Rights and Empire*. London: Routledge.

Duffield, M. (2001) *Global Governance and the New Wars: The Merging of Development and Security*. New York: Palgrave Macmillan.

Dyer, R. (1979) *Stars*. London: BFI.

Dyer, R. (1986) *Heavenly Bodies: Film Stars and Society*. London: BFI.

Eagleton, T. (1975) *Myths of Power: A Marxist Study of the Brontes*. London: Macmillan Press.

Eagleton, T. (1985) 'Capitalism, modernism and postmodernism'. *New Left Review* 152: 60–73.

Eagleton, T. (1990) *The Ideology of the Aesthetic*. Oxford: Blackwell.

Eagleton, T. (2009) *Trouble with Strangers: A Study of Ethics*. Chichester and Malden, MA: Wiley-Blackwell.

Edkins, J. (2000) *Whose Hunger? Concepts of Famine, Practices of Aid*. Minneapolis: University of Minnesota Press.

Evans, H. (2004) 'Propaganda versus professionalism'. *British Journalism Review* 15(1): 36–42.

Eyerman, R. and Jamison, A. (1998) *Music and Social Movements: Mobilizing Traditions in the Twentieth Century*. Cambridge, New York, Oakleigh: Cambridge University Press.

Fairclough, N. (2003) *Analyzing Discourse: Textual Analysis for Social Research*. London: Routledge.

Fearn-Banks, K. (2007) *Crisis Communication: A Casebook Approach*, 3rd edn. London: Routledge.

Fenton, N. (2007) 'Contesting global capital, new media, solidarity, and the role of a social imaginary', in N. Carpentier and B. Cammaerts (eds), *Reclaiming the Media: Communication Rights and Democratic Media Roles*. London: Intellect Books, pp. 225–42.

Fenton, N. (2008) 'Mediating solidarity'. *Global Media and Communication* 4(1): 37–57.

Feral, J. (2002) 'Theatricality: the specificity of theatrical language'. *SubStance* 31(2/3): 94–108. Issue 98/99: Available at: www.brown.edu/Departments/German_Studies/media/Symposium/Texts/Specificity%20of%20Theatrical%20Language%20JF.pdf (accessed 10 May 2012).

Fine, B. (2009) 'Development as zombieconomics in the age of neo-liberalism'. *Third World Quarterly* 30(5): 885–904.

Flynn, T. (1984) *Sartre and Marxist Existentialism: The Test Case of Collective Responsibility*. Chicago: University of Chicago Press.

Flyvebjerg, B. (2001) *Making Social Science Matter*. Cambridge: Cambridge University Press.

Foucault, M. (1972) *The Archaeology of Knowledge*. London: Tavistock.

Foucault, M. (1977) *Discipline and Punish: The Birth of Prison*. London: Penguin Books.

Foucault, M. (1988) 'Technologies of the self,' in L. H. Martin, H. Gutman and P. H. Hutton (eds), *Technologies of the Self: A Seminar with Michel Foucault*. Amherst: University of Massachusetts Press, pp. 16–49.

Franks, S. (2006) 'The CARMA report: Western media coverage of humanitarian disasters'. *The Political Quarterly* 77(2): 281–84.

Friedman, L. J. (2003) 'Philanthropy in America: historicism and its discontents', in L. J. Friedman and M. D. McGarvie (eds), *Charity, Philanthropy and Civility in American History*. Cambridge: Cambridge University Press, pp. 1–21.

Frosh, P. and Pinchevski, A. (eds) (2009) *Media Witnessing: Testimony in the Age of Mass Communication*. London: Palgrave.

Fukuyama, F. (1989) 'The end of history?' *The National Interest* 16 (Summer): 3–18.

Galtung, J. and Ruge, M. H. (1965) 'The structure of foreign news'. *Journal of Peace Research* 2(1): 64–90.

Garofalo, R. (2005) 'Who is the world? Reflections on music and politics twenty years after Live Aid'. *Journal of Popular Music Studies* 17(3): 324–44.

Geldof, B. (1986) *Is That It?* London: Sidgwick and Jackson.

Geras, N. (1995) *Solidarity in the Conversation of Humankind: The Ungroundable Liberalism of Richard Rorty*. London: Verso.

Gillmor, D. (2004) *We the Media: Grassroots Journalism by the People, for the People*. Sebastopol, CA: O'Reilly Press.

Gilroy, P. (2004) *After Empire: Melancholia or Convivial Culture*. London: Routledge

Gilroy, P. (2006) *Postcolonial Melancholia*. New York: Columbia University Press.

Giri, A. K. (2003) 'Reconstituting development as a shared responsibility', in A. K. Giri and P. Q. van Ufford (eds), *A Moral Critique of Development*. London: Routledge, pp. 253–78.

Gourevich, P. (2010) 'Alms dealers: can you provide humanitarian aid without facilitating conflicts?' *The New Yorker,* 11 October. Available at: www.newyorker.com/arts/critics/atlarge/2010/10/11/101011crat_atlarge_gourevitch?currentPage=1 (accessed 1 October 2011).

Gross, D. (2006) *The Secret History of Emotion: From Aristotle's Rhetoric to Modern Brain Science*. Chicago: The University of Chicago Press.

Grossberg, L. (1993) 'The media economy of rock culture: cinema, postmodernity and authenticity', in S. Frith, A. Goodwin and L. Grossberg (eds), *Sound and Vision: The Music Video Reader*. London: Routledge, pp. 185–209.

Grossberg, L. (2006) 'Is there a fan in the house? The affective sensibility in fandom', in D. Marshall (ed.), *The Celebrity Culture Reader*. London and New York: Routledge, pp. 581–91.

Gullace, G. (1993) 'On the moral conception of the Enlightenment'. *The Journal of Value Inquiry* 27(3–4): 391–402.

Habermas, J. (1962/1989) *The Structural Transformation of the Public Sphere: An Inquiry into a Category of Bourgeois Society*. Cambridge, MA: MIT Press.

Hague, S., Street, J. and Savigny, H. (2008) 'The voice of the people? Musicians as political actors'. *Cultural Politics* 4(1): 5–23.

Hafez, K. (2007) *The Myth of Media Globalization*. Cambridge: Polity.

Halavais, A. (2002) 'Part 3: The Rise of Do-it-yourself Journalism After September 11', in *Pew Internet & American Life Project, One Year Later: September 11 and the Internet* (5 September 2002): 31, available online: www.pewinternet.org (accessed May 2012).

Hale, T. and Held, D. (2011) *The Handbook of Transnational Governance: Institutions and Innovations*. Cambridge and Malden: Polity.

Hall, S. (1992/2001) 'The West and the rest', in S. Hall and B. Gieben (eds), *Formations of Modernity*. Milton Keynes: Open University Press and Blackwell, pp. 257–330.

Hall, S. (1997) 'The spectacle of the "other"', in S. Hall (ed.), *Representation: Cultural Representations and Signifying Practices*. London, Thousand Oaks and New Delhi: Sage and Open University, pp. 223–79.

Hall, S. and Jacques, M. (eds) (1989) *New Times: The Changing Face of Politics in the 1990s*. London: Lawrence and Wishart.

Halttunen, K. (1995) 'Humanitarianism and the pornography of pain in Anglo-American culture'. *The American Historical Review* 100(2): 303–34.

Harcup, T. (2002) 'Journalists and ethics: the quest for a collective voice'. *Journalism Studies* 3(1): 101–14.

Harding, P. (2009) 'The great global switch-off: International coverage in UK public service broadcasting'. POLIS, Oxfam, IBT. Available at: www.oxfam.org.uk/resources/papers/downloads/great_global_switch_off.pdf (accessed 7 October 2011).

Hardt, M. and Negri, A. (2001) *Empire*. Boston: Harvard University Press.

Hartley, J. (2010) 'Silly citizenship'. *Critical Discourse Studies* 7(4): 233–48.

Hattori, T. (2003a) 'Giving as a mechanism of consent: international aid organizations and the ethical hegemony of capitalism'. *International Relations* 17(2): 153–73.

Hattori, T. (2003b) 'The moral politics of foreign aid'. *Review of International Studies* 29(2): 229–47.

Henson, S. and Lindstrom, J. (2010) 'Aid to developing countries: Where does the UK public stand? Results and analysis from the UK public opinion monitor'. Brighton, Institute of Development Studies. Available at: www.ids.ac.uk/files/dmfile/IDSUKPOMReport.pdf (accessed 10 May 2012).

Himmelfarb, G. (1984) *The Idea of Poverty*. New York: Knopf.

Hjarvard, S. (2008) 'The mediatization of religion: enchantment, media and popular culture'. *Northern Lights* 6(1): 3–8.

Hodgkin, K. and Radstone, S. (eds) (2006) *Memory, History, Nation: Contested Pasts*. New Jersey: Transaction Publishers.

Hojer, B. (2004) 'The discourse of global compassion: the audience and media reporting of human suffering'. *Media, Culture & Society* 26(4): 513–31.

Holquist, M. and Kliger, I. (2005) 'Minding the gap. Towards a historical poetics of estrangement'. *Poetics Today* 26(4): 613–36.

Horkheimer, M. and Adorno, T. W. (1947/2002) 'The culture industry: Enlightenment as mass deception', in G. S. Noerr (ed.), *Dialectic of Enlightenment: Philosophical Fragments*, trans. E. Jephcott. Stanford: Stanford University Press, pp. 94–136.

Hume, D. (1777/1993) 'Of tragedy', in S. Copley and A. Edgar (eds), *Selected Essays*. Oxford: Oxford University Press, pp. 126–53.

Hutchings, K. (2010) *Global Ethics*. Cambridge: Polity.

Hutchinson, J. F. (1996) *Champions of Charity: War and the Rise of the Red Cross*. Boulder and Oxford: Westview Press.

Hyde, L. (1999) *The Gift: Imagination and the Erotic Life of Property*. London, Vintage.

Ignatieff, M. (2001) 'Human rights, sovereignty and intervention', in N. Owen (ed.), *Human Rights, Human Wrongs: The Oxford Amnesty Lectures*. Oxford: Oxford University Press, pp. 49–91.

Illouz, E. (2007) *Cold Intimacies: The Making of Emotional Capitalism*. Cambridge: Polity.

James, E. C. (2004) 'The political economy of "trauma" in Haiti in the democratic era of insecurity'. *Culture, Medicine and Psychiatry* 28: 127–49.

Jappe, A. (1999) *Guy Debord*. Berkeley: University of California Press.

Jenkins, H. (2004) 'The cultural logic of media convergence'. *International Journal of Cultural Studies* 7(1): 33–43.

Jenkins, H. (2006) *Fans, Bloggers, and Gamers: Exploring Participatory Culture*. New York: New York University Press.

Jestrovic, S. (2006) *The Theatre of Estrangement. Theory, Practice, Ideology*. Toronto: Toronto University Press

Jewitt, C. and Kress, G. (2003) *Multimodal Literacy*. New York: Peter Lang.

Jolie, A. (2003) *Notes from My Travels: Visits with Refugees in Africa, Cambodia, Pakistan, and Ecuador*. New York: Pocket Books.

Jones, B. (2010) 'Katine: an academic review'. *Guardian*, 30 October. Available at www.guardian.co.uk/katine/interactive/2010/oct/30/ben-jones-academic-review (accessed 2 October 2011).

Joye, S. (2010) 'News discourses on distant suffering: a critical discourse analysis of the 2003 SARS outbreak'. *Discourse & Society* 21(5): 586–601.

Kennedy, D. (2004) *The Dark Sides of Virtue: Reassessing International Humanitarianism*. Princeton, NJ: Princeton University Press.

King, B. (1985/2006) 'Articulating stardom', in P. D. Marshall (ed.), *The Celebrity Culture Reader*. London: Sage, pp. 228–51.

King, B. (2008) 'Stardom, celebrity and the para-confession'. *Social Semiotics* 18(2): 115–32.

Kothari, U. (ed.) (2005) *A Radical History of Development Studies: Individuals, Institutions and Ideologies*. London: Zed Books.

Kronman, A. (1983) *Max Weber*. Stanford: Stanford University Press.

Krueger, A. (1986) 'Aid in the development process'. *World Bank Research Observer* 1(1): 57–78.

Kurzman, C., Anderson, C., Key, C., Lee, Y., Moloney, M., Silver, A. and Ryn, M. van (2007) 'Celebrity status'. *Sociological Theory* 25(4): 347–67.

Laclau, E. and Mouffe, C. (1985) *Hegemony and Socialist Strategy: Towards a Radical Democratic Politics*. London: Verso.

Lemke, T. (2001) '"The birth of bio-politics": Michel Foucault's lecture at the Collège de France on neo-liberal governmentality'. *Economy and Society* 30(2): 190–207. Available at: http://mfaishalaminuddin.lecture.ub.ac.id/files/2009/11/BIRTH-OF-BIOPOLITICS_On-Foucaults-Lecture_Lemke.pdf (accessed 2 October 2011).

Le Sueur, J. and Bourdieu, P. (2001) *Uncivil War: Intellectuals and Identity Politics during the Decolonization of Algeria*. Philadelphia: University of Nebraska Press.

Lewis, J. (2004) Television, public opinion and the war in Iraq: the case of Britain. *International Journal of Public Opinion Research* 16(3): 295–310.

Lidchi, H. (1997) 'The poetics and politics of exhibiting other cultures', in S. Hall

(ed.), *Representation: Cultural Representations and Signifying Practices*. London: Open University Press/Sage, pp. 151–222.
Lievrouw, L. A. and Livingstone, S. (eds) (2002) *The Handbook of New Media: Social Shaping and Social Consequences of ICTs*, 1st edn. London: Sage.
Linklater, A. (2007a) 'Distant suffering and cosmopolitan obligations'. *International Politics* 44: 19–36.
Linklater, A. (2007b) 'Towards a sociology of global morals with an "emancipatory intent"'. *Review of International Studies* 33: 135–50.
Lissner, J. (1979) *The Politics of Altruism*. Geneva: Lutheran World Foundation.
Littler, J. (2008) '"I feel your pain": cosmopolitan charity and the public fashioning of celebrity soul'. *Social Semiotics* 18(2): 237–51.
Livingstone, S. (2008) 'Taking risky opportunities in youthful content creation: teenagers' use of social networking sites for intimacy, privacy and self-expression'. *New Media and Society* 10(3): 393–411.
Magubane, Z. (2008) 'The (product) Red man's burden: charity, celebrity and the contradictions of coevalness'. *Journal of PanAfrican Studies* 2(6): 1–25.
Manovich, L. (2001) *The Language of New Media*. Cambridge, MA: MIT Press.
Mansell, R. (2001) 'Digital opportunities and the missing link for developing countries'. *Oxford Review of Economic Policy* 17(2): 282–95.
Mansell, R. (2002) 'From digital divides to digital entitlements in knowledge societies'. *Current Sociology* 50(3): 407–26.
Marks, M. P. and Fischer, Z. M. (2002) 'The King's new bodies: simulating consent in the age of celebrity'. *New Political Science* 24(3): 371–94.
Marshall, P. D. (1984) 'Adam Smith and the theatricality of moral sentiments'. *Critical Inquiry* 10(4): 592–613.
Marshall, P. D. (1997) *Celebrity and Power: Fame in Contemporary Culture*. Minneapolis: University of Minnesota Press.
Marshall, P. D. (ed.) (2006) 'The meanings of the popular music celebrity', in *The Celebrity Culture Reader*. London: Routledge, pp. 196–222.
Matheson, D. (2004) 'Weblogs and the epistemology of the news: some trends in online journalism'. *New Media & Society* 6(2): 443–68.
Mathews, J. T. (1997) 'Power shift'. *Foreign Affairs* 76(1): 50–66.
Mbembe, A. (1992) 'The banality of power and the aesthetics of vulgarity in the postcolony'. *Public Culture* 4(2): 1–30.
Mbembe, A. (2001) *On the Postcolony*. Berkeley: University of California Press.
McCarthy, T. (1990) 'Private irony and public decency: Richard Rorty's new pragmatism'. *Critical Inquiry* 16 (Winter): 355–70.
McCleary, R. M. and Barro, R. J. (2007) 'US-based private voluntary organizations: religious and secular PVOs engaged in international relief and development, 1939–2004'. *American Political Science Association Annual Conference*, 30 August–2 September 2007, Chicago.
McGuigan, J. (2009) *Cool Capitalism*. London: Pluto Press.
McIntyre, A. (1981/2006) *After Virtue*. London: Duckworth.
McLagan, M. (2003) 'Human rights, testimony and transnational publicity'. *S & F*

Online 2(1). Available at: http://barnard.edu/sfonline/ps/mclagan.htm#section1 (accessed 8 August 2011).

McQuire, S. (1998) *Visions of Modernity: Representation, Memory, Time and Space in the Age of the Camera*. London: Sage.

Mestrovic, S. (1997) *Postemotional Society*. London: Sage.

Mills, K. (2005) 'Neo-humanitarianism: the role of international humanitarian norms and organizations in contemporary conflict'. *Global Governance* 11: 161–83.

Mitchell, W. (1986) *Iconology: Image, Text, Ideology*. Chicago: University of Chicago Press.

Moeller, S. (1999) *Compassion Fatigue: How the Media Sell Disease, Famine, War and Death*. London and New York: Routledge.

Mouffe, C. (ed.) (1992) *Dimensions of Radical Democracy: Pluralism, Citizenship, Community*. New York: Verso.

Moyn, S. (2006) 'Empathy in history, empathizing with humanity'. *History and Theory* 45(3): 397–415.

Moyn, S. (2010) *The Last Utopia: Human Rights in History*. Cambridge, MA: Harvard University Press.

Muhlmann, G. (2008) *A Political History of Journalism*. Cambridge: Polity.

Nash, K. (2008) 'Global citizenship as show business: the cultural politics of Make Poverty History'. *Media, Culture & Society* 30(2): 167–81.

Natsios, A. S. (1995) 'NGOs and the UN system in complex humanitarian emergencies: conflict or cooperation?' *Third World Quarterly* 16(3): 405–20.

Nichols, B. (2001) *Introduction to Documentary*. Bloomington & Indianapolis: Indiana University Press.

Nussbaum, F. (2005) 'The theatre of empire: racial counterfeit, racial realism', in K. Wilson (ed.), *A New Imperial History: Culture, Identity and Modernity in Britain and the Empire, 1660–1840*. Cambridge: Cambridge University Press, pp. 71–90.

Nussbaum, M. (1986) *The Fragility of Goodness*. Cambridge: Cambridge University Press.

Nussbaum, M. (1997) *Cultivating Humanity: A Classical Defense of Reform in Liberal Education*. Cambridge, MA. London: Harvard University Press.

Nussbaum, M. (2003) 'Compassion and terror'. *Daedalus* 132(1): 10–26.

Nussbaum, M. (2011) *Creating Capabilities: The Human Development Approach*. Cambridge, MA: Harvard University Press.

Nussbaum, M. and Sen, A. (eds) (1993) *The Quality of Life*. Oxford and New York: Clarendon.

Oliver, K. (2001) *Witnessing: Beyond Recognition*. Minneapolis: University of Minnesota Press.

Orgad, S. (2009) 'The survivor in contemporary culture and public discourse: a genealogy'. *The Communication Review* 12(2): 132–61.

Orgad, S. (2011) 'Proper distance from ourselves: the potential of estrangement in the mediapolis'. *International Journal of Cultural Studies* 14(4): 401–21.

Papacharissi, Z. A. (2010) *A Private Sphere: Democracy in a Digital Age*. Cambridge, UK and Malden, MA: Polity.

Pateman, T. (1989) 'Pragmatics in semiotics: Bakhtin/Volosinov'. *Journal of Literary Semantics* 18(3): 203–16.

Pavlik, J. V. (2001) *New Media and Journalism*. Cambridge, MA: MIT Press.

Payne, A. (2006) 'Blair, Brown and the Gleneagles Agenda: Making poverty history or confronting the global politics of unequal development?' Published by the Department of International Relations, RSPAS, Australian National University. Available at: http://ips.cap.anu.edu.au/ir/pubs/work_papers/06-3.pdf (accessed 20 August 2011).

Peters, J. D. (1999) *Speaking into the Air: A History of the Idea of Communication*. Chicago: Chicago University Press.

Peters, J. D. (2005) *Courting the Abyss: Free Speech and the Liberal Tradition*. Chicago: University of Chicago Press.

Peters, J. D. (2009) 'Witnessing', in P. Frosh and A. Pinchevski (eds), *Media Witnessing: Testimony in the Age of Mass Communication*. London: Palgrave, pp. 23–41.

Phillipson, N. (2010) *Adam Smith: An Enlightened Life*. London: Allen Lane.

Pinney, C. (1992) 'Future travel: anthropology and cultural distance in an age of virtual reality'. *Visual Anthropology Review* 8(1): 38–55.

Polman, L. (2010) *War Games: The Story of Aid and War at Modern Times*. London: Penguin Books.

Poster, M. (1975) *Existential Marxism in Postwar France: From Sartre to Althusser*. Princeton: Princeton University Press.

Puchner, M. (2002) *Stage Fright: Modernism, Anti-theatricality and Drama*. Baltimore: The Johns Hopkins University Press.

Rancière, J. (1999) *Disagreement: Politics and Philosophy*. Minneapolis: University of Minnesota Press.

Rancière, J. (2009) *The Emancipated Spectator*. London: Verso.

Rantanen, T. (2009) *When News Was New*. Malden, Oxford, Chichester: Wiley-Blackwell.

Reese, S. D. (2009) 'The future of journalism in emerging deliberative space'. *Journalism* 10(3): 358–60.

Rifkin, J. (2009) *The Empathic Civilization: The Race to Global Consciousness in a World in Crisis*. New York: Jeremy P. Tarcher/Penguin.

Rojek, C. (2001) *Celebrity*. London: Reaktion Books.

Rorty, R. (1989) *Contingency, Irony and Solidarity*. Cambridge: Cambridge University Press.

Rorty, R. (2008) *Texts and Lumps*. *New Literary History* 39(1): 53–68.

Rose, N. (1999) *Powers of Freedom: Reframing Political Thought*. Cambridge: Cambridge University Press.

Said, E. W. (1993) *Culture and Imperialism*. New York: A. A. Knopf.

Said, E. W. (2002) 'Imaginative geography and its representations: orientalising the

Oriental', in Ph. Essed and D. T. Goldberg (eds), *Race Critical Theories: Text and Context*. Malden, MA and Oxford: Blackwell, pp. 15–37.

Sambrook, R. (2005) 'Citizen journalism and the BBC'. *Nieman Reports* (Winter 2005). Available at: www.nieman.harvard.edu/reportsitem.aspx?id=100542 (accessed 7 October 2011).

Sayer, A. (2009) 'Who is afraid of critical social science?' *Current Sociology* 57(6): 767–86.

Schudson, M. (1995) *The Power of News*. Cambridge, MA: Harvard University Press.

Schudson, M. (1998) *The Good Citizen: A History of American Civic Life*. New York: The Free Press.

Schuurman, F. (2009) 'Critical development theory: moving out of the twilight zone'. *Third World Quarterly* 30(5): 831–48.

Scott, B. (2005) 'A contemporary history of digital journalism'. *Television New Media* 6(1): 89–126.

Sen, A. (1989) 'Development as capabilities expansion'. *Journal of Development Planning* 19: 41–58.

Sen, A. (1999) *Development as Freedom*. New York: Oxford University Press.

Sen, A. (2009) *The Idea of Justice*. London: Penguin Books.

Sennett, R. (1974) *The Fall of Public Man*. London and New York: Penguin Books.

Sennett, R. (1977) *The Fall of Public Man: On the Social Psychology of Capitalism*. New York: Knopf.

Shapiro, M. J. (2002) *Reading Adam Smith: Desire, History and Value*. Oxford: Rowman & Littlefield Publishers.

Silverstone, R. (1994) *Television and Everyday Life*. London: Routledge.

Silverstone, R. (2002) 'Regulation and the ethics of distance: distance and the ethics of regulation', in R. Mansell, R. Samjiva and A. Mahav (eds), *Networking Knowledge for Information Societies: Institutions & Interventions*. Amsterdam: Delft University Press, pp. 279–85.

Silverstone, R. (2007) *Media and Morality: On the Rise of the Mediapolis*. Cambridge: Polity.

Simmons, P. J. (1998) 'Learning to live with NGOs'. *Foreign Policy* 112 (Autumn): 82–96.

Singer, P. (1972/2008) 'Famine, affluence and morality', in T. Brooks (ed.), *The Global Justice Reader*. Oxford: Blackwell, pp. 388–96.

Slim, H. (1997) 'Relief agencies and moral standing in war: principles of humanity, neutrality, impartiality and solidarity'. *Development in Practice* 7(4): 342–52.

Slim, H. (2003) 'Marketing humanitarian space: argument and method in humanitarian persuasion'. Paper presented to *The Annual Meeting of the Humanitarian Negotiators Network*. Talloires, 12–14 May 2003.

Small, D. (1997) 'Development education revisited: the New Zealand experience', in V. Masemann (ed.), *Tradition, Modernity, and Post-Modernity in Comparative Education*. New York: Springer Publications, pp. 581–94.

Smillie, I. (1995) *The Alms Bazaar: Altruism Under Fire. Non-Profit Organisations and International Development.* London: Intermediate Technology.

Smillie, I. and Minear, L. (2004) *The Charity of Nations: Humanitarian Action in a Calculating World.* Bloomfield, CT: Kumarian Press.

Smith, A. (1759/2000) *The Theory of Moral Sentiments.* New York: Prometheus Books.

Smith, A. (1776/1999) 'The wealth of nations', in A.Skinner (ed.), *The Wealth of Nations: Books I–III.* London: Penguin.

Sontag, S. (2003) *Regarding the Pain of Others.* London: Picador.

Stiglitz, J. (2002) *Globalization and its Discontents.* New York and London: W. W. Norton.

Szerszynski, B. (2007) 'The post-ecologist condition: irony as symptom and cure'. *Environmental Politics* 16(2): 337–55.

Sznaider, N. (2001) *The Compassionate Temperament: Care and Cruelty in Modern Society.* London: Rowman and Littlefield.

Taylor, C. (1995) 'The politics of recognition', in A. Heble et al. (eds), *New Contexts of Canadian Criticism.* Ontario: Westview Press, pp. 98–131.

Taylor, C. (2002) 'Modern social imaginaries'. *Public Culture* 14(1): 91–124.

Terry, F. (2002) *Condemned to Repeat? The Paradox of Humanitarian Action.* Ithaca and London: Cornell University Press.

Tester, K. (2001) *Compassion, Morality and the Media.* Buckingham and Philadelphia: Open University Press.

Tester, K. (2010) *Humanitarianism and Modern Culture.* Pennsylvania: University of Pennsylvania Press.

't Hart, P. and Tindall, K. (2009) 'Leadership by the famous: celebrity as political capital', in J. Kane, J. Patapan, and P. 't Hart (eds), *Dispersed Leadership in Democracies: Origins, Dynamics & Implications.* Oxford: Open University Press, pp. 255–78.

Thelwall, M. and Stuart, D. (2007) 'RUOK? Blogging communication technologies during crises'. *Journal of Computer-Mediated Communication* 12(2): 189–214. Available at: http://jcmc.indiana.edu/vol12/issue2/thelwall.html (accessed 11 August 2011).

Thompson, J. (1984) *Studies in the Theory of Ideology.* Cambridge: Polity.

Thompson, J. (1995) *The Media and Modernity: A Social Theory of the Media.* Cambridge: Polity.

Thompson, K. (2008) 'Historicity and transcendentality: Foucault, Cavailles and the phenomenology of the concept'. *History and Theory* 47: 1–18.

Thrall, T. A., Lollio-Fakhreddine, J., Donnelly, L., Herin, W., Paquette, Z., Wenglinski, R., and Wyatt, A. (2008) 'Star power: celebrity advocacy and the evolution of the public sphere'. *International Journal of Press/Politics* 13(4): 362–85.

Thumim, N. (2009) '"Everyone has a story to tell". Mediation and self-representation in two UK institutions'. *International Journal of Cultural Studies* 12(6): 617–38.

Tomlinson, J. (2011) 'Beyond connection: cultural cosmopolitan and ubiquitous media'. *International Journal of Cultural Studies* 14(4): 347–61.

Traub, J. (2005) 'The Statesman'. *The New York Times Magazine*, 18 September.

Tuchman, G. (1973) 'Making news by doing work: routinizing the unexpected'. *American Journal of Sociology* 79(1): 110–31.

Tuchman, G. (1976) 'Telling stories'. *Journal of Communication* 26(4): 93–97.

Turner, G. (2010) *Ordinary People and the Media: The Demotic Turn*. London: Sage.

Utley, G. (1997) 'The shrinking of foreign news: from broadcast to narrowcast'. *Foreign Affairs* 76(2): 2–10.

Vallely, P. (2009) 'From A-lister to Aid worker: Does celebrity diplomacy really work?'. *The Independent*, 17 January. Available at: www.independent.co.uk/news/people/profiles/from-alister-to-aid-worker-does-celebrity-diplomacy-really-work-1365946.html (accessed 10 May 2012).

Vallely, P. (2011) 'How serious is the threat of famine in East Africa?'. Available at: www.paulvallely.com/?p=4087 (accessed 8 October 2011).

Vestergaard, A. (2008) 'Humanitarian branding and the media: the case of Amnesty International'. *Journal of Language and Politics* 7(3): 471–93.

Vestergaard, A. (2010) 'Identity and appeal in the humanitarian brand', in L. Chouliaraki and M. Morsing (eds), *Media, Organizations and Identity*. London: Palgrave Macmillan, pp. 168–84.

Villa, D. (1999) *Politics, Philosophy, Terror: Essays on the Thought of Hannah Arendt*. Princeton, NJ: Princeton University Press.

Virilio, P. (1986) 'The overexposed city', trans. A. Hustvedt, in M. Feher and S. Kwinter (eds), *Zone 1/2: The Contemporary City*. New York: Urzone, pp. 15–31.

Virilio, P. (1995) *The Art of the Motor*, transl. J. Rose. Minneapolis: University of Minnesota Press.

VSO (Voluntary Service Overseas) (2002) 'The Live Aid legacy: The developing world through British eyes – A Research Report'. Available at: www.eldis.org/vfile/upload/1/document/0708/DOC1830.pdf (accessed 1 October 2011).

Walker, A. (1995) *Audrey: Her Real Story*. London: Penguin.

Wasserman, E. (1947) 'The sympathetic imagination in eighteenth-century theories of acting'. *The Journal of English and Germanic Philology* 46(3): 264–72.

Weber, M. (1978) *Economy and Society*. Berkeley: University of California Press.

Wells, K. (2010) 'Memorialising violent death: the ethical demands of grievable lives', in G. Rose and G. P. Tolia-Kelly (eds), *Architectures of the Visual: Embodied Materialities, Politics and Place*. Farnham: Ashgate Press.

Wenar, L. (2003/2008) 'What we owe to distant others', in T. Brooks (ed.), *The Global Justice Reader*. Oxford: Blackwell, pp. 283–304.

West, D. M and Orman, J. (2002) *Celebrity Politics: Real Politics in America*. Cambridge: Pearson.

West, E. G. (1969) 'The political economy of alienation: Karl Marx and Adam Smith'. *Oxford Economic Papers* 21(1): 1–23.

Wheeler, N. J. (2003) *Saving Strangers: Humanitarian Intervention in International Society*. Oxford: Oxford University Press.

Williams, B. (1973) *Problems of the Self: Philosophical Papers 1956–1972*. Cambridge: Cambridge University Press.

Williams, R. (1984) *Television: Technology and Cultural Form*. New York: Shocken Books.

Yanacopulos, H. (2005) 'The strategies that bind: NGO coalitions and their strategies'. *Global Networks* 5(1): 93–110.

Yanacopulos, H. and Smith, M. B. (2007) 'The ambivalent cosmopolitanism in international NGOs', in A. Bebbington, S. Hickey and D. Mitlin (eds), *Can NGOs Make a Difference? The Challenge of Development Alternatives*. London: Zed Books, pp. 298–315.

Youngs, I. (2005) 'Why Live Aid is happening again.' BBC News Online, 31 May. Available at: http://news.bbc.co.uk/1/hi/entertainment/4597363.stm (accessed 10 May 2012).

Yrjölä, R. (2009) 'The invisible violence of celebrity humanitarianism: soft images and hard words in the making and unmaking of Africa'. *World Political Science Review* 5(1): 1–23.

Zelizer, B. (1998) *Remembering to Forget: Holocaust Memory Through the Camera's Eye*. Chicago: University of Chicago Press.

Zelizer, B. (2005) 'Journalism through the camera's eye', in S. Allan (ed.), *Journalism: Critical Issues*. London: McGraw-Hill, pp. 167–77.

Zerilli, L. (2005) '"We feel our freedom": imagination and judgment in the thought of Hannah Arendt'. *Political Theory* 33(2): 158–88.

Žižek, S. (2005) 'Against human rights'. *New Left Review* 34: 115–31.

Index